W9-BJN-478

My Life:

The autobiography of

My Life: A Guided Tour

A Guided Tour

KENNETH N. TAYLOR

with Virginia J. Muir

Tyndale House Publishers, Inc.
WHEATON, ILLINOIS

Library of Congress Cataloging-in-Publication Data

Taylor, Kenneth Nathaniel.
    My life : a guided tour / Kenneth N. Taylor with Virginia J. Muir.
        p.   cm.
    Includes bibliographic references and index.
    ISBN 0-8423-4046-7 — ISBN 0-8423-4047-5 (pbk.)
        1. Taylor, Kenneth Nathaniel.   2. Baptists—United States—Biography.
3. Publishers and publishing—United States—Biography.   4. Tyndale House
Publishers.   5. Bible—Translating.   I. Muir, Virginia J.   II. Title.
BX6495.T395A3   1991
286'.1'092—dc20
[B]   91-20333

Unless otherwise stated, Scripture verses are taken from *The Living Bible* copyright
©1971 owned by assignment by KNT Charitable Trust. All rights reserved.
Scripture verses marked (NIV) are taken from the *Holy Bible,* New International Version.
Copyright © 1973, 1978, 1984 International Bible Society. Used by permission of
Zondervan Bible Publishers.
Scripture verses marked (KJV) are taken from the *Holy Bible,* King James Version.

The poem "Let Me Get Home before Dark" by Robertson McQuilkin on page 383 is
reprinted with the author's permission.
Cover photo © 1976 by William Koechling.

ISBN 0-8423-4046-7, cloth
ISBN 0-8423-4047-5, paper
© 1991 by Kenneth N. Taylor
All rights reserved
Printed in the United States of America

98   97   96   95   94   93   92   91
 8   7   6   5   4   3   2   1

Dedication to Margaret

I want to be different and not simply say, "Dedicated with love to my wife." So, instead, I will tell you some things about her that make her special:

She has been not only a loving wife, but also a friend for fifty years—and for ten years before that, through high school and college days.

She has been my counselor and encourager, and, when necessary, she has pointed out some weaknesses and pricked my pride.

She is the mother of my ten children, and now we have twenty-seven grandchildren.

She worked unceasingly at home during the family years.

She nourished Tyndale House from its earliest days at our dining room table and continued to carry Tyndale responsibilities, through thick and thin, for nineteen years.

She has insisted that I be the spiritual leader in our home, even at times when I didn't want that responsibility. Her own quiet, steady love for our Lord has been a constant inspiration to me.

So I thankfully dedicate this volume to her.

KENNETH N. TAYLOR

Contents

A Word to My Readers ix
Prologue—1940 xi

Chapter 1 *Beginnings* 1
Chapter 2 *School Days* 13
Chapter 3 *High School* 27
Chapter 4 *Preparing for College* 39
Chapter 5 *First Years at Wheaton College* 45

   Poem: "The Cord" 59

Chapter 6 *Margaret* 61
Chapter 7 *The Accident* 69
Chapter 8 *Engaged at Last* 79
Chapter 9 *Some Miracles* 89
Chapter 10 *Life Together* 103
Chapter 11 *Seminary Days* 111
Chapter 12 *An Introduction to Missions* 117

   Poem: "The Rumor" 125

Chapter 13 *A New Job and a Growing Family* 127
Chapter 14 *Housing Frustrations* 137
Chapter 15 *A House of Our Own* 147
Chapter 16 *Traveling the World* 157

   Poem: "She Stood at the Window, Sobbing" 169

Chapter 17 *Moody Press* 171
Chapter 18 *Evangelical Literature Overseas* 181
Chapter 19 *Family Life* 191

   Poem: "Are All the Children In?" Elizabeth Rosser . 205

Chapter 20 *A New Kind of Translation* 207
Chapter 21 *Voice Problems* 217

   Poem: "In Thankfulness for Health" 225

Chapter 22 *Living Letters* 227
Chapter 23 *Tyndale House Grows* 237

    Poem: "What Is in Your Bag?" 253

Chapter 24 *The Living Bible* 255
Chapter 25 *Commendation and Criticism* 267

    Poem: "Street Scene in Iran" 281

Chapter 26 *Tyndale House Foundation* 283

    Poem: "Moving the Hands of God" 289

Chapter 27 *Magazines, Racks of Books,
and Church Bulletins* 291
Chapter 28 *Financial Crises* 303

    Poem: "Hymn of Going Home" 315

Chapter 29 *Living Bibles around the World* 317

    Poem: "Farewell, Forever" 333

Chapter 30 *Tithing and Hospitality* 335

    Poem: "Empty Nest" 345

Chapter 31 *Thoughts about Prayer* 347

    Poem: "The Accident" 361

Chapter 32 *The Past Ten Years* 363

    Poem: "Let Me Get Home before Dark,"
    Robertson McQuilkin 371

Epilogue 373
An Appreciation, by V. Gilbert Beers 375
Chronology of Events in the Lives
of Kenneth and Margaret Taylor 377
Resumé of Kenneth Taylor's Books,
Positions, and Honors 383
Index 389

A Word to My Readers

Autobiographies have always been interesting and helpful to me. I have learned from them how other people have acted and reacted, and I have received many hints as to how my own life can be more useful. Sometimes I have learned about things to avoid, things that have brought others to disaster.

And so, after several years of thinking about it, I have decided that my memoirs may be helpful to others, just as others' have been helpful to me.

However, this is not a story of heroics like *The Cross and the Switchblade, God's Smuggler,* or *The Hiding Place*—three of my favorites. It is the story of an ordinary life with some extraordinary events scattered through it. I fear it is not the exciting reading that some autobiographies are, though I have experienced some dramatic highlights that I will tell you about. It is the story of God's quiet leading, sometimes into exciting events, but more often in day-by-day living.

Many years ago, when I left the work I loved so much at Moody Bible Institute, leaving job security to work full time translating *The Living Bible,* I knew I was taking some risks with the welfare of my large family. I recall remarking with deep feeling to my oldest son, "I'm not sure where I am going, but I know it will be a guided tour." And of course I meant guided by God. And so it has been, just as I believed.

I have not always understood God's leading, and sometimes I understood it but ignored it and got into a lot of trouble as a result; yet I have learned more and more about finding God's guidance.

I have never had a "life verse," but one verse summarizes my heart's desire of many years: "Just tell me what to do and I will do it, Lord. As long as I live I will wholeheartedly obey" (Ps. 119:33-34). I was not always of this mind. But now I recognize how foolish it is to use my own limited wisdom, often influenced by selfish desires, when the wisdom and power of God are mine for the asking. I hope you have come to this same conclusion for your own life, and that this book will help you see the importance of God's investment in you. May you and I both grow more and more quickly into His full purpose.

Kenneth N Taylor

Prologue
1940

I was in my room at the Montreal YMCA, preparing a message for the Inter-Varsity meeting at McGill University that evening. I found myself baffled about the meaning of a chapter in Ephesians, on which I had been asked to speak. I read the chapter several times, without much comprehension. Then I read it slowly, a verse at a time, with no better results. I could understand the words, of course, but I just could not understand the significance of the teaching or make any useful application to my life or the lives of the students.

Suddenly I was overwhelmed with the realization that my Bible reading in the New Testament letters had ever been thus. All my life I had wrestled in vain to understand them. Others could grasp their meaning; why couldn't I? Was I more stupid than my friends who gloried in reading the Word? Frustrated and ashamed, I exclaimed aloud to the empty room, "Why can't somebody translate the Bible so a person like me can understand it?"

Chapter 1
Beginnings

I WAS BORN in 1917 in Portland, Oregon, the gem of the beautiful Northwest, but my earliest memories are of Seattle, Washington, where we moved when I was three years old.

My father was the pastor of the Queen Anne Hill United Presbyterian Church, and we lived next door in the parsonage. Dad's church activities encompassed the usual things that all pastors do—preaching, teaching, baptizing, marrying, and burying. I especially remember the baptizing because of a Sunday afternoon when I was five years old. My older brother, Doug, and Mother and I went with Dad to watch him baptize an infant by immersion in a small tub of water in a wealthy family's living room. On the way, Dad was discussing with Mother the relative merits of trying to hold the baby's mouth and nose closed, risking the squirms and screams, or simply ducking the child quickly and expecting nature to make the baby hold his breath during the moment of submersion. I'm sure I was more interested in the process than the sacredness of the event.

From my earliest memories, I was a believer. Mother and Dad didn't tell Doug and me that we couldn't go to heaven unless we said just the right words of faith. Instead, it was assumed that we loved Jesus, just as they did. However, the way of salvation was clear to us, both from family devotions, as Dad explained the Bible text to us, and because Dad constantly told people he met that Jesus died on the cross for their salvation. Sometimes, especially as I grew older, I found this acutely embarrassing. I remember one time when I got on my hands and knees in the back seat of our Model T Ford when Dad stopped for a hitchhiker. I knew what was coming next!

Punishment was rare in our home, but prompt when needed. Once I maliciously sawed off some branches from a small tree in the front yard. Dad rarely showed temper, but to my lasting remembrance, he picked up one of the branches and used it as a whip! It was only one whack, but I still remember the intensity of the pain. Unfortunately, he didn't follow up with some discussion and a kiss. Perhaps if he had, I would have forgotten it by now.

The only spanking I remember getting from my mother was when, at about age three, I was angry at my brother and steered my tricycle into him, knocking him down. When Mother heard the ensuing commotion, she left her guests in the living room, where she was graciously performing the duties of a pastor's wife, and took me upstairs to perform her duty as a mother.

I have always been troubled by a degree of timidity, and two childhood events may be part of the reason. I was three and a half years old when the family moved to Seattle, going by train from Portland.

We made the trip on a hot, sultry day, and my brother, Doug, and I walked along the aisle several times to get drinks at the water cooler at the front end of the coach. These trips came to a sudden halt when a fat man sitting across the aisle from the cooler scolded us and told us to stay away. I was terrified and sweated out the remainder of the journey. Could such a small event cause timidity that would affect one's entire life? I do not know.

I remember, too, that Mother once threatened to run away when I was not behaving properly. That terrified me, and I recall several occasions after that when she was out of the house, and I was overwhelmed with fear that she would not return. Soon after she made that comment, she went downtown on the streetcar, leaving me with Aunt Ruth, who was visiting us. I was supposed to be taking a nap but lay there sobbing in fear. Aunt Ruth came upstairs to find out what was going on, and I finally told her my fear that Mother wouldn't come home.

On another occasion, after Doug and I were in bed at the parsonage, Mother and Dad went over to the Wednesday evening prayer meeting. Filled with fear about my mother, I got out of bed and, clad in my pajamas, slipped through the darkness to a window where I could look in at the folks seated in the basement fellowship hall. I wanted to be sure my mother was there. But she wasn't! Unfortunately, a wall partly obstructed my view, and she wasn't in sight. I was frantic but went back to bed and lay there gripped with fright until I heard the front door opening and heard my parents' voices. Eventually I came to realize that my troubling fears were unfounded.

A year later another small event happened that helped shape my life. Someone brushed a Bible off the living room table and onto the floor. I remember clearly how my father rushed over, picked it up, and gently put it back on the table. He didn't say anything, but the concern on his face made evident his deep respect for the Word of God and its Author. I've never forgotten it. It is little wonder that from earliest childhood the Bible has held such an important place in my life. How grateful I am for such a godly heritage.

Another memorable event of my childhood was the day Dad brought home our first automobile—a Model T Ford. In cold weather or rain we could snap on side curtains with isinglass windows in them. In 1922 a new Ford car cost $390, but Dad had bought ours used. He was a great admirer of Henry Ford and especially respected the fact that he paid his workers five dollars a day, about twice the prevailing wage. I was not moved by my father's philosophy, but I was excited that we were one of the few families on our block who owned a "machine." I was nervous, though, when Dad took the family for a ride into the countryside and drove thirty or even thirty-five miles an hour!

The driver of that model of car used a crank at the front of the radiator to start the motor, and Dad admonished us boys never to play with it, because the motor could backfire, causing the crank handle to spin backwards and injure an arm.

That Model T gave rise to an incident that made me suspicious of glib talkers. One afternoon Doug and I, six and five years old, were with Dad for an errand in downtown Seattle. We stayed in the car while he went into a nearby store for a purchase. Suddenly a tall, handsome young man opened the car door and told us that our father had given him permission to use the car for an errand. We were to get out and wait on the sidewalk until Dad returned. We were surprised, but we obeyed. Then, just as we got out of the car, the young man saw my father returning and quickly walked away. I guess it was my first realization that bad people don't always look bad.

I must mention a foolish adventure of mine when I was six years old. Getting up before the rest of the family, I decided to fool them by hiding behind the davenport in the living room and then surprise them by my sudden appearance. As soon as I heard footsteps on the stairs, I ducked behind the davenport. After awhile I heard my father ask whether I was still asleep, and my brother said no, I wasn't upstairs. Then pandemonium broke loose: a six-year-old boy was missing! Before long I heard Dad calling the police and reporting a missing child. At that point I felt trapped and afraid to show myself.

Mother and Doug went outside to look for me on nearby streets. Finally sense prevailed, and I crawled out and told Dad about the big surprise I had planned. He seemed understanding, as well as immensely relieved. He couldn't believe I hadn't appeared earlier when I saw how the plan had backfired. Anyway, he sent me out to find Mother, and of course she was overjoyed. That incident made such an impression on me that I can still remember that Mother was wearing a red sweater!

In subsequent years I've had many other great ideas that backfired, and I held on to them far longer than I should have. Still, some of them succeeded. How does one know when to quit? In this case, though, it should have been obvious!

Though Doug was a year and a half older than I, he was kept out of school for a year because of poor health, so we started first grade together. We walked a couple of blocks to school, passing the fire station on the way. We gazed in wonder at the shiny new fire trucks, with the just-retired horses grazing in the small pasture behind the firehouse.

Miss Seymour was our first-grade teacher, and we liked her. A few days after school started she took us to visit the principal's office—an awesome place we children always whispered about because of the punishments we knew were meted out there. The principal was cordial, but he refused to let us see what was behind a certain door, and we knew why—there must be a spanking machine in there! We shivered in terror. (Afterwards, when we were big kids in the second grade, we learned it was his private toilet!)

Dad's tight moral conscience made me uncomfortable at times. One day when I was in the second grade, each child brought ten cents to buy a little mimeographed booklet, a short history of our school. Miss Mott, our teacher, announced as she handed out the books and collected our dimes that one of the books had a star pasted in the margin on page 16. Whichever child had the star would get his ten cents back. We all eagerly looked, and to my delight I was the lucky one!

I rushed home after school to share the good news with my family but was dismayed to find no enthusiasm from my father. He gravely explained to me about gambling and told me to take the ten cents back to the teacher. I did, but not very happily. As I look back on it now, I think my dad may have overreacted, but I agree with his general point of view. I am sick at heart when I think about the billions of dollars thrown away by needy families who participate in state lotteries and bet at the race tracks and other sports events.

My father and mother were both devoted Christians from childhood. My mother, Charlotte Huff, was born in 1884 in Hastings, Nebraska, and came to Oregon with her parents, two sisters, and three brothers when she was in high school. After completing high school she taught for several years and then attended college—unusual for women of her generation. She graduated from Oregon Agricultural College (now Oregon State University) in Corvallis in 1912, with a major in home economics. Her application at age twenty-nine to a foreign mission society was, to her lasting regret, turned down, apparently because she was too old.

My father, George Nathaniel Taylor, was born in 1874 in Canisteo, New York. His father was a partner in a furniture factory, but he was forced to close the plant in Canisteo during the depression of 1884. Four years later he died of tuberculosis. Dad was the oldest child, with a brother and two sisters. He was a student body leader, but he dropped out of high school to help support the family after his father's untimely death. My grandmother took a job as a maid in a wealthy home, quite a shock, no doubt, after being the wife of a well-to-do manufacturer.

As a young man, my father became a traveling salesman, selling windmills, screen doors, and windows. At one point in his early career he wrote advertising copy for various patent medicines.

Dad's custom as a salesman was to refrain from traveling on Sundays and to stay in a hotel wherever he was and attend church (preferably Presbyterian). On Wednesdays he always went to the local prayer meeting. It was at a prayer meeting in the Congregational Church in Corvallis that he met my mother. He was forty years old at the time, and she was thirty. Soon his bachelor days ended as he and Mother were married in 1914.

In Dad's travels before marriage he had noticed as he visited churches along the way how little money was going to foreign missions. Also, most of the support for the annual budget seemed to come from the wealthy, but little from the average member. Dad kept thinking about this and wondered if it would help to have all the members of each church sign up at the beginning of the budget year to make a pledge for that year. The more he thought and prayed, the better the idea seemed, but what could he, an unknown traveling salesman, do about it?

Dad met with a denominational official and sold him on the idea. It was eventually passed up the ladder, and Dad was invited to meet with Henry P. Crowell, chairman of the Quaker Oats Company and one of the most influential and respected Presbyterian laymen of his day. They became friends, and Mr. Crowell accepted Dad's idea and carried it to the Presbyterian hierarchy. It was put into practice across the nation under Dad's title, "The Every-Member Campaign." Giving rose dramatically, and foreign missions were given a great boost.

I mention this about my dad because his was a creative idea formed through observation of a need and prayer as to how to meet that need. I feel that I inherited some of this gift of being able to observe a need, analyze it, pray, and act.

Somewhere along the line Dad felt called to be a pastor. He was not seminary trained, but he was an ardent Bible student, spending hours every week reading his worn Scofield Reference Bible and checking out the notes and references. He was, in fact, one of the most knowledgeable people I have known in Bible doctrine, as well as in pious living in the best sense of the word. Dad was ordained by the United Presbyterian Church in Kenton, Oregon, on May 8, 1919—my second birthday.

I don't think Dad was any better than average as a preacher, but he was liked for his friendly manner. I do recall that Mother used to tell him not to scold in his sermons and not to talk so loudly. Although he wore a formal Prince Albert coat in the pulpit, he was informal and folksy in his preaching. He was, in summary, a man of God whom I greatly loved and admired. His influence on me has been profound throughout my life. I've often regretted that my children didn't know him until he came to live with us in his eighties, when he had become forgetful and eccentric.

Strangely enough, I do not remember my mother as clearly as I do my father. She was serious but not severe, thoughtful, quiet, and pleasant. She too was an active Christian and much loved by her Sunday school class of high-school girls.

Dad was always strong for using "the eye gate," as he called it, along with "the ear gate." By this he meant that people remember more of what they see than what they hear. He used this principle in his chalk talks in Sunday schools.

He drew a line down the center of a blackboard, with a cross in the middle. As he talked about heaven, he wrote the word "Heaven" on one side and added such words as "Angels," "Happiness," "God," and "Love." On the other half of the blackboard he wrote "Hell," "Sin," "Satan," "Death," and similar dark words. He asked this question: "Which side do you want to be on? Jesus died on the cross for you. Do you want

Him as your Savior, to give you all the good things and save you from the evil ones?"

Then Dad announced his own choice—he would choose for Jesus—and wrote his initials on the "Heaven" side of the board. He offered the chalk to any others who wanted to put their names there. Over the years, many children did this, and I was one of them.

Another approach my father used in personal evangelism was to ask, "When is your birthday?" Using the month and day, he opened a Gospel of John (or his worn pocket Testament) to the chapter and verse determined by the birth date. My birthday, for example, is May 8. May is the fifth month, so he opened to the fifth chapter of John and pointed out verse 8. He read it to me and talked about it. John 5:8 says, "Jesus saith unto him, Rise, take up thy bed, and walk!" (KJV). It is part of the story in which Jesus heals a man who had been bedridden for thirty-eight years.

Dad pointed out to me that the story involved much more than the healing of the man's paralysis. There was also the great miracle of his standing unassisted and walking without the trial and error of learning, after long, long years of lying still. He made the application that Jesus had not only forgiven my sins and healed my broken relationship with God, but He could help me walk all the way, throughout my whole life. And Dad was right!

I did not inherit my father's ability for sharing his faith. Perhaps this is not something that is inherited. Is personal evangelism a special gift given by our Lord to some more than to others? I do not know.

I remember so well the time many, many years later, when I attended a Campus Crusade seminar for business people. After my arrival, I found out to my horror that part of the program was to leave the conference grounds, go out and find someone, and tell him or her the good news that Christ died for our sins and redeemed us for heaven. I almost literally clenched my teeth to make myself carry out the assignment. I started out across a nearby park to find someone I could talk to, hoping against hope that no one would be there—but of course, someone was!

A young black man was sitting on the ground, leaning against a tree, so I went over and sat down beside him and tried to open a conversation with a few comments about the weather. He didn't make much response to my overtures. Finally I took courage and asked him if he ever read the Bible. He said no, so I told him some things it says, especially its promises to those who believe. He was somewhat interested, but not to the point of making a life-changing decision. When I left him I had mingled emotions: sadness because of his little chance for happiness, hope that the tiny seed I had planted would grow, and elation that I had carried out a hard task. That was, in fact, a turning point in my life. I had discovered that telling strangers about our Lord was not an impossible thing for me to do, and after that it became less intimidating— though never easy.

My father set a wonderful example not only in his character and in telling others about Christ, but also in the field of journalism. Another early memory is of Dad sitting at the typewriter, writing and rewriting what he called his "ad copy." Each week he wrote an interesting five-inch, single-column ad and placed it in the *Queen Anne News*. There was always a tantalizing headline of the "Man Bites Dog" variety, then he would share the gospel in clear, easy-to-understand terms. He ran these ads in the format of news stories on the sports page, because he was trying to reach men. He paid for the ads out of his tithe. It took him two or three hours each week to write his message and then boil it down so that the gospel advertisement was no longer than five inches when printed. This involved much scratching out and revising. I suppose I began to learn the art of writing by observing him at work.

Later he enlarged this ad ministry to a string of weekly newspapers in Oregon and Washington. He continued his newspaper evangelism until shortly before his death, thirty-five years later. After the first few years the ads were paid for by wealthy friends.

My father's model of reaching out to the general public with the gospel through journalism made its mark on me. One of my growing aspirations after college would be to become a Christian journalist. I remember Dad used to say to me, "If the Apostle Paul were alive today, he would use the newspapers to reach the millions." I believe he was right.

Chapter 2
School Days

WHEN I WAS seven years old we moved from Seattle to Beaverton, Oregon. Dad had accepted a position as fund-raiser for Albany College, a Presbyterian institution at that time, located near Portland. He also became the part-time pastor of the Beaverton Congregational Church.

Beaverton was a town of twelve hundred, and its board sidewalks were quite a curiosity to us city children. The Denney family lived a block away. Mrs. Denney had been one of Mother's best friends in their college days. Four of the six Denney children were close to our ages, and we quickly became good friends. They had a four-passenger platform-swing in the backyard, the kind with seats facing each other. By pushing with our feet against the suspended platform, we could propel the swing to delightfully alarming heights.

The Denneys had a cow and some chickens. We bought milk from them at ten cents a quart and eggs at eleven cents a dozen. A dime in the 1920s was worth more than a dollar today, so prices haven't changed all that much!

My eighteen-year-old cousin Phil from Idaho came to live with us for several months one autumn and winter, to go to a business college in Portland. His capacity for fun, his character, and his stability were a model to me, his much younger cousin. Despite his advanced age he managed to play hide and seek and similar games with us youngsters—especially when a girl closer to his age occasionally joined us! The open heart and open house attitude of my parents was a good heritage and example for me in future years, one that I, in turn, have helped to pass along to my own children.

We had some rabbits in hutches in the backyard, with a new litter of six to nine bunnies twenty-eight days after the does were mated. A few months later we butchered the young rabbits. Some we ate, and some we sold to neighbors at fifteen cents a pound. I don't know whether Dad got us into the rabbit business to help the family budget or to teach us the elements of business as we bought grain and hay to feed them. Perhaps it was to teach us "the facts of life," as we placed the bucks with the females to mate. Rabbit raising was a good experience, except on Saturdays, when we had to clean out the hutches.

The Barnum and Bailey Circus came to Portland every year. My parents would take us to see it, though some of my friends weren't allowed to go. Their parents considered the circus to be evil, perhaps because of the skimpy clothing of the female performers and because of the life-style of the crew. We heard a rumor that kids could get free tickets by carrying pails of water to the elephants, but we lived too far away to be able to take advantage of that opportunity.

My childhood days were relatively good days for public morality. Movies were free of profanity and explicit sex, divorce was rare, the magazines at Dean's Drug Store were clean. True, one of the stores in town carried dime novels, which we were not allowed to read. Illegal drugs were unknown in our small town. In those Prohibition days alcohol was not used very much, at least in our community, although we knew about the speakeasies in Portland, where liquor could be bought.

I never experimented with smoking and was shocked one day when I was in my early teens and my mother remarked, "I hope you boys never learn to smoke." I was appalled! How could she even dream that I would betray her in that way?

We didn't yet know the full extent of tobacco's devastating effects on heart and lungs. Nevertheless, I remember my father's statement that every cigarette smoked was a nail in one's coffin. There seemed also to be some spiritual basis for the taboo in our home and our church, although when I once asked my pastor why it was wrong to smoke, his answer was vague. But now we have statistical evidence to reinforce the argument that our bodies, which belong to Christ, should not be unnecessarily endangered.

I listened on the radio to the championship fights of Jack Dempsey and Gene Tunney and to the gently ethnic humor of "Amos 'n' Andy." I think I had quite a normal childhood.

Ballroom dancing was the rage of the day, but our church and my family were dead set against it. Square dancing was permitted by some churches, although it might be called "folk games" to avoid the use of the word "dancing." As a prepubescent child I couldn't follow all the emotions of the argument, but it seemed clear to me that someone's wife should not be in another man's arms, and that it was wrong for unmarried folks to be enjoying physical contacts that, it was explained to me, were to be saved for marriage. Maybe my parents overdid this part of my moral education—though I really don't think so, for they may have saved me from a lot of potential evil. I remember my dad's prayer that God would save his boys from "the moment of sin that could ruin their entire lives." At the time I didn't know what he meant, but God did, and He answered the prayer.

How quickly conditions have changed during my lifetime. During my high-school days I didn't know a single instance, or even hear a rumor, of a girl's dropping out of school because of pregnancy, let alone having an abortion or staying in school until full term, as often happens today. I suppose there must have been students who were immoral, but I heard no talk of such things. Divorce was exceedingly uncommon, and I don't remember any schoolmate whose parents went through that experience.

At our home we had family Bible reading and a prayer time each morning before we left for school. Dad always encouraged us to read the Bible for ourselves, too, and to do it every day. I remember how earnestly he told us, "If you boys don't get God's Word deep into your hearts and do what it tells you to, you'll never amount to much for God." I knew he was right, but the Bible was hard to understand, since we had only the King James Version in those days, and its seventeenth-century language was strange to my ears.

Doug possessed a spiritual depth that was sometimes an embarrassment to me at school. He had declared from age six that he was going to be a missionary in Tibet. In the classroom he sometimes bowed his head and closed his eyes, and even from my seat across the room I could tell he was praying about something. Fortunately, no one else noticed. But one morning our teacher came over to my desk while Doug had his eyes closed and asked me if he was ill. I gulped and said his eyes were probably hurting him. She let it go at that, and so did I!

Honesty in an autobiography is necessary, so I must add another childhood memory that doesn't please me, because it indicates a character trait of covetousness that in one form or another has often plagued me through the years. We were on a vacation trip—Mother, Dad, Doug, and I—and had stopped for lunch on a farm owned by a friend of my father. The farmer suggested that Doug and I try our luck fishing for trout in the stream near the house. He outfitted us with poles, hooks, and bait and showed us where to stand. So we stood, and stood, and stood. Finally I tired of the sport and quit, grumbling. Doug kept on while I played around. Suddenly Doug had a fish on his line and triumphantly pulled in a beautiful ten-inch brown trout! The prize was cooked for Doug's lunch. He generously offered me a piece, but I, sulking over his success, refused it!

Once when we were on a family vacation on an island in Puget Sound, Doug and I found a raft on the beach in front of our rented cottage. We enjoyed paddling and poling it near the shore, but we suddenly realized that we were getting out too far from the beach. Mother was on the shore, calling us to come in. We tried to paddle the raft toward shore but didn't make much progress, for the tide was going out, and we and our raft were going with it, out to sea. Mother waded out as far as she could, swam the rest of the way, and finally reached us. She was exhausted on arrival, but after resting a bit against the edge of the raft, she began slowly swimming it ashore, where we eventually arrived in good condition. Even after so many years I'm grateful to God for her safe arrival at the raft and her strength to get us back to the beach.

The next day another crisis occurred. Doug and I went along the shore to where a wooded hill jutted out across the wide beach. We climbed to the top and after an hour of playing went back down—only to discover the beach wasn't there! The tide had come in and we were trapped. But scarcely had we discovered our plight when we saw our rescue team. Mother, in her fashionable knee-length bathing suit, was working her way toward us through the water along the edge of the hill, and Dad, who was not a swimmer, scrambled overland through the brush. They had realized our plight before we did and set out to find us. Soon a relieved and happy family was making its way along the top of the hill to a place beyond the water's reach where we could climb down to the beach again. Later I would reflect upon the apt parallel between that experience and God's plan to rescue us even before we knew we were lost.

My interest in missions came early, because missionaries came frequently to the church my father pastored. Some were from Africa, China, or South America, and some from American home mission organizations. One man I especially remember was speaking in churches to raise money for the survivors of the Turkish slaughter of the Armenians. Entire Armenian villages in some areas of Turkey had been wiped out as the people tried to flee but were cut down by the swords and guns of mounted horsemen. We children in the Sunday school were glad to give our dimes and to be led in prayer for refugees.

I don't remember how our family heard about some missionaries in India at a place called Dolebe Hill, but we prayed for them every day at family devotions. Then a most unfortunate thing happened. Dad wrote a letter to the missionaries there, telling them that our family prayed for them regularly. After a long time Dad got a letter back with a lot of strange-looking foreign stamps. He opened it at the family prayer time and read it to himself. He seemed confused and wouldn't read it to the family for awhile, but finally he did. The missionary was very abrupt and said not to write him anymore unless we sent some money with the letter—even a dollar would have helped—and that they didn't have time to write to people like us. Dad said, "Pshaw," which I think was the closest he ever came to profanity. The rest of our family kept on praying for them for awhile, but I didn't, and finally everybody just quit.

Fortunately, that one sour experience didn't negate the logic of being concerned about the world's need for the gospel. Out of those early experiences of contacts with missionaries who visited our church, there developed a longing to help them and to spread the good news about our Lord. It was probably that childhood exposure to missionaries that became fertile soil for various missionary projects with which I became involved in later years. And no doubt those early influences helped guide Doug into his long and fruitful career as a medical missionary in Africa.

A school playground incident when I was in the fourth grade helped me lose some of my timidity. The school bully had spread fresh manure from a nearby pasture on the door-knob of the girls' entrance to the school, and my brother, the moralist, told him he shouldn't have done it. Angered, the bully challenged Doug to a fistfight after school. But there was a rule at our house that the preacher's boys shouldn't get into fights, so I was surprised at Doug's nonchalance. He countered with an offer of a wrestling match. I was scared for him, but he declared that he was as old and as big as the other boy and should be able to pin him.

Quite a crowd gathered for the big event, and they went at it. Doug quickly got on top and was ready for the pin when the other boy gave a great push, struggled to his feet, clenched his fists, and demanded, "Get up here and fight like a man."

Doug walked away. Some of the spectators called him a coward, but some supported his protest of the sudden change of rules. Something important happened to me that day, and I began to be less fearful of physical harm.

Still, not long afterwards, when a boy who was mad at me challenged me to a fight, I refused. He called me a preacher's kid and spat in my face. I can still remember the humiliation of wiping off the spit as I walked away.

When the Congregational Church called a full-time pastor, we had to move from the parsonage. For five hundred dollars Dad bought a wooded acre a couple of miles east of Beaverton. He paid a contractor four thousand dollars to build a modest, six-room house. Now Doug and I walked a quarter of a mile to catch a school bus for our last two years of grade school and all through high school.

I went to Sunday school, as did most of the children in our

town and countryside, and I experienced some strong spiritual growth as a result. My Sunday school teacher was Mr. Doty, and I owe much to him. If this is being read by a discouraged Sunday school teacher, let me encourage you. You may be affecting young lives in ways you'll never know.

One Sunday Mr. Doty introduced Mr. Nunn from the Pocket Testament League, who told us how much good it would do us if we read the Bible every day. We all thought it was a great idea, and when he offered a free New Testament to any boy or girl who would promise to read it daily, we all lined up and got copies from him. I read some of it that afternoon, but it was hard to understand. Nevertheless, I kept trying to keep my promise of daily reading, but I think I broke my vow about 300 of the next 365 days!

My difficulty became especially acute when I finally got out of the narrative section—the four Gospels and the book of Acts—into Romans and the other Epistles. The sentence structure was often twisted and the meaning obscure, and it was just hard work to read. I didn't get very much out of it. Yet my parents and Doug seemed to have no such problems and even reveled in the reading. I thought it was normal for my mother and father to enjoy it, because they had been reading it all their lives, but it made me jealous and almost angry that Doug was getting so much more from his regular Bible reading than I was from mine.

Doug was both an exasperation and a model to me spiritually. An example of this occurred one summer when we were young teenagers, and Dad decreed that Doug and I spend two hours a day, except Sundays, clearing trees and brush from the back of our acre. I enjoyed the work, especially when we dynamited the stumps of the trees we had chopped down for our wood-burning furnace. As I look back on it, I am amazed that my parents let us handle and use the dynamite, especially the little copper caps half-full of ignition powder that could blow a hand off. The caps were crimped with pliers onto the black fuse (and sometimes, in youthful bravado when schoolmates were around, crimped with my teeth!).

We bored a narrow hole down beneath the stump, using a special auger. The next step was to cut a slit in the stick of dynamite and press the copper cap, attached to a foot of fuse, into the dynamite. Then we put the dynamite stick into the hole beneath the stump, lit the fuse with a match, and ran!

One morning I was eager to get our two hours of work behind us before starting out on a hike with Doug through woods and fields to Rainy Mountain, a few miles away. Doug, however, insisted on having his personal Bible reading and prayer time first. Well, I got mad! That was carrying religion a bit far. I still don't know whether I was really so impatient to get going on the day's work, or whether I was impatient with myself and frustrated because I had so much trouble keeping at my daily devotions while Doug didn't. I complained to Mother, but she was unsympathetic with my plight and told me to leave him alone. It seemed as if everybody in the family got along better with God than I did.

Actually, Bible reading continued to be a frustration to me for many years. I went to a Christian college and had the same problem there. I took the required Bible courses, read the assignments, and got reasonably good grades on the lectures, but devotional reading was always difficult. Moreover, my college roommate, Tom Lindsay, heading for the Presbyterian ministry, had a regular daily Bible reading program, and this too made me upset because he seemed to enjoy it! He was a constant reminder to me of my own failure in this regard, though also a help to me by making me realize the error of my ways.

When I was eleven years old I began to wish for a younger brother or sister, and one day I spoke about it to my mother. Since I raised rabbits, I suppose I thought reproduction was a simple matter. It may or may not have been because of my request, but a few months later Mother told Doug and me that we would be having a baby in the family sometime that summer. Mother was forty-five years old, but I didn't realize then that she was past the usual age for bearing a child. I happily looked forward to the baby, as we all did.

One evening early in August, Mother said the time had come, and she and Dad left for the hospital in Portland. That night Doug and I slept on blankets out in the backyard. Early the next morning Dad wakened us to say we had a baby brother named Lyman Waldo.

For the next five years, until Doug and I left home for college, Lyman was an important part of all our lives. He remembers that as soon as he was able to tag along after Doug and me, we tolerated his presence pretty well! We missed a good bit of his childhood when we were in college. But despite the age difference, we enjoyed our little brother.

I don't know exactly when I became a Christian, but I remember when I made a public affirmation of my belief. One Sunday night at the church youth meeting when I was perhaps twelve years old, Mr. Doty, the sponsor of the group, asked us if we were sure we were Christians. He reminded us that each of us needed to make a personal decision about accepting Jesus Christ, who had died for our sins. He asked if we remembered when we had made "the big decision," as he called it, and I didn't. He suggested that if we wanted to be sure we had done so, or wanted to do it then, to stand up. So I stood up along with several others. This public testimony was an important event in my life.

Doug and I went to a church youth camp for a week one summer. It wasn't too much fun, though, because the main recreation each afternoon was a game of softball. Softball wasn't popular in Beaverton, and we had rarely played it. One afternoon one of the counselors, a pastor, was picking the mixed teams of boys and girls. Doug and I were chosen last because we had played so poorly the previous day. Two more girls were needed to balance one of the teams, so he used us to fill the quota, remarking that we didn't play much better than the girls anyway!

Actually, I think he was angry with us for arguing with him at the Bible class that morning about whether or not the Bible was true. He didn't think so, and I suspect our arguments were not well thought out. He also told the class that the italics in the Bible were at places where wormholes had obliterated the text in the original manuscripts, and the translators had to guess what words had been written there! But Dad had once explained to us all about translating, so we knew the counselor was wrong.

When I was in the eighth grade, Grandmother Taylor come to live with us for awhile. Grandmother was about seventy-five years old and had been a widow for many years. She had lived with my Aunt Bertha in Chicago and then for a few years with my Aunt Ruth and Uncle Claude. Now it was our turn to have her with us.

I liked Grandma Taylor a lot. She had a lively sense of humor, and she seemed reasonably happy in our home. I did notice, though, that she was inclined to intrude somewhat into the discipline of her grandchildren. Once when Doug and I were leaving the house to attend a party at church she said, "Well, be good and you'll be lonesome," which my mother found a bit shocking. Grandma often took subtle digs at Mother, who never acknowledged them, and there was no real camaraderie between the two women.

When Doug and I were in college, Grandpa Huff, my mother's father, came to live with us. There wasn't room for both grandparents, so Grandma Taylor returned to Aunt Bertha's to live.

Grandpa Huff was in his seventies when he came to us. He

had been a farmer for many years. He was a gambler at heart, my father said, and had made several bad business decisions. Now, in his final years, he had nothing left. I recall one of the events that led to his financial ruin. Doug and I were in eighth grade and spent a few days on Grandpa's farm, which was primarily a cherry orchard. The picking had begun, and on the evening of our arrival a truckload of beautiful cherries had gone to the nearby cannery.

But the following day a well-dressed young man from the cannery came to talk to Grandpa. When the man drove away, Grandpa was very angry. He called together the thirty or forty pickers and told them that no more cherries would be picked because the cannery said there were worms in them.

So the crop rotted on the trees, and the farm disappeared into the hands of the bank. Grandpa had taken a chance on getting a bigger profit by not spraying the trees. He saved the cost of the spray, but lost everything in the gamble. I have a lot of sympathy for Grandpa Huff because I've made some disastrous business decisions during my lifetime. The temptation to take dangerous risks should be recognized for what it is, and one should use safeguards, such as seeking counsel from competent advisers.

While Grandpa was living with us, he wasn't physically strong enough to help in our backyard garden, and I don't think he was interested in helping around the house. So he sat in a chair in the living room or in the front yard, dozing most of the time, maybe thinking back on his busy farm days and perhaps reproaching himself for the business mistakes that had left him penniless.

Grandpa never spoke about religion. He had no apparent interest in the church and never attended services with us. During our family prayer times, when it was our custom to kneel by our chairs after breakfast, Grandpa sat with unbowed head and open eyes. Each of us prayed short prayers except

Dad, whose prayers were longer and tended to cover the world, the political situation in Washington, the Union Gospel Mission meeting he was to lead that night, his sons' future, ethics and morals in general, and all the missionaries he knew. Through it all, Grandpa sat erect, making a clicking sound from time to time with his teeth. He never spoke against the church, but given my youth and my reticence to discuss religion—especially with Grandpa—I never asked him what he was thinking and how he felt.

All of the Ten Commandments were taken very seriously in our home, including the observance of Sunday. On that day we didn't go to the store, the gas pumps, or to work, nor did we even shine our shoes (that was done on Saturday evening). Sports, swimming, and lawn mowing were not done on that day. I recall that though I was our high school's star miler and county champion, I once had to miss a track meet because it was held on Good Friday. Taking walks, automobile rides to make Sunday afternoon visits to friends, reading, and board games were on the approved list. No one talked much about these rules; it was just understood that some things we did on Sunday and some things we didn't do. One very hot Sunday afternoon when we were camped on the shores of a lake, my father suggested that we go to the beach and cool off by going for a "quiet swim." I remember being shocked by his violation of one of the traditional taboos.

Chapter 3
High School

DURING THE SUMMER before Doug and I started high school, we were full of anticipation. My father insisted that I take both Latin and public speaking, so I bought a used Latin textbook before school started. A previous owner had expressed his own misgivings about the subject by writing inside the front cover the familiar lament:

> Latin is a dead, dead language,
> As dead as dead can be.
> First it killed the Romans,
> And now it's killing me!

Dad had a friend named Harry West who was a millionaire. "He has a daughter named Margaret who will be in your class," Dad said. "Be sure to look her up and get acquainted."

I wondered what the daughter of a millionaire would be like, but in the rush of activities during the first days of school I forgot about her.

Several days later I asked a friend if he knew who Margaret West was. He pointed her out to me; she was sitting in the next row a few desks away. Even from a distance she seemed very nice—and she was pretty, too—so I went over to get acquainted."Are you Margaret?" I asked her. "I'm Ken Taylor, and my father and your father are friends."

She hadn't heard about me from her father, but thirteen-year-olds don't stand on ceremony, so it didn't matter.

That night I reported to my father that I had accomplished my errand, and it crossed my mind that it had, after all, been a rather pleasant duty to fulfill. Later Dad told me that Margaret's father was no longer a millionaire, because he had made some bad investments in those depression days of the early 1930s.

Doug and I waited for the school bus at a gas station near our home, where the friendly proprietor let us use his office as a waiting room. He was a would-be writer, and once while he was outside pumping gas, I read a few pages from a manuscript on his desk. It made my hair stand on end. I think this must have contained about as racy a bedroom scene as publishing standards of the time allowed. My innocent mind was badly sullied for a long time afterwards. I am sorry for young people today who have that kind of thing paraded before them continually via books, TV, records, videotapes, and movies.

Both of my parents expected and encouraged Doug and me to do our best in school, and we worked hard to perform up to their expectations. I enjoyed my classes and got good grades, often straight *A*'s. This meant that I got a blue report card instead of the usual white one that most of the students got. Since the cards were passed out in the study hall, everyone could observe who got the blue ones, and they could either envy or congratulate the recipients. An even more tangible reward was that a blue card entitled the student to a day off from school and to be excused from taking final exams.

I was motivated by competition with my brother, who habitually received blue cards too, and with other friends, including Margaret West. The algebra class was one of my favorites, partly because I enjoyed math, and partly because I could stand beside Margaret when the class was sent to the black-board to work out a problem.

During my freshman year and the following summer, I grew several inches in height, and Coach Warren thought I was a prime candidate for the football squad. But, much to my disappointment, Dad would not agree. He had read reports of permanent injuries and even deaths from football accidents, and he didn't want me to take the risk, minimal as it was. It didn't occur to me to argue and try to change his mind, as he and I both assumed he knew best. Thinking back on this, I wish I had had this opportunity for rough-and-tumble team competition. I think it would have helped me get acquainted with another side of life—vigorous physical competition plus team loyalty and interdependence.

One morning I learned that a two-mile cross-country race was being organized for the lunch hour that day. Several of my friends were going to run, so I decided to try it too. I had never done any competitive running before, and this was long before jogging was a popular exercise, but it sounded like fun. I borrowed a pair of gym shoes that fit fairly well, and at the crack of the gun I was off, running through brush, around trees, and on country roads. We were to circle around the designated course and finish at the football field. To my complete surprise, I came in first, and Coach Warren promptly invited me to try out for the mile run on the track team. I made the team and won my full share of points in the track meets with other schools.

Only a few weeks into my freshman year I had heard about a Saturday night Bible study for high schoolers at the home of Mr. and Mrs. Gordon Fraser. Doug wanted to go and check it out, and I went along. A dozen or more of us were there, welcomed graciously by Mrs. Fraser and stimulated spiritually by Mr. Fraser's thoughtful, well-presented exposition of Bible prophecy. I found it especially enjoyable because my new friend Margaret West was there. For all these reasons, in whatever order, I became a regular at the weekly meetings.

After a few months the class grew too large to be accommodated in the Frasers' small living room, so we began meeting in the more spacious McMinn residence. Mr. and Mrs. McMinn were quite different in temperament—she vivacious and he very quiet—but they were as one in their devotion to the Lord and in their desire to serve Him.

We young people greatly enjoyed being in their tastefully decorated home, which was surrounded by Mrs. McMinn's carefully maintained rock garden. She had a charming Tennessee accent, never before heard in my little world, and Mr. McMinn's warm, smiling silence ministered to us even apart from the teaching ministry.

Who can forget the vivid impressions of those happy times of fellowship, learning, singing, and enjoyment—and the hot cider and doughnuts afterwards? I cannot even estimate the great value those evenings had in my spiritual growth and outlook. Besides the teaching by devoted adults, the knowlege that other kids our age loved the Lord was a stabilizing influence in our constant struggle to relate to God and to the indifferent world around us. I feel sure that next to the guidance of my childhood home and my own parents, this weekly gathering through four years of high school was among the highest, strongest influences in my life.

Not the least of the good things about the Bible study was that Margaret was there too. We enjoyed much conversation and bantering, and our acquaintance grew rapidly. This was boy-girl friendship at its best, with as yet little thought of romance.

One Christmas, following a party, the young people walked to a home a few blocks away for refreshments. Margaret and I lagged behind the others. I enjoyed being with her and I especially remember "helping" her across some wet spots on the pavement by holding her hand as we jumped!

One day I was out of school with a high fever. This was very unusual for me, as I was seldom sick. Mother solicitously provided hot soup and sympathy throughout the day. The young people were going to have a social at church that night, but I felt too ill to attend. When Doug came home from school in the afternoon, he gave me all the news of the day, including the fact that Bob Denney had invited Margaret to the social. I became more and more depressed about missing the party. It wasn't that I objected to her going with Bob, for our friendship hadn't progressed to the point where I had any exclusive claim on her company, but I felt sad that I wouldn't be there to enjoy being near her.

The more I thought about it, the less ill I felt, and I finally decided I was able to go. Shakily, I got out of bed, took a shower, and got dressed just as Mother arrived with more soup. I suppose she wasn't deceived by my insistence that I felt much better and was able to go to the party, but true to my parents' usual way of never referring to our interest in girlfriends, she didn't comment. I went to the party and actually did feel better and better as the evening progressed.

Because of Dad's insistence, I reluctantly agreed to take a class in public speaking. I suppose he insisted on it because he knew its importance from his preaching experience.

"Sure, it's useful," I agreed as we talked about it, "but it makes me nervous to get up in front of people and talk to them."

"I know, Son," he said, "but you'll be more useful to the Lord if you learn to do it well."

"Some people have the talent for speaking and some don't," I objected.

"If you don't, you can learn," was his final word as he put an end to the discussion.

So I found myself in Mr. Webb's public speaking class, with several other scared students. As it turned out, Dad was wrong in thinking I would get over my nervousness, but entirely right in knowing that public speaking is a useful art, whether the speaker is comfortable or not.

Mr. Webb asked Doug and me and some of our friends to try out for the freshman debate squad, and soon we were deeply involved in the issues of the day, such as "Should chain stores be abolished?" and "Should the United States join the League of Nations?"

Mr. Webb's policy was to have us debate both sides of a question, sometimes taking the negative side and sometimes the affirmative. "You need to develop the arguments on both sides so you will know what the other team is going to say before they say it," he insisted.

Debating was one of the highlights of my high-school years. The freshman-sophomore squad debated mostly among ourselves, but in my junior year I was on the varsity squad, participating in debates with other schools throughout the county and district. My partner that year was Ivan Bierly, a seasoned debater from the senior class. He was a marvelous colleague in every way—intelligent, perceptive, a convincing speaker, and a born leader. I learned much from him, and together we won many debates and tournaments and were applauded as much for our forensic prowess as the athletic teams were for their skills.

In my senior year Ivan had graduated, and I had a new debate partner—my friend Margaret. She had not had any prior experience in debating, but she was a leader, having been our class president and president of both the Torch Honor Society and the Girl Reserves. One Sunday afternoon I telephoned her to ask if I could come over and review some debate material with her, and she seemed happy to have me do this. The family car was in use, so I walked the two and a half miles. At her home, we sat in the library, poring over the debate material and discussing strategies. In the previous year Ivan and I had never found it necessary to compare notes very extensively, but with Margaret it seemed quite important!

Margaret Dickman was another favorite classmate. She was Ivan Bierly's girlfriend and was much fun to be with on debate trips and at speech contests, where she always captivated her audiences. The first semester of our senior year she and I vied for the honor of being elected student body president. This office was a high honor at our school. Since we had never had a girl president, I assumed I was to be the winner. To my chagrin, she won an easy victory. In those days to be beaten by a girl was a disgrace! But with her kind help I won the election the second semester.

A big event of each year was the district debate tournament and speech contest at Astoria, about a hundred miles away. A busload of debaters and speech class students went by school bus. Returning home that evening, with the tensions of the day behind us, everyone felt relaxed and playful. The girl sitting next to me dared me to get her shoe off. Of course, such a challenge could not be ignored, and the tussle began.

Unfortunately, I felt not only the high excitement of the chase but also some moral discomfort because of the emotions that accompanied physical contact with a pretty girl, so I let her win and boast about it to all our fellow passengers. Like all other boys at that age—and for many years afterwards—I found lust a difficult problem to deal with. It could happen without plan or intent at any moment.

I prayed many times for purity of mind, and no doubt prayer helped. But I helped myself, too, as best I could. As a young man and even after my marriage, I disciplined myself not to stare at attractive women and avoided situations where temptation would be hard to handle. I sometimes stood with my back to the sidewalk, staring into a store window, if a particularly attractive young woman was walking along ahead of me or coming toward me on the sidewalk. More than once I walked across the street to avoid the terrible lure of gazing, and even then I had to keep my eyes straight ahead to keep from glancing.

One particular oratorical contest turned out to be quite dramatic. Students from several schools were competing in the contest at the Grange Hall in Huber, a few miles from Beaverton. I had spent a lot of time planning and writing my oration before memorizing it. The theme was the moral disintegration of America, a topic that was important in the early thirties, after the Roaring Twenties. After giving facts and figures to prove my point, I reached the climax as I described a sturdy oak tree. I told of a storm that arose and how the huge tree fell. Upon examination the reason became evident. The core was rotted out, and impending death was hidden there for many years until suddenly, under the stress of the storm, the mighty tree toppled. The moral was, of course, that America still looked strong on the outside but was rotting away within, filled with corruption and disease, and it would eventually crash.

On the night I delivered my oration, a heavy storm swept the area. This was especially impressive because we so rarely had violent storms in Oregon. The wind howled and the rain fell in sheets upon the galvanized roof, producing a steady drumbeat. Just as I reached the climax of my speech, the part where the oak tree toppled with an earthshaking crash, a tremendous clap of thunder shook the Grange Hall and all the lights went out! Even as my gestures showed the tree's fatal collapse, a flash of lightning through the darkness illumined me there on the stage with outstretched arms, and at that moment the lights came back on. Great applause greeted me from the startled crowd, and I won the coveted award.

Shortly before graduation, our senior class party was an evening of roller-skating at a rink in Portland. While I was skating with Margaret, our skates tangled and we both fell. With brutal frankness she remarked that I skated like a horse.

Our first real date, if you can call it that, was for the debate banquet at the end of my senior year. Of course Margaret would be attending also, since she and I had been partners all year. Parents of the debaters were invited to the banquet too.

"Will your folks be there?" I asked her. She said they wouldn't.

"Want me to pick you up on the way?" I inquired.

"Sure," she replied. "What time?"

And so it was settled; I had a date. It might be more accurate to say that the family had the date, for Doug and my parents were going too. Doug had had the car that afternoon and was delayed in getting home. The time to call for Margaret came and went, and I was really pacing the floor. To be late for Margaret's and my first date seemed to me a terrible disaster.

Dad tried to soothe me. "Being patient is the hardest thing in the world," was his platitude as he observed my mounting concern. But his reassurance did nothing to ease my anxiety.

Doug finally arrived, fifteen minutes late, and we took off. Margaret was ready, looking beautiful and composed. She seemed a bit surprised at the carful of family, but my tension was eased by her cheerfulness and poise. It turned out to be a good evening.

While Margaret was important to me during high school, most of my recreation and companionship centered in my friendship with other boys. One of my best friends was Bob Denney. Bob was a classmate through high school and on through the first two years of college. Other good friends were Don Walker, Elman Johnson, Carson Murray, Marvin Stalder, Arnie Garnett, my debating partner Ivan Bierly, and, of course, my brother Doug. These and many other friends figure prominently in the good times I remember so well.

Bob was often the leader of our escapades and sometimes

caused me concern with his daring. At one of our church group's Saturday afternoon picnics at Roamer's Rest, a swimming and canoeing center on the Tualatin River, Bob discovered a diving board on a cliff twenty feet above the river. I watched in horror as he walked out to the end of the board and jumped in. He waved as he emerged and shouted for me to do the same. I was terrified of even the normal high-diving board at the swimming pool, and I couldn't imagine doing what Bob had just done. But peer pressure was powerful, so with a fluttering heart and a lump in my stomach that felt like ice, I walked to the end of the plank and stared wildly at the placid river below. Bob vigorously beckoned me on, but I hesitated—then turned around and walked back to safety, my stomach now sick for being chicken.

Another time Bob, Elman, and Charlie West decided on an exciting, harebrained scheme. They would take Elman's dad's new Hudson Supercharger to a railroad crossing, maneuver it around so the tires were on the tracks, then let out the air to soften the tires so they would stay on the rails. Then they would drive it down the tracks to the next crossing. I declined to be involved, partly because my parents wouldn't like the idea if they had known, and also because I couldn't imagine anything but total disaster for Mr. Johnson's car if a train came along and couldn't stop in time. Actually, the prank worked out fine, and then I wished I had been braver!

I had hoped to be class valedictorian that spring of 1934, but the class, with faculty approval, voted to have four speakers, including Margaret West, Margaret Dickman, and me. Margaret still remembers that the floor burns on her arm from our tumble at the skating rink were plainly visible because her graduation dress was sleeveless.

I used the speech about the oak tree for graduation night— though without nature's sound effects to assist me—and the next day the mother of one of my classmates insisted that my father must have written it because it was so good. What a blow!

High school graduation was a traumatic experience for me. The ceremony was held in the school gymnasium, and as a class speaker I sat on the stage. I looked out through the high window above the crowded bleachers, where the sun was setting in a crimson sky, and I felt that it was the end of the world—that life could never again be so sweet. But of course I learned, like most graduating seniors before and since, that the best was still ahead.

Chapter 4
Preparing for College

THE SUMMER AFTER graduation was a time of big decision about college. Whether to go to college wasn't the issue, nor even an option. My father had deeply felt his lack of education and credentials all his life, especially as a pastor. Like many others of his generation who had not been to college, he believed that college was a must for his children.

I had planned to go to Oregon State, but one Sunday evening a gospel team of athletes from Wheaton College in Wheaton, Illinois, came to minister at Central Bible Church, where our family had been attending for three years. I remember that two members of that gospel team were Grant Whipple and Harv Chrouser, men I would get to know well in years to come. They were an inspiring group and gave good testimonies about how and why they had become Christians. They encouraged young people in the congregation to consider sending in applications to attend their school. I didn't give it much thought because I wasn't interested in going to school "way back East," as we Oregonians thought of Illinois.

To my dismay, Doug sent for a catalog and soon made his decision to apply. At first I felt sort of abandoned, because from first grade through high school we had been in the same class. I finally decided to apply to Wheaton also, even though I was reluctant to leave the safe nest of home, friends, and familiar surroundings.

We soon received notification of acceptance by the college, along with the information that tuition was seventy-five dollars a semester. There were no men's dormitories, but rooms were available in private homes near the campus at weekly rates of $1.75 to $2.00 per person. We heard of other Wheaton College students in the Portland area and learned from them that the standard car-share expense to or from Wheaton was fifteen dollars per passenger, a reasonable amount in those days when gasoline cost only about twenty-three cents a gallon.

So Doug and I spent the summer of 1934 trying to raise the necessary money for the first year. We got jobs at thirty cents an hour working at an iris farm—hoeing, watering, planting, and digging bulbs to fill customer orders. I enjoyed working outside and was interested to see new hybrid varieties of iris being developed.

Doug told me of a conversation about the Lord he had had with the owner. He had invited Doug to come over for a spiritualist séance on a Sunday afternoon, where contacts were presumably made with the dead. Of course Doug didn't go, and he wrote our boss a long letter, telling him about the good news of Christ and the dangers of dealing with the occult.

Whenever I stopped work to get a drink of water, I noticed that the owner happened to come out of the office, and he saw me away from the wheelbarrow and hoe. One Saturday evening, as he handed me my eighteen-dollar paycheck (for six ten-hour days at three dollars a day), he told me I had been goofing off too much—walking around instead of working—and that I needn't come back on Monday. Getting fired was a blow to my pride, especially because I was a very conscientious worker.

Bob Denney, who also planned to go to Wheaton, got me a haying job on his uncle's farm. This was hard physical labor, making haystacks, then piling them onto the horse-drawn hay wagon. When the wagon was full, we drove to the barn, where a special hayfork lifted the hay up the outside of the barn and through a door under the eaves, dropping it to the haymow below. Later in the summer the work changed to picking up sheaves of wheat that came from the harvester and were left lying in the field. We pitchforked them onto wagons that took them to the threshing machine.

That was the beginning of summers in the hayfields for the next three years. The hours were long, and the work was hard, hot, and dusty. Baling hay was the hardest of the jobs. Wages began at nineteen cents an hour, but with experience and promotions we could progress to thirty-five cents. My job, with a partner, was to pitch the hay up to a platform on the baler, where another worker pushed it into a square hole. A mechanical chunker crushed the hay down into the hole and the compressed hay came out as a bale. Every half hour the pitching team would "rest" by trading places with the team carrying the 150-pound bales away and stacking them four high in the field. Half an hour later, back to pitching hay onto the baler platform!

My first day on the baler crew nearly became my last. By midmorning I was so exhausted that I didn't see how I could possibly keep going, but I couldn't think of quitting. To make matters worse, I showed poor judgment about the timing of lifting the hay to the platform. My experienced partner started to lift, but I didn't, deciding to wait a moment for the platform to be cleared of our previous deposit of hay. The sharp-eyed foreman, protective of every second, rushed over and bawled me out.

"Listen!" he roared at me. "You have an experienced partner there, and when he says 'lift,' you lift, or we'll get someone who will." I humbly agreed and have since thought it was some of the best advice I ever received. In a new situation, don't argue with old hands!

As that summer after high school drew to an end, our social life became more active. There were several farewell gatherings as we prepared to leave for nine long months. The church youth group, of which I was president, had a big going-away party, and so did the Saturday night Bible class. Special friends had their parents invite us for dinner, and I had to say good-bye to Margaret.

Our preparations for college were simple, since we had little to take besides our bedding and a few clothes. We shipped these ahead by freight train. Dad made arrangements with Alex Hamilton, a Wheaton College upperclassman who lived in Portland, for Doug, Bob Denney, and me to travel with him in his Model A Ford roadster—room for the driver and one passenger in the enclosed front and two more in the open rumble seat behind the rear window, out in the cold, heat, wind, rain, or dust. We all thought it sounded like fun.

The day finally came for the actual leave-taking. Dad and Mother were obviously upset—Mother quietly grave, Dad trying to act happy-go-lucky but doing poorly at concealing his feelings. When we got to Alex's house, we got our first look at the little roadster and realized just how small it was for the four of us. I recall that as we were loading the car, Dad walked to the end of the block and back, all alone, too upset to wait with us beside the car. Sensitive to his feelings, I knew he was crying out to God for his sons, committing us to God's mercies, not only for the trip to Wheaton but for the unknown future ahead of us.

We three passengers drew straws to see who had the privilege of spending the first hours in the rumble seat with our feet on the luggage and our knees uncomfortably close to our chins. Then the moment came, and we drove away. I can still see the family group bravely standing there, five-year-old Lyman vigorously waving good-bye.

Yes, good-bye to childhood. I knew life would never be the same again. I felt forlorn to be leaving behind forever the fun of high school days and the security of our wonderful home. I began to realize then what I have now finally accepted, that change is inevitable and each of us is essentially alone with himself—and with God—in his own changing world.

We drove the two-lane highways at thirty-five to forty miles per hour for much of the way, stopping only for gas and meals and continuing through the nights. We changed drivers every hundred miles and managed to enjoy the trip despite being crowded.

The first night of driving was especially beautiful, with a full moon and eerie landscape beside the mighty Columbia River and later the plains of eastern Oregon. I thought a lot about Margaret and was somehow comforted that she was seeing the same moon and perhaps thinking of me. Already I missed her, but I realized that what Dad had told me was likely, that one usually marries a college schoolmate, and high-school friends are seldom seen again.

After a couple of days and nights of sitting up in the car, trying to sleep, we all decided to look for a cheap hotel in the next town and try to get a few hours of rest. The usual rate for a room was fifty cents per person, and we thought we could afford that. We parked in front of a hotel, and Doug went in to inquire about the accommodations. He came back looking confused and told us the price was five dollars each—completely ridiculous. Finally it dawned on us naive country boys that we were in the red-light district! We hurried away and found a park beside the railroad tracks, stretched out on the ground, and were wakened only twice during the night by freight trains thundering by a few feet away.

At last our long trip ended as we entered the outskirts of the small town of Wheaton, population about seven thousand. Since it was too late in the day for the college offices to be open, we ate some sandwiches and slept all night in a woods bordering the highway. My poignant memory of that occasion is of hearing a song on the car radio: "Everybody Loves My Margarita." Margaret was two thousand miles away at her home, having had to postpone college for a year for financial reasons. I was already homesick and physically exhausted, and my spirits drooped to a new low.

In the morning we drove to the campus and found the registrar's and dean's offices, where we enrolled and got our room assignments. Doug, Bob, and I found ourselves a block away from the campus at the home of the Mackenzies—an elderly, godly couple who treated their student renters as guests and friends. The two-dollar weekly rate was reduced because the three of us roomed together.

Our college years had officially begun.

Chapter 5
First Years at
Wheaton College

ON CAMPUS we soon found several other students from Oregon, some from the state of Washington, and even more from California. We were certainly not the only ones who had made the long trip east to attend this famous Christian college. Our provincialism became clear to us at the first student prayer meeting when we heard testimonies from those who talked of coming "out west" to Wheaton. I think we had thought of Chicago and New York as being just a few miles apart; however, we found that some of our new eastern friends seemed not to have heard of anything west of Chicago! I was fascinated and delighted by hearing southern accents for the first time, especially when they came from pretty southern girls.

I found that many of my new schoolmates had a devotion to Christ far deeper than my own. At home I had been one of the spiritual leaders of our youth group. Now I was challenged to spiritual depths I knew little about, despite my godly background.

This sense of my spiritual need was intensified a few days later when the annual autumn evangelistic meetings were held, with lengthened times of daily chapel and a special preaching service each evening. Dr. Harry Ironside challenged us to lives of commitment and integrity, and I began to realize my need to commit my life to Christ with new intensity and to face pride, lust, and all manner of other inward sins. Privately confessing them in the prayer times, I asked God's help in cleaning them out. It wasn't, for me, an instant deliverance, but to be made freshly aware of these concerns of God regarding my life was salutary and a giant step of progress.

But there was one area of my life that I didn't open up to God for cleansing. I still had as a life goal to become rich and famous. Following Doug's example, I was on a premed track. He planned to be a medical missionary, but I saw the practice of medicine as a probable way to become rich.

Freshmen soon discovered the sophomore rule that they must wear distinctive caps, called dinks, at all times for two weeks when outside on the campus. This minor hazing was enforced by the sophomore kangaroo court. For men, the penalty for being caught without the dink was the "spat" machine, which meant crawling between the legs of a line of sophomore fellows who whacked the unfortunates as they passed through. The secret, as I found from experience, was to crawl fast enough that the sting was minimal.

The main event on Friday nights was attending one of the six literary societies—three for men and three for women. We freshmen found ourselves being invited to meetings and recruited for membership, and most new students soon joined the society of their choice. The meetings were a mixture of formality and fun. Everyone stood when the black-robed president of the society solemnly strode down the center aisle of the crowded room and gaveled the meeting to order. Members rotated each week in giving a devotional thought, an extemporaneous speech, or a humor number, or in taking part in a debate or leading the parliamentary drill using *Robert's Rules of Order* as our text.

I had enough money in hand from childhood savings and summer earnings to handle only part of the first year's costs. So I reported to the college employment office where Wheaton residents phoned in for students to mow lawns, put up storm windows, and do other odd jobs. But the year was 1934, and the Great Depression meant that more students needed jobs than there were jobs available. So I was grateful for each hour or two assigned to me.

Most of the students left campus to return home for the Christmas vacation. I was so homesick that I wrote in my diary I thought I would go bats. But driving home with other students would have cost fifteen dollars, and I had only seventy-eight dollars left for the rest of the year. I wondered if I should have stayed out of school for a year and earned more money. Our parents sent Doug and me five dollars each for Christmas, and Mr. Doty, our former Sunday school teacher, sent one dollar.

Doug and I picked up as much work as we could find and ate cold meals in our room at the Mackenzies'. We were grateful to spend a few days with Aunt Bertha and Grandma Taylor in Chicago and eat proper meals. When we returned to the campus, we found a large box of goodies for us from the McMinn Bible class—cake, cookies, cheese, jam, and candy—which we shared with Bob.

Probably Margaret had made some of the cookies. We were writing to each other every week. If her letter was a day late in arriving, I was well aware of it.

Our freshman class was high-spirited and enthusiastic, and we decided that instead of a *senior* class gift to the college, which was the custom, we would give a *freshman* class gift. Several of us went to talk to the dean about it, and he suggested building a gate at the west entrance of the campus. We were immediately off and running. I don't remember whether I volunteered or was otherwise appointed by the class officers to head up the program, but I eagerly took on the task. Gradually our ideas took shape, and we planned a beautiful stone gate, consisting of graceful, curving walls framing the main driveway leading to Blanchard Hall, Wheaton College's historic administration building.

With guidance from the business office, we got bids and selected an expert stonemason. One of our classmates who had some architectural experience prepared the drawings. We used the same Indiana limestone that had been used in building Blanchard Hall, and the finished product was a wonderful addition to the campus. When the gate was dedicated, we put a list of the class members, a freshman dink, and a copy of that week's college newspaper, the Record, into a blue Mason jar and sealed it behind the cornerstone.

When the gate was rebuilt fifty-four years later, some of my classmates and I had the fun of opening the cornerstone, taking out the jar, and finding everything in perfect condition!

The traditional football rivalry with nearby North Central College was intense. One night someone had the idea of several carloads of us driving over to Naperville, home of our arch-rivals, and tearing down their goalposts. I can't remember now why this appeared to be such a brilliant idea, but at the time it seemed clearly inspired, and the midnight raid took place.

The usual tension of rivalry at the game the next day was heightened by this goalpost incident. A few fists flew, resulting in penalties against both teams. I don't remember who won, but after the game our president, Dr. J. Oliver Buswell, and the president of North Central were in an animated and indignant discussion over some of the events of the game and were even shaking their umbrellas at each other. Seeing the two men arguing, I jauntily walked between them and pushed them apart with a cocky admonition, "Gentlemen, stop your fighting!" Then I fled into the safety of the crowd before President Buswell could more than glimpse my back!

When I tried out for the basketball team but didn't make it, I tried out for the wrestling squad, in the 165-pound class. I soon found that my enjoyment of the sport exceeded my skill. Still, I improved, and by my junior year I was able to earn my letter, but not easily. At the tryouts the day before the meets with other schools I usually lost to teammate Wes Berghouse, who had natural ability and strength. As a result I seldom represented the school in my own weight class except for a time or two when Wes was sick. For this reason I sometimes tried out at the 175-pound spot.

John Frame was our 155-pound man. Once when he had to be absent, the coach asked me to take off ten pounds and replace him. This proved difficult, since I was tall and slim, but by half starving for a week and sweating off the final pounds by climbing behind the asbestos-covered steam pipes in the boiler room of the heating plant, I barely made the weight by check-in time, an hour or so before the match.

A huge steak for lunch tasted good but was apparently too late to restore my strength. All I could do in the match was to keep crawling off the mat, dragging my opponent with me. Finally the referee called, "Wheaton, stay on the mat or forfeit," so I stayed and soon found myself staring at the ceiling, locked in the iron grip of my opponent. I heard the referee's fateful three slaps, announcing that I was pinned.

I learned a lot from the daily wrestling workouts. This individual sport, one against one, teaches the participant a lot about self-reliance and endurance in the face of painful weariness. He learns too about the necessity of long hours of preparation for a few crisis minutes of the actual match. I believe these lessons helped me in the task that lay in the yet-unknown future, the long hours and years of sitting at the translator's desk. A wrestler is also a member of a support team, even though the final competition is individual, and he has the encouragement of other members of the squad in success or in defeat.

The first year of college was a great adventure in broadening my outlook in many ways. I met students from almost every state in the union, and I was exposed to a variety of political opinions. I even sat in some bull sessions with fellows who thought President Franklin Roosevelt was a great man! This came as a surprise, because I had been brought up to believe that the welfare programs Mr. Roosevelt pushed through Congress threatened the work ethic that had made America great. I had been led to believe that the New Deal would destroy the moral fiber of the nation and bankrupt it economically.

At the inception of the Social Security system in 1935, I heard my father declare that the payout would far exceed the income, and the nation would find itself hundreds of millions of dollars in debt that it could never repay. What a prophet! But he was thinking too small. We did not foresee billions, let alone trillions of dollars of debt. Yet I don't know what he would have suggested that we do about those who are jobless, homeless, and hungry.

The fun-filled, exciting freshman year at Wheaton came to an end in June, and the obvious question was how to get a summer job. We could always go back to the Oregon hayfields, but I heard that some students had sold Thompson Chain Reference Bibles the previous summer and had made more than enough money to cover their expenses for the entire academic year. These students were soliciting other students to travel door-to-door in some of the southern states, and the financial aspect appealed to me. I attended one of the meetings held to explain the project to potential recruits. I wasn't deterred by the ten- to twelve-hour days, six days a week, for I faced that in the hayfields too, but I was indignant when I heard that part of the sales pitch was to disparage the Scofield Reference Bible, from which my Dad had—for good or ill—learned his theology.

I suspect that another equally powerful deterrent to my taking the job was my timidity about selling anything to anybody. This trait of personality or character has perplexed and disturbed me all my life, especially when I have wanted to witness to others about our wonderful Lord and all He has done for me. For whatever reason, I declined the opportunity and decided to go home for the summer. I looked forward to being home and particularly to seeing Margaret again.

Finding transportation to the West was the next task. Bob, Doug, and I decided to investigate the system known as "driveaways," whereby automobile dealers hired drivers to drive new cars from Detroit to dealers' showrooms in faraway cities. The three of us made arrangements to join a caravan going to Portland. We got a ride to Detroit with a fellow student and picked up our cars.

Most of the other fifteen drivers in the caravan were professionals, who spent all summer with the agency, driving to various cities and returning by bus to Detroit to start out again. They were a rough bunch, but our supervisor, Al, was a tough leader and tolerated little nonsense in driving. The cars stayed in line, with enough distance between us on the two-lane highways to allow faster-moving cars to pass us, one by one, and eventually get beyond the caravan.

At night, however, the drivers were less disciplined. We stopped at cheap hotels or campground cottages. We college students enjoyed a good night's sleep after long, hot days on the road, but the professional drivers were out on the town. One morning Al woke us about five o'clock and told us to hurry to our cars and be on our way. We learned that one of the drivers had raped a young woman and Al had spent the night paying off her parents and the sheriff. The sheriff let the fellow out of the local jail and told us to get out of town before some kind of vigilante group could swing into action!

That summer, like the rest of my college summers, was full

of hard work and long hours in the hayfields. We looked forward to occasional Saturday night picnics, campfires, and canoeing with friends from the Bible class still held at Mr. and Mrs. McMinn's home.

During my workday I rubbed shoulders with a class of men I had previously known little about. They were mostly unmarried men in their thirties, and their Monday morning reports of their weekend escapades made my hair stand on end. As a preacher's kid, brought up with other young people who didn't do that sort of thing, I had been protected from knowing very much about unregenerate human nature. These men seemed to have no thought for anything but sex, and no farmer's daughter was safe from their stares and vulgar comments.

Once when the crew spent the night in a hayloft, one man in particular kept us all awake with his dirty stories. I finally told him to shut up or I'd punch him. He didn't, so I did! It was probably fortunate for me a general fight didn't break out.

Through these experiences I learned a lot about the depravity of human beings, including myself, and I observed the danger of letting one's thought life be corrupted by exposure to the lusts of the flesh. Out of these experiences has come my aversion to pornography in every form—on the newsstand, in the movies, and the incessant exposure to soft pornography on TV. The other realization from that summer was that these men I was working with were just like me, and I was as they were except that God had been gracious to me in giving me a Christian home. I felt for them in their emptiness and the futility of their lives. And I realized that although they had no veneer, those of us who do are no better than they.

Thus my world opened up to a vision of the lostness of humanity in a way that had never occurred to me before. I have realized the truth of the statement, "There but for the grace of God go I."

The final evening before leaving again for college, I went

over to Margaret's house and we talked—about my personality and all the things wrong with me. I was the one who brought up the subject, and Margaret, instead of reassuring me, added to my sorrows by her agreement that I had a long way to go!

She was going to attend Oregon State College (now Oregon State University) that fall, and during our conversation that night she told me that, unlike the previous year, she was not going to write to me—something about "making new friends." We were sitting side by side on the kitchen counter, eating apple pie and talking, when Margaret's mother came in. She laughed and said, "I don't think you children can settle the world's problems tonight," and seemed to be suggesting that I go home, so I did. I was depressed because I wouldn't see Margaret again for nine months, and I think she was a bit sad too.

The two-thousand-mile trip back to college for my sophomore year was very interesting. Bob, Doug, and I put an ad in the Portland paper, offering to share expenses to Chicago, and a woman replied. Thinking she was a college-age girl, Dad was alarmed, for to him it was unseemly for unchaperoned fellows and girls to cross the country together. He was relieved to find that she was middle-aged. She was also, we soon found out, a terrible driver and a real battle-ax. She would let loose great strings of profanity whenever we had a flat tire or blowout, which was rather frequently. Once, while we were changing a tire, she became angry about something and picked up the tire iron and hurled it at me. Fortunately for me, I saw it coming and ducked, but unfortunately for her car, it left a body dent. This of course made her even more angry.

Because of her unsafe driving I suggested to Bob and Doug that we do all the driving, and they fervently agreed. When the tire was changed, I got behind the wheel and explained our decision to her. She ranted and raved but was helpless and finally huddled in the back seat, cursing at us. We were too young or at least too inexperienced to know how to probe her bitterness toward life or help her spiritually, though we lamely tried to. Somehow I think this experience made me aware in a new way of the vast world around me, where turmoil has no solution because God is unknown or ignored. From time to time through the years I have thought of that woman and her needs and then the millions, even billions, she represents.

The 1935 school year got off to a good start with the fall evangelistic service. These services were a great help to my spiritual growth all through the college years. Although they were called "evangelistic," they were for Christians, too, as the speakers aimed at the Christian majority, helping us grow in the grace of our Lord Jesus Christ. They always made an appeal for us to face ourselves squarely and give up anything that was holding us back from God. One of my problems was that I longed to be popular. I wasn't unpopular, but I longed for more popularity among my fellow students. During one meeting, the evangelist pleaded with us to yield ourselves to God, and I struggled hard before I could finally say, "All right, Lord, I commit to you this desire that I know is holding me back. Please take it away." The emotional high that came as a result was, I suppose, partly psychological and partly spiritual, but the long-term result was cleansing, though the answer didn't come overnight.

I constantly juggled my time between studying and doing odd jobs when I wasn't in classes. Occasionally, when I had no money to pay a room bill, I would have to write home. By return mail would come five or ten dollars out of my parents' already tight budget. Dad kept track of these loans in a little black notebook.

The big break for my fortunes came at Christmastime, when Bob Denney—ever the entrepreneur—decided that since we hadn't the time or money to drive to Oregon and back, he would buy a used car and drive students to their homes in the East, charging enough to pay for the gas and still have some profit left over for college expenses. (There was no thought of such minor matters as car breakdowns and loss from the operation.) He bought an ancient Lincoln with pull-down jump seats between the front and back seats, and a luggage rack on top. Six students could fit in comfortably.

I determined to follow his example. A classmate told me about her uncle, who owned a huge, imported Italian car of uncertain vintage. She offered to make an appointment for me to ask him to rent me his car for the trip. With some fear and trembling I visited him and tried to impress him with my virtues.

Then he asked, "What would you do if the car stalled and you couldn't get it started? Would you wait for parts to come from Italy? Who would pay for them?"

And so the interview ended. I have often been grateful for his refusal, though I was foolishly disappointed and a bit angry with him at the time.

Meanwhile, Bob had been scouring the used-car lots on my behalf and came back with the world's best deal. The salesman said he would sell me an old Lincoln limousine like Bob's for $100 and would buy it back at the end of the trip for $125.

Thus equipped, I set out on my trip south to Virginia with a group of six young women. I stayed in some of their homes and met with a lot of southern hospitality. I learned, too, about the lingering anguish of the Civil War, which was then only seventy years in the past. In one home I overheard an early-morning, back-fence conversation outside the guest room window. My host was saying apologetically to his neighbor, "He's not really a damn Yankee though. He's from out west in Oregon!"

The trip back to the campus after the vacation days was notable for a leak in the radiator that required stopping every few miles for a refill. We arrived on campus at three o'clock in the morning during a bitter, sub-zero January night, and after delivering my passengers I tumbled into bed—forgetting that the radiator was filled with water instead of antifreeze. The next morning, when I tried to start the car to return it to the used-car lot for my refund, I found that the water had frozen inside the block, cracking it. I finally sold the car for fifty dollars and took a step in learning the price of carelessness.

Vicariously, too, I learned about people—or at least about the used-car salesman who promised $125 at the end of the trip. Bob had bought his car from the same man for the same price, with the same promise. But when Bob took the car back to him, "market conditions had changed," and the new offer was for $75. Any fool would have expected this, but I was still trusting that what a man said was what he meant, and it took me a few years to become a realist about the human condition.

A never-to-be-forgotten event in our sophomore year was a chapel service that lasted all day and far into the night. At the conclusion of the regular chapel period, one of the students stood up and asked permission to say a few words. He spoke of his own spiritual coldness and hardness of heart and of his longing for a closer walk with God. After he finished speaking, a great hush came over the auditorium. The chapel leader announced the end of the meeting, but no one stirred. With everyone else, I found myself so spiritually disturbed that I could only sit and pray in silent pain at my own heart condition in my relationship with God. Someone in the balcony above me began to pray aloud, and after that another student went to the platform to use the microphone and told of his longing to be more pleasing to God.

Another followed him, and soon a line formed; many wanted to make public statements of confession and penitence. God's Spirit was being poured out upon us individually in a most remarkable way. Students who were not Christians came to the Lord that day, and others, including myself, gave their lives afresh to Christ. Many hours went by before all who wanted to speak had had opportunity to say what needed to be said. The campus was very different in the following weeks. I found that while all my spiritual problems were not solved, I had made great strides forward.

The Cord

The slim electric cord, plugged in,
Contains enormous power:
The organ sings, machinery whirs,
The lights come on,
And blankets warm the bed.

A Greater Power, if plugged in,
Will warm my heart:
Love, joy and peace grow strong,
And my small talent
Grows and pulses with keen life.

When not plugged in,
The organ stops.
No pounding of the keys or treadles
Gives the slightest sound of music
To the waiting ears.

When not plugged in,
The Greater Power also stops.
Love, joy, and peace grow dim.
Life languishes.
Sickness comes,
And Death.

Why waste my life?
I'll take the cord and plug it in,
Rise up
And live.

K.N.T.

Chapter 6
Margaret

WHILE MY COLLEGE life consisted of mountain peaks of youthful confidence, independence, and comparative freedom from responsibility, I was conscious of a personal valley—deep and constant—paralleling the peaks. That was my relationship with Margaret. Though she was two thousand miles away, she was ever present even in my campus dating. She stuck by her word that she wouldn't write to me. Was she making new friends? Were they Christians? I had no way of getting the answers.

I was in love with her but wasn't at all sure she was the girl I should ask to marry me. My plan was to marry a perfect person who had no peers, someone everyone could recognize as an angel. Whenever I was attracted to a girl on campus, I began to run through a mental inventory, analyzing that girl's good points as compared to Margaret's. I could always find excellent qualities that I thought Margaret lacked, and my mind was in a whirl.

One day a classmate said, "Taylor, you look like you've lost your last friend." I realized that my inner turmoil was hurting not only myself (and Margaret) but was having an effect on other people too. I discussed my problem with a friend, a senior big-man-on-campus type. His response was brusque: "Look, if you *could* find a perfect girl, she wouldn't marry *you!*"

But I kept looking. And whenever I found someone who got higher points in my rating system, the fact that I loved Margaret threw me into another depression, for how could I abandon the one I loved in favor of someone else even if she were more perfect? I even consulted a highly respected faculty member about the subject of finding God's will. He tried to be helpful, outlining scriptural principles and describing some of his own experiences, but the conversation did nothing to solve my problem.

Walking back to my house, I prayed, for the millionth time, "God, help me know what to do—to continue my friendship with Margaret or to develop a deep relationship with someone on the campus." No answer. No voice. No vision.

In desperation and disgust, I said to God, "My plight is like that hedge over there across the street—impenetrable. No way through. Look! I'll show you!" And to demonstrate to God my impossible situation, I walked across the street to the hedge.

"See, God," I exclaimed, "I can't get through. I can't find the way. I am exhausted with trying."

Just as I arrived at the hedge, I saw a hidden pathway through it, where I suppose students had worn a shortcut—invisible until one was at the spot. I walked through in a daze, silent before God. Yes, God would show me the way. But when? And meanwhile, what should I do about social relationships at school? So the battle went on.

At home again during the summer after my sophomore year, my friendship with Margaret was renewed. Late in the summer I suggested to her that she transfer to Wheaton from Oregon State College, where she was majoring in home economics. Because she was using lipstick and fingernail polish, I thought she was getting "worldly" and that a year at Wheaton College would help her spiritually. But I didn't tell her my motive. She was reluctant to change schools because Wheaton didn't offer a major in home economics. Another problem was that she was hoping to qualify as an exchange student in China during her junior year. On the other hand, she was in love with me, and she assumed that my suggestion indicated I was finally becoming serious about our relationship.

While she was deciding whether to transfer, I had a memorable, life-changing experience. It came about in an unexpected way on a Sunday afternoon. After church and the family dinner I picked up a book that looked interesting, *Borden of Yale '09.* It was about a college student, Bill Borden of the Yale University class of 1909. I became fascinated as I read, because he had such great love for God and for his fellow human beings. Those were qualities I longed to have in my own life. I was eager to see how he got that way, so I could find the answer and follow his example.

Bill Borden came from a wealthy home. His father had left him a million dollars, far more money in those days than today. But Bill didn't cling to his riches, because he had given himself to God, and he felt that everything he had was a trust from God. He gave away hundreds of thousands of dollars. I was aghast. Since childhood I had thought of being a millionaire as one of life's highest goals, even though in my case it was an impossible one. But here was Bill Borden, a college senior, giving away great wealth.

He was a spiritual giant in other ways too. He frequently talked with his classmates about God—that He had a plan for their lives, including the forgiveness of their sins through faith in Christ. I don't think I had ever talked with an unbeliever about Christ at that time, and the thought terrified me. Perhaps this was a reaction to my father's almost embarrassing readiness to tell others about the Savior. Yet here was my new hero, Bill Borden, preaching at a gospel mission to down-and-outers. He would go there on Saturday nights and put his arm around men who came forward, telling them about Christ's willingness to forgive and help them.

I also admired Bill's experience on the Yale wrestling team; he knew some of the agonies I had experienced when pinned to the mat.

As I read more about this millionaire, athlete, and spiritual giant, I became uneasy. I found he was thinking of becoming a missionary! Now that was something I had decided I would never be—not because I had prayed and decided on the basis of knowing God's will, but because I just didn't want to go. I didn't want to give up the good things of life in America, and I didn't want Bill Borden to do it either!

Nevertheless, he did just that. After Yale University he attended Princeton Seminary and became greatly concerned about Chinese Muslims, for whom little was being done by mission societies. After being ordained in Moody Church, his home church in Chicago, he applied to the China Inland Mission and was accepted. He was assigned to a western province in China heavily populated by Muslims. In preparation for that assignment he went to Egypt to study the Arabic language and Muslim literature. As I read this, I became increasingly uncomfortable. Suppose God called *me* to be a missionary. Would I go? I wasn't willing to face the question and tried to put it out of my mind.

Then I read that Bill became ill after only a few weeks in Egypt. But I had read missionary stories before and I knew of wonderful miracles of healing because people trusted in God. Well, I was entirely unprepared, as I turned the page, to find that Bill's fever grew higher and higher.

"Dear God," I prayed in the intensity of following the story, "*don't* let him die."

But he did die. God let Bill Borden die. I was overwhelmed by shock. Then a cold, hard resolution gripped me. "If that is the way God treats a man wholly devoted to Him, then I want no more of such a God." It was a terrible moment as I deliberately turned my back on God. It was as if I were stepping off a cliff and plunging to the rocks below.

At that moment, God showed His grace to me in a way almost beyond my ability to tell it. He reached out and grabbed me and pulled me back. I can't explain what happened, but suddenly I found myself on my knees beside the chair where I had been sitting. I was praying in deep contrition, "Lord, here is my life. Take it and use it in any way you want to."

I have never turned back from that decision—a decision that completely changed my life's direction. It was a decision that made it possible for God to lead me onward in a "guided tour" for the rest of my life.

But as I entered my junior year, my future was still shrouded in uncertainty, especially so far as Margaret was concerned. At my urging, she had decided to come to Wheaton for one year. I reacted to her decision with both pleasure and concern, realizing that she was expecting that we would "go steady," and I was far from ready for that. Socially, it was a dreadful year for both of us. While I dated her occasionally, most of the time I virtually ignored her. Our infrequent dates left us depressed, both of us realizing that I had betrayed her by what really amounted to false promises about my intentions. As a transfer student, she had left her good life and friends at Oregon State and found it difficult to make a place for herself on a new campus.

She dated other men occasionally, but she decided against joining a literary society, the heart of the Wheaton social life, and spent Friday evenings studying alone. Our relationship hit an all-time low when I invited another girl to the annual Washington Banquet in February—definitely the climax of the year's social calendar.

In other ways, my junior year was a good one, full of fun and excitement. Class rivalry was strong, and we were very anxious to disrupt the Senior Sneak by finding out where they were going to spend their secret weekend. We spent many dollars telephoning all the resorts within a two-state radius, pretending we were seniors inquiring about some detail of the weekend. Finally, to our elation, we got the desired response from the reservation desk of one of the resorts.

After chapel on the morning the seniors were to leave, we held a public meeting and triumphantly announced to the student body that we had discovered the seniors' intended hideaway. The seniors expressed great anger and sorrow at our brilliant conniving, but the next day we learned we had been taken! The seniors had set us up by arranging with one of the resorts to which they were not going, to give us the false lead when we called. This ruse had successfully thrown us off the scent. Meanwhile, they were off to some undisclosed destination, leaving us to be the object of ridicule.

However, we quickly bounced back. Another tradition was that sometime during the year the seniors buried a fruitcake in a metal container somewhere on the campus. The cake was to be dug up by the senior cake committee in an appropriate public ceremony during the last days of the school year. Tradition required that the juniors make every effort to find the cake before the crucial day.

Our aggressive class was determined to win and went about the seemingly hopeless task of scrutinizing every square inch of the thirteen-acre campus. We looked for mounds, fresh soil, or indentations in the grass. We checked out anything that looked the least bit suspicious, by pushing a metal rod down into the soft earth, moist with the spring rains, hoping to hear or feel a thud that would reveal the presence of the metal box.

Many of us were out on the campus most of the night for

several nights, checking out suspicious spots, but to no avail. The last night before the seniors were to dig up their cake, several of us despondent juniors were gathered at our residence, The Zoo, when John Frame charged up the steps, carrying a round copper cakebox with the cover soldered on.

"Eureka!" he shouted. "We've found it!"

Naturally, we had a triumphant ceremony the next day as we presented the cake to the crestfallen seniors.

In retrospect such pranks seem a bit silly, but they were a wholesome and innocent part of college life in those relatively untroubled years just before World War II.

At the end of the school year I decided to hitchhike all the way to Portland. I was both nervous and excited, and I would have been more so if I had known what lay ahead!

Chapter 7
The Accident

CARRYING A SMALL canvas zipper bag, I trudged across town to Roosevelt Road and headed west. Within a few minutes a farmer in a Model T Ford stopped for me, and I was on my way home. That ride was a false start, however, because he took me only a dozen miles before turning off from my route, and I was back on the highway again. But the next car that stopped was a new 1936 Buick, with a forty-year-old, no-nonsense driver who liked to travel at eighty miles an hour whenever road and passing conditions permitted. I didn't enjoy the speed at first, but I got used to it. He and his wife were going to Cheyenne, Wyoming, halfway to my destination.

This Jewish couple had heard of Wheaton College and were curious about the school and its "strange rules," as they expressed it. (We didn't dance, smoke, drink, play cards, or go to movies.) In a very faltering way I tried to tell them about faith in Christ, but although they didn't argue, they weren't interested. With a feeling of relief that I had discharged my duty, I changed the subject.

By evening we had made it about halfway to Cheyenne. They were surprised and shocked that I planned to hitchhike on through the night, and they offered to pay for a cabin for me at a tourist camp where they stopped, so that I could go on with them the next day. I accepted their offer with pleasure.

What intrigued me most was their concern for my welfare. To my knowledge, it was the first time I had ever talked to Jews, who were viewed with antagonism by many in those days. I had been brought up in a home where there was no trace of anti-Semitism. Yet, strangely, I felt disdain for Jews—perhaps as a result of peer pressure. Public opinion expressed in newspapers often made snide remarks about them, and Henry Ford, Sr., was notorious for his anti-Semitic attitude. How easily even Christians can be swayed by the world's attitudes.

The next evening we arrived in Cheyenne, and they offered to get me a room in the hotel where they were staying. Eager to get on home, I declined and bade them farewell.

As night began to fall, I stood impatiently waiting for my next ride. Eventually a rancher in an old pickup truck stopped for me, much to my delight. Unfortunately he went only thirty miles or so before turning off to his ranch, a few miles off the highway. I almost asked him to let me go with him and stay in his barn, but I didn't know how I'd get back to the highway in the morning.

So once again I stood and waited—and waited. Cars were few, and in the blackness of the night the drivers couldn't observe that I was only a harmless college boy, so they sped by. Soon the high plateau became chilly, and I was very tired and cold. Thinking some sleep would make me better prepared for the increased traffic in the morning, I walked out into the sagebrush wilderness and lay down on the hard, uneven ground to try—unsuccessfully—to sleep.

I began to hear, far in the distance, what I thought to be the howling of wolves. I suppose that if Wyoming once had wolves, they were by then long gone and what I heard were coyotes. But I was scared. Then I was attacked by giant mosquitoes, lusting for human blood. I thought I felt my face swelling from their bites, so I got up and dumped out the contents of my zipper bag. I put my head inside and zipped the bag up to protect my head from the attacking hordes. Even that failed, as mosquitoes worked their way past the zipper at my throat, into the bag, and onto my face where now I couldn't even swat them. I was in a state of despair—cold, miserable, and frightened. Would I get pneumonia? What if the howling came closer? Where could I hide? Could enough mosquito bites kill a person? And it was so dark—and so cold!

What does one do in a situation like that? I prayed. "Dear Lord," I cried aloud, "help me. What shall I do?"

In reply, something happened that I had never experienced before and never since. I didn't hear a voice, but I felt such a strong urge to get back out to the road that it was irresistible. I jumped up, unzipped the bag from my head, stuffed my things back into it, and rushed to the road. Surely, I thought, God was speaking to me; a car would come by and pick me up. But there was nothing there—no car coming, only blackness and silence. Not knowing what to do, I stood there uncertainly. What was this strange impelling force I was feeling?

Then, far in the distance, I heard the sound of an approaching car. Eagerly I waited as it came closer and closer. I waved frantically as it sped past and disappeared again into the night. I was crushed and confused.

However, another car was coming! Again I waited and waved hopefully, and again it sped past. But then I saw its red brake lights come on as the driver slowed and stopped. A door opened, and someone stepped out and shouted back to me, "Is that you, Taylor?"

It was Bob Harrah, a Wheaton College classmate, driving to Portland with three other students. We were both too surprised to realize what a miracle had happened. I opened the back door and got in. A girl moved over to make room for me—it was Margaret! After our stormy year together at Wheaton, Margaret was not at all pleased to see me. I had thought it was cold outside, but it was nothing compared with the chill in that back seat!

Sandy Campbell was driving and Mary Soltau was in the front seat to keep him awake. After a short time, I fell asleep. An hour or two later we were all jolted wide awake by a crash of metal against metal, as an oncoming car sideswiped ours. We began to career wildly as we skidded past a telephone pole, missing it by inches. I shall never forget the sensation of seeing the road in the headlights moving away from us, then back, then away as we skidded completely around. Margaret was screaming so I grabbed her and held her in my arms, trying to protect her, even though I had no idea what the next seconds might bring. The car and the five of us landed upright in a six-foot ditch.

Climbing out unhurt, we fellows raced back to the other car and found that miraculously no one was hurt there either, except for a bleeding hand that had gone through a broken window. The kids in the other car were University of Washington students going to Chicago. Apparently one or both of the drivers had gone to sleep, and the cars sideswiped each other at the midline, sending both spinning into the ditch, one on each side of the highway.

Returning to our car, we thanked God for His mercy and for guardian angels' care over us. We slept fitfully in our car during the rest of the night. At last the sheriff arrived and took us to Wamsutter, where there was a telephone and telegraph station at the depot stationmaster's office.

Bob telegraphed his father the unhappy news about the accident and waited for instructions. Margaret and Mary wired their families for money so they could continue to Portland by train. The next passenger train was not due until evening. I did not want to desert my friends while plans were being sorted out, so I stayed with them.

In the afternoon, despite the heat, Margaret and I went for a walk through the sagebrush. Strangely, campus tensions did not carry over to Wyoming. We were comfortable with each other. She was relieved to be putting her year at Wheaton behind her.

Margaret and Mary finally boarded the Portland Rose. Bob and Sandy were still waiting for the insurance adjustors when I took off to continue hitchhiking on Route 30. Rather thoughtlessly, I did not telegraph my parents. I suppose I had a childish desire to walk in on them and surprise them with the big story of my adventures—the hero returning home in triumph! However, someone else called them, so they got the message that I had been in an accident, and that's all the information they had during a couple of days of painful anxiety.

I was fortunate—or the Lord helped me—and the first car I hailed stopped. The driver was going to Portland and wanted someone to help drive.

That summer of 1937 was like the previous ones, full of hard work in the hayfields, with occasional interludes of Saturday picnics followed by canoeing on the Tualatin River. Margaret and I were on good terms—such good terms, in fact, that she talked about the possibility of coming to my graduation the next spring. She would get a job waiting tables at her dorm and save the money to pay for her train fare. I could look forward to getting letters from her again.

All too soon the summer was over and it was time to return to college. Margaret went back to Oregon State for her junior year, and I said good-bye to her and to family and friends and headed back to Wheaton for my senior year.

It was a good year, filled with debate team victories, social life, student politics, and even some studying. Debating occupied a lot of my time during that year. Dr. Clarence Nystrom was our debate coach. His wife, Gertrude, though not very much older than we were, was like a mother to the entire team and was a special help to me in her cheerful kidding about my "girl back home."

The varsity debate squad, consisting of Thomas Lindsay, Harold Lindsell, Roger McShane, and me, had debated together for three years, and we made a nearly unbeatable team. We went to several out-of-state tournaments that year. In February we made a long-planned trip, going as far south as New Orleans. We had debates every day, often more than one, and on Sunday we assisted in Sunday school and church services in Baptist and Presbyterian churches. We were gone two weeks.

In the autumn of my senior year I helped organize another literary society, the Naitermians, and became its president the second semester. As a premed student, I was majoring in zoology, and that year I became a lab assistant in the zoology department. I helped squeamish girls dissect pig fetuses, and I even taught the zoology classes a few times when our professor, Dr. J. B. Mack, was ill.

I dated different girls, being careful not to be seen with any one girl too often. It was good to be getting regular letters from Margaret. But in late March there was an enigmatic letter from her. She said she wouldn't be coming for graduation after all, and, further, not to expect any more letters. Period. What had I done? Or what had she done? She didn't say she had fallen in love, but maybe that was it. I was baffled. Her not coming for graduation did not bother me so much, but not writing—ever!

About the same time, I received an even more crushing blow. We senior premeds had taken aptitude tests preparatory to applying for medical schools. When the test results came back to Dr. Mack, he notified his other students of their good success, but he sent me a note asking me to make an appointment with him. As I came into his office, he graciously stood up and asked me to be seated.

"Mr. Taylor," he asked, "I wonder if you would not prefer

to get a Ph.D. and teach biology, rather than be a doctor?"

I should have guessed what he was trying to tell me, but I didn't, so he had to be more direct. He said I had failed the medical aptitude test, and no medical school would admit me with such a low grade. Doug had passed. John Frame had passed. Grace Vanderpoel had passed, along with several other classmates who were headed for medical professions. But I had failed. How could that be? I was an honor student. I was shocked and disappointed, and I left his office in a state of bewilderment and depression.

It was a long time before I came to realize that I was being given clear guidance about what God wanted my future to be. I should have been grateful instead of disappointed. This was one of my first lessons in trusting God when He closes a door to my own desires. Now I can thank Him that I did so poorly on the test and that He turned me to another path, even though at the time I had no idea what that path would be.

Because of good grades, character, and campus activities, a certain number of seniors each year were eligible for election by the faculty to the Scholastic Honor Society, Wheaton's equivalent of Phi Beta Kappa. The announcement was made one morning in chapel, and both Doug and I found ourselves among the twelve elected, along with several of our special friends. Some who didn't make the list were bitter because their grades were better than mine. In some cases, perhaps the problem was that they concentrated too much on academic achievement and didn't participate in other campus opportunities.

My years at Wheaton College were filled with friendships that have lasted through the years. Many of my classmates have had distinguished careers and have become well known. Carl F. H. Henry came to Wheaton as an experienced newspaper journalist, then became a theologian and the founding editor of *Christianity Today* magazine. Harold Lindsell became dean of the faculty and a distinguished professor at Fuller Seminary and followed Henry as editor of *Christianity Today.*

My other debate partners, Tom Lindsay and Roger McShane, became outstanding Presbyterian leaders, as pastor and seminary professor respectively. After rearing her family, Margaret Bailey Jacobsen (now Margaret Voskuyl) has served as Christian education and missions director at Lake Avenue Congregational Church in Pasadena, California. John Frame is an expert in tropical diseases. He identified the virus of the often fatal disease of Lassa fever. Sam Moffett became a missionary in Korea, as did Del Mackenzie, who married Sam's brother Howard. Another missionary statesman from my class was Dayton Roberts, a leader in the Latin America Mission. Arthur Volle and Donald Boardman served their alma mater for decades as professors. We treasure our friendship with them and their wives, Ruth and Betty, who were also classmates. These are just a few of my friends who were given unusual opportunities in Christian service.

The four wonderful years came to a glorious end one June morning in 1938 when we graduated, our joy somewhat tempered by the knowledge that most of us would not see each other again. For a sensitive person like myself, parting with close friends made it a hard morning.

Dad and Mother came for the ceremonies, and it was a proud time for them. Doug and I enjoyed introducing them to our many friends. Dad went on by train to visit the towns he had lived in as a child, while Mother rode back to Portland with Doug and me in a driveaway car. Unfortunately, the man who arranged our transportation assigned two college-age girls to ride with us. This crowded the car and also made it impossible for me to have the personal, in-depth conversations with my mother that I had hoped for after being away from home for most of four years.

Not knowing where else to turn for immediate employment, I had another long, hot summer of hard hours in the hayfields. I had little time and energy for social diversions— and not much interest, either, since Margaret was spending the summer with her sister in Texas. Apparently she was trying to forget me by putting as much distance as possible between us. I tried to forget her, too, but with no real success. In fact, the mental whirl was all the greater, with college behind me and no coeds around to choose between!

Meanwhile, my medical school plans having crashed in Dr. Mack's office, I tried to rebuild my plans for the future. Should I follow Dr. Mack's suggestion of teaching zoology or biology? That would require attending graduate school. Or perhaps I should specialize in genetics, a field of study that particularly interested me? Or should I go to seminary, as Dad suggested, for a good foundation for whatever I later decided? What about journalism? Perhaps I should forget the professions and go into business? How fortunate I was to have a variety of interests and opportunities open to me. It was years before I knew enough of life to understand that most people in the world scratch desperately for daily bread all their lives, at whatever menial tasks can be found. It didn't occur to me then, in my youthful optimism, that God might lead me into dark, hard years instead of into bright ones—and either way would be equally within His full, loving plan for my life.

After the hay-baling and wheat-threshing season ended, I returned again to the iris nursery. (Apparently the boss forgot, or overlooked, the fact that he had once fired me.) I had long, dreary hours to think as I stared at God's beautiful creations in the long rows ahead of me. Doug began his first year at the University of Oregon Medical School, and Bob Denney was preparing for his career, first as a cattleman and later, with his brothers, in the logging business.

And I? I was hoeing iris.

Chapter 8
Engaged at Last

ONE DAY WHILE I was hoeing and dreaming in a back field, I was surprised to see Mr. West, Margaret's father, making his way through the field in his business suit. He was concerned about me, not because of Margaret but because it was characteristic of him to be concerned for others. He offered me a job as a refrigerator salesman in the company he owned. I was in a dilemma. I was scared to death of selling, but I knew it would be good experience. And, I hoped, the commissions would be better than the pay for hoeing iris. So I thanked him and said I would report for the new job after a couple of weeks' notice to my boss.

Two weeks later I arrived at Mr. West's place of business, dressed in my one and only suit and very frightened. He introduced me to his sales manager, wished me good luck, and retired to his office. The sales manager suggested that we talk in his car, which was parked in front of the store. He was angry.

"Mr. West had no business hiring you," he said. "I have no need of your services. I'm sorry."

I can't describe the utter relief that surged through me at that moment, like being saved at the last moment from being thrown to the lions. With a joyful heart I drove home, but I soon realized that I was now jobless as well as purposeless.

While I was unemployed, so was Dad. His work for Albany College had been terminated while I was in high school—at the depths of the Great Depression. After Dad had been unemployed for two years, Mr. West, who was chairman of the board of the Union Gospel Mission, had asked him to serve as superintendent of that mission on Portland's skid row. Then Dad had been "retired" by the mission just weeks before coming to Wheaton for Doug's and my graduation. Just when things were getting extremely difficult financially, he received a legacy of a thousand dollars from a former parishioner in Seattle who remembered him in her will.

At sixty-five Dad could not easily find a job suited to his abilities. Occasionally he did supply preaching on a Sunday. And I recall his spending a day harvesting potatoes, picking them off the ground where the plow had turned them up. It broke my heart. Then he had an opportunity to take over a Raleigh route—selling staples such as tea, coffee, spices, and home remedies from door to door. It would have provided a secure income and would have given his friendly personality a rich opportunity for expression. It was, in fact, a God-sent opportunity for regular employment again.

Unfortunately, at about the same time, there arrived a mailing soliciting salesmen to sell aluminum cooking ware by getting friends to host dinners cooked in the sample aluminum pots and pans. The "guaranteed" earnings from sales to the dinner guests would be from seven hundred to a thousand dollars a month (at a time when one hundred dollars a month was a good wage and a two-bedroom house and lot sold for five thousand dollars).

Especially unfortunately, Dad asked me for my advice. He thought his college-educated son would have wise words, little realizing that college teaches facts but not necessarily wisdom. So I voted for the incredible income instead of the assured living. My deep regret still lives within me to this day, for if he had taken the Raleigh route, the next few years might have been happier for him and Mother.

One day soon after Dad began his aluminum sales business, I came home to find Mother near tears. She had been depressed for several days, and now the reason became clear. She was almost out of money for food and household expenses. Dad's efforts had failed to turn up a single sale and had left the household budget even deeper in the hole because of the cost of the food for the elaborate demonstration dinners.

My advice had resulted in complete disaster for him and Mother. I learned—or began to learn—two important lessons: to be very cautious about giving advice, and to be wary of advertising claims.

I'm sorry to say I didn't learn an even greater lesson—that the love of money is a root of all evil. My advice to Dad was based on my own values at that time, not his. My philosophy was to take the big and "easy" money, not the hard daily slogging.

Someone told me about aptitude and interest tests that might help me select an agreeable career. These were a new development and were not routinely given to college students. I took the tests, which showed that I had high interest and potential skills in journalism, the Christian ministry, and as a school administrator. The tests seemed to rule out some areas I had considered, such as law and teaching, and I hoped God wouldn't call me to be a minister or missionary—even though I would be obedient if He gave that direction. Journalism appealed to me, perhaps because of my father's interest. I tried to figure out the steps that would lead to a journalism career. An interview with an editor at the Portland *Oregonian* didn't give much hope—many would-be cub reporters had applied for jobs ahead of me.

Then it occurred to me—God leading my prayerful think-ing—that a side door to journalism might be through writing advertising copy in an advertising agency. But there were long lines of the unemployed in Portland and across the nation, and a college degree was no guarantee of finding a job.

I turned to the yellow pages of the telephone directory and copied the addresses of all the agencies listed. The next morning I started out to interview my prospects. It was an interesting experience.

The first ad agency I went to seemed to be a one- or two-person office and the man said his secretary had just quit and could I type and take shorthand? Well, I had taken a semester of typing in high school, but I could not take short-hand, and he said he must have someone with shorthand.

At the next place there was nothing. At the third place the man said he didn't have anything at the moment but would take my name and address. The next day he called me and told me he might have something for me, though not at his agency. One of his clients, the Hirsch-Weiss Clothing Manufacturing Com-pany, was looking for someone to learn the business.

I went over to see Mr. Weiss, the owner. He was a kindly, elderly Jewish gentleman who said that none of his children was interested in the company. He wanted to train someone in all aspects of the business—someone who would eventually become president and chief executive officer! He seemed to like me, and I liked him. He said he would first put me on the road for a few months of selling, then into the factory where the cloth was manufactured. Then I would go into the tailoring shop, the business departments, and so on through the com-pany. What an opportunity!

He said to go home and write him a letter of application in longhand. (He believed he could read character from the handwriting.) However, I knew he wouldn't be able to read my writing very well, so I wrote my letter on the typewriter and mailed it to him. A day or two later he telephoned me, quite upset, and asked why I had not written my letter by hand, as he had instructed me to. Nevertheless, he asked me to bring my parents in, as he wanted to meet them. So I knew he was serious.

As I thanked the Lord for this marvelous opportunity, a strange feeling came over me that I ought to give further consideration to my parents' idea that no matter what I did in the future, I should have a seminary education. Also, the more I thought about it, the more I wondered whether I ought to go into full-time Christian work of some kind rather than into business. But if I signed on with Mr. Weiss, it would need to be a lifetime commitment, in fairness to him. So after a couple of days of thinking and praying about it, I finally decided to decline his offer, and I went back to tell him.

He was glad to see me and said I could start right away at fifty dollars a month—not a very large salary, but that was hardly a problem in view of the vast potential. It was harder than I thought it would be to explain to Mr. Weiss that I was a committed Christian and felt I ought to go to seminary and maybe become a minister. He seemed very thoughtful and, I thought, almost sad as he said, "Well, Mr. Taylor, you and your God know best." He shook hands with me, and I never saw him again, but I remember him as a godly man of character.

Bob Denney, now attending Oregon State, told me when he was home for Christmas that if I was interested in Margaret, I'd better decide in a hurry. She was dating a man on campus and Bob thought it was serious. Not knowing what else to do, I decided to register for graduate work in zoology at Oregon State in the spring term. I would be near her again, and perhaps I could decide whether to commit myself or get her out of my mind forever. After being on campus a few days without seeing her, I telephoned and asked her for a date.

"It must be springtime again," she said testily—which it

was. She meant that about once a year I seemed ready to make a commitment, and then, after a few weeks, I backed off. Her answer to my request for a date was a definite no. "If you ever make up your mind, let me know," was her parting shot as she hung up.

During that term I walked her home from the library once. We had no actual dates.

Back home during spring break, I knew I could wait no longer. For several hours I hiked through fields and woods, turbulent with the thoughts that were no different from the ones I had had all during my college years, and perhaps even back into high school.

Do you love her? I asked myself.

Yes, of course! I replied.

Then why don't you ask her to marry you?

Because I might meet someone I like better, came my reply, for the hundredth time.

Well, you have to decide. I knew that.

I knew it was now—or never. My heart cried out yes, but my mind was weary with thinking about possible problems. Why couldn't I be normal like most people and fall desperately, hopelessly in love? Or was I in love? Certainly the thought of her marrying someone else was devastating. But were our interests similar enough? Was she as "spiritual" as *X, Y,* or *Z?* What about her personality? *X* and *Y* were warmer; *Z,* more spiritually mature.

It was, I suppose, three hours later that I cried out in final despair to the Lord, "O God, I'm so confused and I can't put off the decision any longer. I will ask her tonight. O God, don't let us make a mistake. Please, God, *please.*"

I turned back home, full of despair. I confided my intentions to Doug. "Doug, I'm going to propose to Margaret tonight."

"Well, it's about time!" was his only comment.

After supper I telephoned Margaret to ask if I could come

over. She said it was not convenient, as they had guests for the evening. I was not to be deterred. Surely the guests would be gone by ten; what if I came then? She finally said yes, I could come. But there was no enthusiasm in her voice, and her greeting when I arrived was strained.

"Let's go for a ride," I suggested. We drove along Terwilliger Boulevard, not saying much. I stopped the car when we came to a scenic turnout overlooking the city of Portland. The lights of the city were bright, but my mind and heart were dark, and the words I had intended to say didn't come.

"Can we start dating again?" I finally asked.

She was slow to reply. "Not unless you have marriage in mind."

My resolution to be bold had wilted, but I managed to say I probably did.

"I'll have to think about it for a few days," was her reply.

Two days later she called and asked me to come over. There was a lightness in her voice that gave away her reply, and my spirits brightened. We agreed that dating, with serious intentions, was now the plan.

Soon after we returned to the campus, Margaret was babysitting on a Friday night, and I joined her. I wanted to sit by the fire and talk. She wanted to study—and did! My moodiness did not improve when I learned she had a date to go bicycling the next morning. She reminded me there was no reason not to. The fellow who had invited her wasn't even a special friend, but bicycling for a couple of hours in the country appealed to her.

When the baby-sitting was over, I walked her home across the tree-lined campus. My heart raced. Finally I haltingly said, "I don't know how to say this, but will you marry me?" No dramatics!

And after waiting for that question for half a dozen years, she said, "Yes!" We sealed the pact with our first kiss. Almost immediately I lost interest in my graduate studies of genetics, dropped out of school, and returned home.

We agreed not to tell our parents immediately about our engagement, as it would be too much of a shock. In fact, I was being so guarded that I asked Margaret not to write me every day. What would my parents think?

About this time I had a letter from Stacey Woods, who was working with Inter-Varsity Christian Fellowship in Canada. My college classmate Ted Benson had given him my name. The IVF movement had begun among British university students years earlier and was now being developed in Canada. Its purpose was (and still is) to provide a forum for Christian students on college campuses for Bible study and prayer to strengthen each other against negative peer pressures and anti-Christian teaching in the classroom. There was also some emphasis on evangelism. In Canada there was a branch of this work in high schools, called the Inter-School Christian Fellowship. Inter-Varsity also operated camps in the Muskoka Lakes area of Ontario.

Stacey's letter was an invitation to join this ministry, first by being a cabin leader at Pioneer Camp that summer, then during the school year to travel from town to town in western Ontario to organize Bible study groups in high schools. It would mean getting the permission of principals and speaking in school assemblies.

The camping part got my attention right away. One of my dreams while baling hay and hoeing iris had been to begin a Christian boys camp on one of the Oregon beaches, but I hadn't known how to go about it. I learned later that it was at this time that several Christian camps were in their early stages. As often seems to happen, God was speaking the same message simultaneously to several of His people, including me.

Speaking in school assemblies and organizing Bible study groups for students did not appeal to me, even with all my training and experience in speech. But remembering the great benefit my friends and I had had from the weekly Bible class at the McMinns', I could hardly say no to this opportunity.

To take this job would obviously defer seminary. But I felt, and Dad agreed, that the practical experience would be a good background for seminary later. The pay was fifty dollars a month plus travel expenses.

I went back to Corvallis for Margaret's graduation. She received honors for having the highest grade point average of all the students in the school of home economics. Her family was a little surprised when, following the convocation, she invited me to join them in a picnic on the banks of the Mary's River.

Before I left for the summer, we needed to tell both sets of parents that we were engaged. Margaret said I would have to go through the protocol of asking her parents. That surprised me.

"Why can't we just tell them?" I asked.

"We could," she replied, "but we might as well get off on the right foot with them."

It was agreed that I would talk to her father at his office the next day. I didn't think I'd have any trouble with him, so I breezed in and told him our story.

He thought it was a good idea, although he advised that we not marry for a couple of years, until I had a job. I explained that I wanted to go to seminary for four years before marrying and had just accepted a one- or two-year job with Inter-Varsity Christian Fellowship in Toronto, Canada.

Then came his bombshell: "Go and talk to my wife," he said. That was something I had hoped he would not do, as Margaret's mother had never been overly friendly toward me, and I was a bit afraid of her. She was, in fact, a wonderful woman of German descent and very reserved. For some reason we had never hit it off, just as my parents hadn't been as cordial as I wished toward Margaret. My parents' problem, as I learned later, was that they had heard somewhere, erroneously, that

Margaret danced, which was regarded at our house as extremely worldly.

With trepidation I went to see Margaret's mother. It was a lovely June morning, and she was pruning some vines in her extensive flower gardens on their large estate. After a few minutes of talking about the weather and the garden, I told her, "Margaret and I are planning to get married."

"I'm sorry to hear it," was her terse reply. "Have you talked to my husband?" I stammered that I had and that he had agreed. Soon I found myself in the car, shell-shocked, and on the way home.

I called Margaret that night and reported the situation to her. She thought it best that I not try to see her that evening, so I used that time to tell my parents, knowing their disapproval in advance. They had watched the rocky friendship for several years and, like Margaret's mother, wondered if it could be a happy marriage.

My dad's comment was a bit brusque. "If you love her enough to marry her, why are you here tonight instead of being with her?" So then I had to explain about Margaret's mother.

Unfortunately, my questionings and doubts didn't melt away. Years of indecision had worn ruts in my thought processes, and the ecstasy I should have felt was only partial. Fortunately, Margaret did not know I was still judging her and comparing her with everyone else. As I left her to go to Canada, she had a loveliness and glow in her eyes that thrilled me, but at the same time I was troubled by my own doubts.

Chapter 9
Some Miracles

MY FIRST assignment at Pioneer Camp was as a counselor to a cabinful of teenage boys. This proved to be challenging, as the camp was not very well managed. I was only a novice swimmer myself, but I was given the responsibility of teaching beginners. Some of them improved by experience, but they gained little from my instruction! I recall an embarrassing day when the father of one of the campers arrived to visit his son. I could see that he was very angry as he watched his son flounder around during the swimming class. He had expected better results for the high fees he was paying. I lamely promised that I would try harder, but he walked away, shaking his head and muttering under his breath.

On one of my afternoons off, I went for a walk down a trail that led through a thick woods. Noticing an interesting geological formation about a hundred yards away, I left the path and climbed over a tree-covered hillock. After inspecting the interesting rocks, I turned back to find the trail, but it had disappeared. I searched in vain, trying to figure out how I had become confused. After a long and rather frightening time, I finally found the trail again.

As I was hunting for the trail, I thought how easily I could find the right way if I were a bird and could look down through the trees. This reminded me that God's perspective was even better—He could see the trail from beginning to end as He watched my fruitless search. As I lay on my cot that night, thinking over the events of the day, I realized more clearly than ever how foolish it would be to try to run my own life. God sees both the beginning and the end, and everything in between, and He is happy to tell me what to do and where to go if I am willing to obey. I vowed to try harder to be willing to do His will, not my own, as I walked along the trail of my life. Yes, it would be a safely guided tour, if I would only let Him be the guide.

The after-supper mail call was wonderful on the days when Margaret's letters came. I would go down to the dock, get a canoe, and paddle out to the center of the lake to be alone (and escape the mosquitoes). Ceremoniously, almost reverently, with fast-beating heart, I would open the blue envelope and read the beautiful writing. No question about it; I was in love.

The summer of 1939 passed quickly, and fall came. Along with two other new Inter-Varsity staff members, I had expected some training. We really had very little idea of what we were to do, but no one seemed to have time to tell us. We were given a list of high schools scattered over a hundred-mile area and were told to visit the principals and ask to speak for thirty minutes in a school assembly. Then we were to find a faculty sponsor and begin weekly Bible studies with students in a classroom. Fortunately, some of the principals were familiar with the annual routine and could tell me what was expected. They referred me to the faculty member who had been the sponsor the previous year, or helped me find one who might be interested.

But in some schools the principals had no interest. I recall one who quickly told me that a group could meet only if a faculty sponsor volunteered, but I was forbidden to contact the faculty about it. He even escorted me to the exit and watched me leave the building, lest I talk to a faculty member on the way!

Our director, Stacey Woods, lined up people from his own denomination, the Plymouth Brethren, to be my hosts in the various towns I visited. Usually this was a happy experience, although occasionally I was shocked at the gossiping that took place about other brothers and sisters. One afternoon I arrived by train at a town near Toronto, where I was to speak at the high school the next morning. I was met at the station by the man who was to be my host. However, his wife had become ill, so he had made arrangements for me to stay in another home. This turned out to be quite an adventure.

Apparently these two families represented very different, and definitely not harmonious, branches of their denomination. When we arrived at the home of my new hosts, the man who had met me at the train took my bag to the porch, cautiously rang the doorbell, hurriedly shook hands with me, and scurried back to his car and drove away!

My host, a burly, middle-aged man, came to the door and ordered me in. He introduced me to his wife and teenage daughter. As he did so, he announced in her presence that his daughter wasn't saved. He said, "You can lead a horse to water, but you can't make it drink." The girl said nothing; apparently she was used to this treatment. I asked her father later, in private, whether he would let her attend the weekend conference with other Christian young people, where there would be an evangelistic emphasis. He snorted a loud negative and said, "They're all just a bunch of hypocrites. None of them knows the Truth."

During supper he kept holding forth about all the other Christians in town, how ignorant of "the Truth" they were, and how unspiritual. At their family devotions he handed out

Bibles and told me to read from a chapter in Hosea. I couldn't find Hosea, and he roared with laughter and derided me for pretending to be able to help young people become better Christians when I couldn't even find the book of Hosea!

However, perhaps the Lord demonstrated His sense of humor later that evening. I excused myself rather early from the tense family gathering and went up to my room to prepare for bed. When I finished in the bathroom and was ready to go back to my room, I couldn't get the door open. I kept working away at the key in the lock, and finally my host came up to see what was wrong. My plight amused him, and he ordered his wife to get the ladder and climb up the outside of the house. Soon she appeared at the window. As I stood there in my shorts, she told me how to jiggle the door and the lock in a certain way, and I was free! My host was outside the door to greet me, and from then on the ice was broken. In fact, he even let his daughter come to the Christian camp weekend.

Much as I longed to go home for Christmas, I could see no way to finance such a trip. Dad came to my rescue. He arranged with a Portland car agency for me to drive a new car from Detroit. I had not seen Margaret for six months, and in my eagerness to get home I decided to drive nonstop day and night, except for meals. Not only was I eager to see Margaret and my parents, but I'm afraid my foolish decision was prompted partly by the fact that Bob Denney had once made such a nonstop trip. I thought if he could do it, so could I; then I'd be a hero. I'm not sure to whom I thought I would be a hero, nor why it seemed necessary, but those were my thoughts.

The beginning of the trip was uneventful. I warded off sleepiness with caffeine tablets, since I didn't drink coffee. I picked up a hitchhiker or two to combat the loneliness, but for the most part I found it a battle of concentration to keep going and not pull off the road for a little sleep. The occasional food and gas stops along U. S. Route 30 were welcome diversions.

In western Idaho I looked at my highway map to see why Route 30 seemed to be turning north instead of going straight west. Yes, the map showed the highway looping north and west, which I thought would be out of the way. Then I spotted a small road that went straight westward. Why not take the more direct route, saving a hundred miles or so and two or three hours of time? Of course! It was the only logical thing to do.

What didn't occur to me was that if this was such a great idea, my "direct route" would be marked as a major highway, and many other cars would be turning off of Route 30 just as I now did. But I actually believed I had found an answer that had escaped the less perceptive general public! With elation over my discovery I drove on westward into the night. All went well for several miles. The road was paved, and there was no traffic at all, so I could sail along—Columbus discovering a new route to India.

But soon the pavement ended and I found myself on a washboard gravel road that shook the car terribly at any speed above twenty miles per hour. I stopped and looked at the map again, was reassured, and drove on. Tenacity is a good trait, but sometimes one must say, "I made a mistake," and turn back before the mistake is compounded. But not me! I had already come forty-five minutes from Route 30, and I couldn't consider driving another forty-five minutes to get back there.

So I went on, varying my speed in an effort to minimize the bumps in that awful road. Nothing helped. I was responsible to get the car to Portland in good condition, and I knew these road conditions could damage it. I slowed down to a snail's pace and crept forward through the night.

Next I began to experience some kind of hallucinations, probably from lack of sleep. At one point I saw a deer jump out from the side of the road. Just before I ran into it, it disappeared into thin air. Later a man was walking along ahead of me in the beam of the headlights. Overjoyed to see another human being, I prepared to stop and give him a ride, but before I reached him, he was gone. I realized I was having a problem and needed some sleep, but that would spoil my determination to make a no-sleep, two-thousand-mile drive, so I kept on.

Suddenly I was all attention. I glanced at the gas gauge and was shocked to see the needle hovering near empty. For hours I hadn't passed a house or ranch, let alone a gas station. I pulled out the map again. To my tremendous relief it showed a town that looked to be not far ahead. I went on, feeling hopeful, though I feared the gas pump would be closed for the night. But perhaps the attendant lived near the premises and I could wake him up.

Just before dawn my headlights picked up buildings ahead. No one was up yet; the few houses were all dark, so I parked at the side of the road to wait for morning. I must have dozed for awhile, but when I awakened, the morning light showed me an incredible sight. The houses were utterly dilapidated—unpainted, weatherbeaten, and obviously abandoned! It was a ghost town, existing now only as a dot on my map.

What should I do? The map showed that I still had at least a hundred miles to go before I would reach a main road. How could I go a hundred miles on an empty gas tank? I could think of only one solution: drive as far as possible, then abandon the useless car and walk as long as it took to get help.

You may be sure I prayed much as I drove away from the shanties. The gas gauge now registered empty. I had no idea how much reserve the tank might hold. I was exhausted, hungry, and fearful, despite my prayers. I was also full of remorse and chagrin about my foolish assumption that everyone else was wrong in following Route 30 and that I was the smart one when I cut across!

Then it happened. Don't ask me what, or how; just accept

my simple statement that a miracle took place. I looked again at the gas gauge, and it registered half-full! I stared at the gauge, incredulous, but there it stayed. Still only half believing, though now filled with hope and thanksgiving, I plunged on. After several hours I came to a busy crossroad, with cars in sight in both directions and, soon, a gas station.

Why do these rare, dramatic miracles happen? I've been in other situations where it seemed that a miracle was just as badly needed, but it didn't come. Why does the Lord answer prayer at times with a dramatic healing, for instance, but more often doesn't? I'm confident it is not because one person's faith is greater than another's. In the incident just recounted, I had no faith at all. No, I think the occurrence of miracles is bound up in the profound mystery of the providence, the sovereignty, the will of God, and of prayers of parents and friends as well as our own.

In the end I had not shortened my driving time by leaving Route 30, and I arrived home so weary I was almost disoriented. I stopped at Margaret's home on the way to mine, but she wasn't home when I drove up in front of her parents' big brick house. So I went on.

When I told my story at home, the miracle of the gas supply was overlooked, and I was chided for taking the risk of going to sleep and having an accident like the one in which I had been involved when traveling through the night with my Wheaton College friends two years before. I was not a hero after all.

After six months apart, Margaret and I had a wonderful few evenings together during the holidays. Her Christmas present to me was a hand-knit red sweater that was a favorite for many years.

Then it was back to Ontario and what had now become the grind of visiting schools, speaking at assemblies, teaching Bible classes, and doing my best to lead high-school kids into stable Christian lives. At the time, I could not tell how much of the seed sown actually took root or nurtured young faith, but in subsequent years I have met or heard of several who credit my ministry in Canada with growth and fruitfulness in their lives. I hope any discouraged Christian worker who reads these comments will take heart, being reminded that labor for Christ is never in vain.

During the year of speaking and leading Bible studies in high schools, I also visited McGill University in Montreal to encourage the Christian student group there. I roomed at the YMCA near the campus. One afternoon I was in my room, studying the Bible in preparation for leading the weekly student meeting that evening. I found myself baffled about the meaning of a chapter in Ephesians, on which I had been asked to speak. I read the chapter several times, without much comprehension. Then I read it slowly, a verse at a time, with no better results. I could understand the words, of course, but I just could not understand the significance of the teaching or make any useful application to my life or the lives of the students.

Suddenly I was overwhelmed with the realization that my Bible reading in the New Testament letters had ever been thus. All my life I had wrestled in vain to understand them. Others could grasp their meaning; why couldn't I? Was I more stupid than my friends who gloried in reading the Word? Frustrated and ashamed, I exclaimed aloud to the empty room, "Why can't somebody translate the Bible so a person like me can understand it?"

At the meeting that evening, I used a few sentences from the chapter as a basis for some wide-ranging devotional generalizations. I hope some of the students were helped. As for myself, my deep discouragement increased. Even today when I read occasionally from the King James Version, I have the same difficulty in understanding and applying it. Perhaps the Lord veiled my mind to help me see the possibility of a clearer translation—but that came many years later.

A pleasant break in the routine came in March 1940 when staff member Charlie Troutman asked me to go with him to Quebec to look at a site that was being considered for another Inter-Varsity camp. We traveled by train and were met on that cold, snowy winter morning by a farmer who took us by horse-drawn sled across the frozen lake to the home of the local doctor, who owned the land we wanted to use.

As we waited in the doctor's living room for him to get his boots on, a young man came to the house to report that he thought he had appendicitis. The doctor took him into the kitchen to examine him. He soon reappeared to tell us he would need to operate, and that it would be half an hour before he would be able to join us. Soon we heard gasps and groans from the kitchen table as the youth gagged on the chloroform. Then all was quiet, and before long the doctor was ready to go, leaving the patient to his wife's care. I couldn't help speculating whether the doctor had used a kitchen knife for the rather impromptu operation!

Between the closing of schools and the beginning of summer camp in Quebec, I had time for another trip home to Oregon. Unfortunately, I did not have enough money to make the trip, but then another miracle jumped into place! A member of the Canadian Inter-Varsity board called one day and asked if I would be interested in a free round-trip ticket to Vancouver, British Columbia. From there it would be an easy bus trip to Portland . . . and Margaret.

All I had to do was to watch over a middle-aged Chinese man who was traveling across Canada under bond not to leave the train. He was a wealthy businessman from Cuba going home to China, but he was not allowed an entry permit into Canada. Therefore, the immigration staff needed someone to travel with him and prevent his sneaking off the train. I was to be the guard. I gladly took the job.

The only problem I had was in communication, since neither

of us spoke the other's language. I had some difficulty in keeping him out of the women's washroom. I kept saying, "No! No!" and he would obediently repeat, "No! No!" as he walked in!

Margaret was working as a consumer representative for Northwestern Electric Company, so we had only evenings to be together, and there was no round of parties as there had been at Christmas. Our engagement seemed to be falling flat with our being separated most of the time. I didn't pay much attention when she told me what she had been able to buy and put away: sheets, towels, a sewing machine, and tableware.

Personally, I wasn't thinking about marriage in concrete terms. For me it was a rosy glow in the future and not something to rush into. While I didn't talk about it and maybe wasn't even conscious of my feelings on the subject, I wasn't all that anxious to be married. In my immature opinion, the romantic excitement would probably last only a couple of years, and then—I didn't like to think about the "then." I preferred to survive on the rosy glow a while longer.

However, there was one mountaintop experience that June. A literal one.

Anyone in Oregon with mountain-climbing instincts and ability sooner or later climbs eleven-thousand-foot Mount Hood, near Portland. Margaret had made the climb with a hiking club when she was thirteen, but I had never done this. So we planned to climb on a Saturday with her brother Charlie and his friend Rachel. We started up the south side before sunrise in order to get as far as possible before the sun softened the snow underfoot.

After hiking for eight hours, we reached some sulfur springs, and Rachel said she was too tired to go further. Charlie said he would wait with her while Margaret and I climbed the last few hundred feet. We continued until we came to a cable that had been provided to guide climbers around a rocky crag and on to the top.

But I thought it would be fun to be different. I suggested to Margaret that we go around the rock the other way and clamber to the top across a couple of ice ledges. We would have to be very careful not to slip and fall. Margaret seemed willing to let my judgment prevail, and we started out.

I suppose the plan might have been successful except for the cloud that suddenly blew in against the mountaintop, enveloping us in heavy fog that made it impossible to see more than half a dozen feet ahead. I realized we had to backtrack in a hurry, but Margaret was huddled against the ice cliff we had been chopping our way around, immobilized by fright and frozen by the icy wind that came with the fog. My panicky urgings for her to take a step at a time backwards went unheeded as she clung silent and shivering to her pre-carious perch. I knew we were in deep trouble but didn't know what to do.

Then it occurred to me that I might be able to go back to the trail and up to the top, throw a hiking rope to Margaret, and pull her up. It was a foolish idea that doubtless would have killed us both, but I found my way back to the path and the cable and got to the top. In the dense fog I couldn't see the edge of the cliff and didn't know where she was. Although I called and called, there was only silence.

I desperately cried out to God for His help and, finding my way through the cloud to the cable again, I slid back down and made my way fearfully out to the ledge where Margaret was still clinging. I chopped wider steps in the ice below her and, realizing it was her only chance, she finally found the courage to lower herself a step at a time to safety.

Going down the mountain through the soft snow, I remem-bered other times when my life had been preserved. One day, as a child, I was playing in a narrow clay cave in a hillside near our home. I had to crawl in to get to the more spacious interior. Tired of my play, I was crawling out backwards when a great boulder, weighing perhaps fifty pounds, fell from the clay ceiling to land an inch or two in front of me, where my head had been just a split second before.

On another occasion, when I was in high school, several of us were hiking up to Wahtum Lake, high above the Columbia River. It was a seven-mile hike, and the rocky trail switched back and forth as it climbed to the top. Suddenly I heard something crashing toward me down the mountain, and I saw a huge boulder coming straight toward me. There was no time to run. But at the last instant, it hit another boulder just above me, bounced over me, and went crashing on its way.

Did Satan's messengers try to kill me? Did God's angels hold them back?

Soon it was time to say good-bye again to Margaret and my family. I headed for the camp in Quebec that Charles Troutman and I had checked out in March. Charles later wrote about an incident that happened during that summer of 1940.

The younger campers were taken on an overnight hike on the longer, easier climb up the mountain. Unfortunately a heavy rainstorm caught them in the early stages of ascent, so they took refuge in a sugar camp. After supper they continued with the climb until they were high in the mountain.

That evening when they were having their campfire, Ken Taylor suddenly appeared. He had been left in charge of the whole camp when the camp director had gone to town to get supplies. With his characteristic diligence, Ken felt he had to make sure of the campers' safety, in view of the storm that had passed through the area. He had scaled the face side of the mountain to reach the campers by the shortest route. When he discovered all was well, he headed back down the mountain by the same route.

The concern Ken showed for the campers' safety, inspiring him to come up that treacherous route by himself in the rain and return in the dark, made a deep impression on the boys. Ken Taylor was a real hero.

At last someone thought of me as a hero—and I hadn't even been consciously trying to impress anyone!

Chapter 10
Life Together

AFTER SPENDING the summer of 1940 at the Inter-Varsity camp in Quebec, I headed back to Oregon. I would be there only a few days before leaving for my first year at Dallas Theological Seminary in Dallas, Texas. Dr. Louis Sperry Chafer, a friend of my father, was the founder and president. Dr. Chafer was Dad's hero among theologians, along with Dr. C. I. Scofield, author of the Scofield Reference Bible notes that had given my father his theological education. Some former students and graduates of the seminary told me tactfully that I would receive more benefit from friendships and interaction with fellow students than I would find in the classroom. They were implying that with a couple of outstanding exceptions, the faculty scholarship was not strong.

But with my Dad's urging, I had applied and been accepted and was on the way, except to stop in Portland for ten days with my fiancée, parents, and friends. Ahead of me were four years of seminary, then marriage.

Margaret had stopped in Dallas when she was on vacation in Texas during the summer and had tried to find a job. I would be working part-time for Inter-Varsity, but we could afford to get married while I was in school only if she also had a job. However, she had had no success.

I took a bus from Toronto to Wheaton, where I joined my college roommate, Tom Lindsay, and his wife, Barbara, who were driving to the West Coast. Along the way they urged that Margaret and I get married right away. "Why wait?"

I did not voice my private fears about marriage, since I could honestly say, "We can't afford it."

It was fun to be with them and reminisce about our college days. Margaret had invited Tom and Barbara to stay at her home, and I joined them for dinner the night of our arrival. Margaret seemed unusually quiet through the evening. When it was time for me to leave, we went out on the front porch for a good-night kiss.

"Didn't you get my letter?" she asked.

"What letter?"

"The one I sent to you in Wheaton."

No, I hadn't received it. "Was it something important?"

"Yes! I heard from Dr. Lincoln at the seminary. I have a job there! We can get married next week!"

Married! Next *week?*

It was too late in the evening to discuss the ramifications of her announcement. And, Taylor-like, I didn't say anything about it to my parents that night.

The following day Margaret and I drove to the Oregon coast with Tom and Barbara, and our possible marriage was almost the sole topic of conversation.

If it was finances that had been the true barrier to marriage after eighteen months of engagement, that barrier was gone. We would have a combined income of one hundred dollars a month, and, with care, two people could live on that amount. Now I didn't have to make a decision, but only to get over the shock of being married in a few days, not a few years! We were both twenty-three years old.

Margaret favored a small wedding at her home, with only relatives and the closest of friends invited. I thought we should have a church wedding and invite everybody we ever knew. But how could all the arrangements be made in seven days, with invitations to be printed, addressed, and mailed?

A complicating factor in our planning was the wedding of Elaine McMinn and Don Mortimore the following Friday, to which our families and all our friends were invited. Dr. Jack Mitchell, their pastor and mine, was to perform their ceremony. Margaret's sister Ruth and brother Charlie were among their attendants. To upstage their wedding by having ours a day earlier, on Thursday, would not be fair, but we had to be on our way to Dallas by Friday night to be in time for classes.

Margaret's idea of having a small private wedding seemed to be the only solution, but then Elaine and her mother came to the rescue by suggesting a double wedding with Don and Elaine. And so our wedding was set for the next Friday, September 13, 1940.

The next few days were a whirlwind of activity. Margaret shopped every store in town to find an end-of-the-season wedding dress. We got our license, telephoned our relatives to invite them to the wedding, bought wedding rings, and ordered two hundred wedding announcements, which Margaret's mother would mail after the wedding. I asked Doug to be my best man, and Margaret asked her friend Jerry Shipley to be her maid of honor. Mrs. Denney, in charge of the flower arrangements for Elaine and Don's wedding, was glad to make two more old-fashioned bouquets for Margaret and Jerry from the assortment in her large flower garden.

On Thursday a little package I had been anxiously awaiting arrived in the mail. It was an engagement ring I had bought in Canada. Margaret had never said anything about not having a ring for the year and a half we had been engaged, but I had thought she should have one during the four years I would be at seminary. Little had I dreamed it would arrive just in time for our wedding.

We had planned to travel to Dallas by bus to save money, but Margaret's father took the matter into his own hands and made reservations for a private room on the train for Friday night and the bridal suite in a San Francisco hotel for Saturday and Sunday nights. It was his wedding gift.

The evening of our wedding came with breathtaking speed. I packed my few belongings, and the family stood together at the front door of our home for Dad's final prayer. As he prayed, I felt Mother's hand over mine. I was surprised and a little embarrassed, for our family was not given to any outward expressions of our love for one another. Being brought up with so much repression of emotion was poor preparation for marriage.

When we got to the church, I joined Don and our grooms-men in the vestry. Following tradition, I had not seen Margaret all that day. We lined up, first Dr. Mitchell, then Don and his attendants, me, Doug, and Charlie West, and took our places at the front of the church. Then the brides and their bridesmaids were coming down the center aisle, each bride on her father's arm. Margaret was radiant in her floor-length white chiffon dress with its short train.

Dr. Mitchell gave a brief homily. Don and Elaine repeated their vows, and then it was our turn. I was holding Margaret's hands and saying, "I, Kenneth, take thee, Margaret, to be my wedded wife, to have and to hold from this day forward. . . ." Did I know what I was promising? How could anyone know? It was such a momentous step. Dr. Mitchell first pronounced Don and Elaine man and wife, then Margaret and me. "Till death do us part," we had just said. We had no time to daydream or fantasize. It was over. We were going back up the aisle, smiling self-consciously at friends and relatives.

We did not have time to participate in a wedding reception,

as the ceremony was at eight o'clock in the evening and our train left an hour and a half later! Following the recessional, we said good-bye to Margaret's grandparents, aunts, and uncles. Margaret's mother welcomed me, her newest son-in-law, with a kiss. Margaret quickly changed from her wedding gown to a new blue dress, and I returned the black shoes I had borrowed. Then we drove off to Union Station, only a few blocks away, followed by our parents, brothers, sisters, and closest friends.

Even as we stood in the station waiting room with friends and loved ones around us, I was assailed with the same old doubts and uncertainties. Had we made the right choice? Had *I* made the right choice of a life partner? Had we acted too impulsively? These agonizing thoughts must have shown on my face, because my Uncle George took me aside to tell me, "Marriage is wonderful, but you look as if you've lost your last friend! You're going to spoil everything for everybody. Get back over there and smile." So I did, though my heart was in turmoil. No wonder Margaret's mother had not been happy with our engagement. She was perceptive enough to recognize that I didn't really know my own mind.

A friend of Margaret's father was an official of the railroad and had arranged with passenger agents along the way to offer their services. Their special attention began in the dining car the next morning. With our limited budget we had chosen the least expensive combination for breakfast. But then the steward approached us, telegram in hand. He inquired if we were Mr. and Mrs. Taylor. Margaret blushed, and I said yes. Then he gave us the good news that our bridal breakfast was free, with the compliments of Southern Pacific. So we quickly reordered!

That evening we arrived in San Francisco, where we had decided to spend the weekend touring the 1940 World's Fair. One of the most interesting exhibits to us was the one featuring

Irwin Moon's "Sermons from Science," sponsored by Moody Bible Institute of Chicago. In 1940, evangelicals were just beginning to make a public impact in secular society. An example of this was Charles E. Fuller's "Old Fashioned Revival Hour," which was sweeping across the nation's airwaves and making Christians proud of the public recognition given "one of our own."

The remainder of the trip to Dallas was punctuated by the fun of being met by station managers at every stop along the way. I remember too how warm the uncooled coaches were, and the difficulty of sleeping while sitting up. The realities of life had begun.

As the train moved south, we made out a tentative budget based on our combined monthly income of one hundred dollars. The first item was tithe, ten dollars, followed by rent, food, utilities, and books. We weren't sure whether any money would be left over for clothing. The seminary did not charge tuition but relied on gifts from friends of the school to cover faculty salaries.

When we arrived in Dallas, we found a furnished apartment on the second floor of a large house that had been divided into several apartments. It was just one room with a small kitchen annex and a bathroom that we shared with the occupants of the adjoining apartment. The rent was twenty dollars a month. Our neighbors were two rather hardboiled nurses who worked at Baylor University Hospital.

One fall day we picked up pecans from a roadside tree. It was then that we found we had nighttime intruders—rats that rattled the pecans noisily across the kitchen floor to a hole in the wall! We trapped three in one night. The first two times I disposed of the bodies in the garbage can behind the house. The third time, tired of interruptions to my sleep, I wrapped the dead rat in newspaper and put it in the hall. In the morning we were awakened by a scream outside our door. One of the nurses thought my package was her morning newspaper, but when she picked it up, the rat fell out at her feet! We were treated to a recital of her amazing repertoire of curses.

The professors at the seminary were all dedicated men, and I learned valuable spiritual lessons from each of their lives. As in many institutions, their teaching abilities varied greatly. Much to our shock and dismay, our Greek prof couldn't remember all the letters of the Greek alphabet when he wrote them on the board the first day of class. Another teacher simply read the textbook to us in class, and another majored in outlines for us to memorize. Several of the first-year men left at the end of the semester, transferring to Princeton Seminary. Although I sympathized with them, I decided to stay. Today Dallas Theological Seminary is outstanding in its scholarship and is one of the largest and most important evangelical schools in the nation, bearing little resemblance academically to the school of fifty years ago.

Wedding gifts arrived throughout the fall, and it was fun to open them. We received quite a few cash gifts, but we were careful not to spend any of the money, as we had no immediate needs, thanks to Margaret's foresight in having stocked up on sheets and towels. Dishes were included in the apartment furnishings. Grandmother Taylor sent us sets of crocheted doilies, assorted sizes. They were put away until someday in the future, when we might acquire some fine china to go with them. We never did get that fine china!

Chapter 11
Seminary Days

MY PART-TIME JOB with Inter-Varsity was similar to the one I had had in Canada, but now I was to work exclusively with colleges and universities. I found the work extremely difficult. In general, the atmosphere on college campuses was antireligious. Most Christians were strongly denominational and were not interested in meeting for Bible study with an interdenominational group. Relatively few students came from nondenominational churches, and most of them seemed fearful of openly identifying themselves as Christians.

So my work was generally disappointing, despite some encouraging exceptions. No doubt I was a large part of the problem. I was timid about personal evangelism myself, so I was ineffective at giving the kind of strong leadership the Christian students needed to get them started sharing their faith with others.

When summer came, Margaret and I had to decide how to spend the vacation months. I was feeling a call toward Christian journalism as a career, and that surely would necessitate specialized training in writing. I thought of quitting seminary and going full-time to a university with a strong journalism school. But I continued to believe that seminary was a good background to a career in Christian journalism. Another possibility was to take summer school journalism classes. But with no income, how could I?

Then I came up with an almost unthinkable suggestion: Margaret could get summer employment at Inter-Varsity's Pioneer Camp for Girls in Canada, across the lake from the boys' camp where I had been a counselor. I would live in Chicago, get a part-time job, and attend summer school at Northwestern University's Medill School of Journalism. Deciding to be separated for the summer was terribly hard, but it seemed the only way. So that is what we did.

I found a job as a night telephone switchboard operator at Norwegian American Hospital, which provided room and board and a weekly wage. I learned a lot from my writing courses at the university. Although I was terribly lonely for Margaret, I had opportunity for some good times with my Wheaton College classmate John Frame, who was interning at another Chicago hospital.

Although it seemed as if the summer would never end, Margaret and I eventually had a joyful reunion, and we drove to Oregon to spend a few days with our parents before returning to Dallas. Dad West had sent me money to buy a used car in Chicago so we would have transportation home, then he would sell the car in Portland. A Christian friend of mine, a mechanic, tuned up the car. Unfortunately, he forgot to replace the oil cap after changing the oil. He discovered his error an hour after I had left his shop. He knew our proposed route, so he jumped into his car and chased us for a hundred miles, hoping to catch up with us. Unable to find us, he gave up and returned to Chicago, hoping we wouldn't get into mechanical problems.

Meanwhile, we were indeed running into difficulty. A few hundred miles out of Chicago, the motor began to knock.

When we stopped at the next town, I found that the pistons needed to be replaced. Fortunately, I had enough cash to pay for this, but a couple of hundred miles later the same problem recurred. Again we stopped and found a mechanic who informed me that the pistons installed at the other garage were the wrong size and of an inferior brand!

An interesting sidelight to this story is that, using my writing skills newly acquired at summer school, I wrote the offending garage and demanded a refund. Eventually I was reimbursed half the cost of the repairs. I couldn't afford to lose even half of the money, but the incident encouraged me to think that God had given me an ability to write persuasively. Perhaps I should pursue journalism as a career following seminary, rather than going into the ministry. This may seem like a tenuous hook on which to hang a career, but God often guides with unspectacular means to bring about major results.

Dad West was more than a little dismayed when he saw the junker I had bought with his money. I had been trying to save him money by buying the cheapest car I could find, without thought of how he would resell it. We had only a few days of visiting family and friends in the Portland area before taking the train back to Dallas. This time no station agents gave us the glad hand!

Back on campus we moved into a married students' studio apartment. We had our own bathroom now, but the walls were so thin that we knew what our neighbors on either side were doing at all times, and we were aware of our own lack of privacy.

Then came Sunday, December 7, 1941. I vividly remember the interruption of a church service I was listening to on the radio and the announcement of the massive destruction of the United States' fleet at Pearl Harbor. President Roosevelt's speech to Congress was broadcast to the world the next morning. Congress quickly and almost unanimously declared war on Japan and on Germany. Some of the seminary students in the Army Reserve left campus that afternoon.

Registration of all young men for the draft quickly followed. We seminary students were deferred until graduation, when we would go as chaplains. Some volunteered as privates, but I did not, electing to continue with my preparation.

In the middle of the school year I was offered the job of dining hall manager at the seminary. It paid a small salary in addition to board and room. I was quick to accept. Margaret, with her training in foods and nutrition, could make out the menus and I would do the purchasing. The excellent black cook and his wife needed little supervision. The job had all the earmarks of a less stressful way to get through school than the Inter-Varsity campus ministry.

We soon experienced other stresses, however. Students are notorious for complaining about food service, and some of my seminary classmates were no exception. They thought the soup was "slop"; the steaks were all cooked medium instead of to individual specifications; the salads weren't fit for rabbits; we didn't provide enough variety—and so on.

Actually, the food was quite good, considering the amount of money we had to spend, so I didn't let the complaints bother me. This dining room experience was good for me because I learned some lessons about trying to avoid a critical spirit. My job as a Christian is to help others, and this is usually done best by encouragement and building up, not tearing down. I still need more practice in praising, however, instead of being a critic.

One spring afternoon in 1942 Margaret and I went out for a walk. Margaret kept lagging behind and finally said, "Don't walk so fast. We can't keep up with you!" For a moment I didn't catch the significance of that remark, but then I realized it was an announcement. She was pregnant! I was as excited and happy about her pregnancy as she was. We had not talked much about having a family, though I thought we might have two or three children, while Margaret somehow had the goal of six! She had grown up with three sisters and three brothers (and two other siblings had died in infancy). Anyway, our first child was on the way.

That summer we managed to get home to Oregon again and we lived with Margaret's parents. The shipyard in Portland was building freighters to get supplies overseas. I was hired as a journeyman carpenter, with union dues automatically deducted, and my pay suddenly jumped from the thirty cents an hour I had earned in the hayfields to $1.10. Everyone was happy, especially the shipyard owners, as they were working on a cost-plus basis. This meant that the more people they hired, whether needed or not, the more extra profit they received. My estimate is that there were three times as many of us as were needed.

My first assignment was to construct a wooden privy on the top deck. Never having constructed anything before, I worked at it for two days. When I finished, it was obviously tilted to one side, as I had not allowed for the slope of the deck, but the boss said it was okay. The next day, however, it was gone! Someone had changed his mind and had it torn down, and one was now being built on a lower deck.

On one occasion the foreman told most of us to go down into the ship and hide because an inspector was coming. The foreman didn't want him to see all of us standing around trying to find something to do. I was puzzled about the ethics of this situation, but I was also afraid of being fired, so I swallowed my conscience and followed the crowd. I was already under suspicion because when there was work to do, I tried to do it as fast as I could. I was told to slow down, because if everyone worked fast, the ship would be built several months ahead of schedule, and we would all be out of jobs. Quite a change from the hay-baling philosophy of "work hard or get out"!

Margaret was in full blossom with her pregnancy and prettier than ever when we returned to Dallas. One morning in early December she wakened me at five o'clock, and we walked the four blocks to the hospital. After twenty-four hours of hard labor, Margaret gave birth to our first little daughter. We named her Rebecca. What a wonderfully happy day it was!

We had some savings from my shipyard work to pay the doctor and hospital charges, and we dipped into our wedding gift money to buy a crib, playpen, buggy, and a used washing machine.

Chapter 12
An Introduction
to Missions

ALTHOUGH I HAD seldom been effective in personal witnessing for Christ, I was sincerely committed to trying to give the good news of His love to those in darkness. One method I thought of while at the seminary was to mail tracts addressed to boxholders on some of Dallas's rural routes. Margaret and I used our tithe to pay for the mailings and postage, and we enclosed a postage-free business reply card inviting those who received the tracts to ask for a free copy of the Gospel of John. We were able to get free Gospels from a tract society, and soon we were gratified and encouraged as we received scores of responses. Some who replied checked that they had "received Christ," and we prayed for them.

I thought of trying to find someone with enough money to sponsor the cost of such mailings all across the nation. I had no contacts with wealthy people, however, and even if I had known them, I would have been too timid to ask for their help. So although the project was successful, it died for lack of follow-up.

Because my time in Dallas was my first experience of living in the South, it was there that I first became aware of the plight of "colored" people, as they were then called. I had heard about segregation and more violent forms of persecution in southern states, but I knew nothing of it firsthand. One day I went to a Dallas post office to buy some stamps, and a black man was in line ahead of me. When he noticed me, he jumped aside and got behind me. Of course I felt bad about that.

On another occasion Margaret and I got on a city bus where the front "whites only" section was filled. The bus driver went back where the blacks were sitting and slammed down the "whites only" sign above the window of their seats. They immediately jumped up and stood at the back of the crowded bus. We heard a rumor that the sheriff had twelve notches on his gun handle, one for each "nigger" he had killed.

As I think back on those experiences now, I am surprised that it never occurred to me to dream about social justice and to think about what I or anyone else could do about it. It was twenty years later, in the 1960s, that activists—people willing to demonstrate, march, and die—made enough impact on society and government to bring about significant change in segregation and other discriminatory practices. Racism continues, and many reforms still need to be achieved, but much progress has been made.

It was during seminary days that I began to be more serious about my prayer life. Our one-room apartment didn't provide adequate privacy for prolonged personal prayer, so I began to take occasional prayer walks through the neighborhood. Since Dallas Seminary is in a residential area, the fields and woods I would have preferred were not available. I didn't take these walks on a regular daily schedule, but the outings were frequent enough to help me learn how wonderfully God answers prayer.

It was also during my seminary days that I became more and more interested in missionary work, although I didn't feel called to become a missionary myself. I began to read books about the idea of indigenous missions. At that time it was relatively common for missionaries to become the pastors of "native" churches. A better procedure is for those churches to be self-supporting rather than having their expenses paid by mission societies. The ideal is for missionaries to work themselves out of their jobs and move on to new territory, leaving behind a self-directed, self-supporting church whose members are not dependent upon money from America or other prosperous countries.

These ideas are common in mission work today—though not always practiced—but in the forties they were still mostly theory. The missionary was usually the pastor of the church he started for his local converts. Missionaries feared that new Christians, being inexperienced and relatively uneducated in the Scriptures, might lead the church into error. That does sometimes happen, but recent history has shown that those early fears were exaggerated. I was especially gratified to hear of some missionaries in Mexico who were practicing these principles.

The Christmas vacation of 1942 would begin two days after Margaret came home from the hospital with baby Rebecca, and some of my fellow students invited me to go to Mexico with them during the school break. Without giving any thought to how Margaret might feel about my absence at that time, I jumped at the chance to make the trip and observe indigenous missions at work. Margaret was under doctor's orders to rest in bed for another week, so I arranged with the wife of one of the other students going to Mexico to stay with her and the baby.

Margaret didn't say much about my plan, but I realized much later how hurt she was by my lack of sensitivity to her need to have me with her during those earliest days of parenting. As I look back on it, I am astounded at my thoughtlessness. I know now that it has often been a problem for me through the years to make good judgments about priorities. I still am not always sure how to balance personal relationships with "the Lord's work." But I am well aware that in that particular situation I made a significant error.

The trip to Mexico was my first visit to a Third World country. I was intrigued to see the Mexican culture and environment but was greatly moved by the economic and spiritual poverty I saw. Catholic churches were everywhere, but the people's religion didn't seem to carry over into sexual morality or spiritual vitality, at least for the men. This seemed to me directly related to the fact that Bible reading was strictly forbidden to the laity in those days.

We saw evidence of real godliness in some of the Protestant missionary outposts and particularly in the growing Pentecostal movement. This was somewhat confusing to me, because Pentecostalism was still anathema to our fundamentalist seminary, as well as to my home church and in my home training. I have come to realize how wrong we fundamentalists were in refusing fellowship with charismatic groups, for in many parts of the world they are leaders in making the gospel known.

In Mexico City we spent our first day or two doing the usual tourist things like going out to see the pyramids and visiting the cathedral. But my mind was set on visiting Eglon Harris, the missionary I had heard about who was trying to teach the Christian nationals to "run their own show." He lived in a town several hours away by a night bus trip. I was timid about going alone, not knowing Spanish, and none of the other men was interested in accompanying me. In fact, they thought it was a foolish venture and advised against it.

The bus was to leave at 6:30 that evening, but I was tired and wanted a good night's sleep instead of sitting up all night during a bumpy ride. I pondered and prayed and struggled with the question but, characteristically, couldn't make up my mind.

Six o'clock came—and I was several minutes away from the

bus depot. In desperation I did something I don't recommend: prayerfully I opened my Bible at random, put my finger down on the page, and looked to see what the verse said. In substance it said, "Take not the advice of thy friends"! So I ran for the bus and found a seat.

Some of the passengers had crates of chickens with them, and one had a small pig in the aisle, tied by a rope to the seat. The bus driver knew my destination because of my ticket and awakened me from a fitful sleep in the middle of the night. I climbed off the bus and found a hotel. In the morning I went to find Mr. Harris.

Mr. Harris's father had come to Mexico as a railroad engineer fifty years before and had begun a Plymouth Brethren meeting. Fifteen years prior to my visit, the little handful of believers had blossomed to three hundred. Then a financial crisis shut down the mills of their town, sending most of the people back to their villages. So now groups were meeting in fifty-seven villages, with as many as two hundred people in each one, and with Sunday schools averaging one hundred students. In addition, Mr. Harris printed 150,000 copies of a four-page gospel leaflet each month for distribution in Mexico and in Central and South America.

Mr. Harris's devotion to Christ was genuine and heartwarming. His example challenged me, and it made me think more seriously than I had before about whether God might want me and my family as missionaries. This was a sobering thought, but I felt glad that I was not automatically rejecting it, as I always had before. This indicated spiritual progress, and I was glad I had decided to make the visit.

A day or two later my seminary colleagues and I visited Cameron Townsend, founder of Wycliffe Bible Translators. He and his wife, Elvira, lived in a small trailer in Tetelcingo. While the Summer Institute of Linguistics was several years old, Wycliffe Bible Translators as a separate but closely linked organization was new. Its purpose was, and is, "to put the Word of God into all the tribal tongues of earth in which it does not yet exist." We shared the Townsends' joy when learning that fifty-one young people had already volunteered for this Bible translation work. Today this number has grown to more than six thousand, working in 305 languages.

The trip back to Dallas was uneventful except for one incident, when we got out of the car in a small Mexican town and were soon surrounded by children begging for money. They were good-natured about it, but they crowded around us in such numbers that we could hardly move, so we got back into the car and hurried away. Their needs were almost overwhelming, though I found it easy to put them out of my mind as we drove across the border to middle-class America.

As my third year of seminary drew to a close, I was still completely unsettled about what my career path should be. I had no sense of call to become the pastor of a church but was full of interest in Christian journalism.

We stayed in Dallas that summer of 1943 rather than going back to Oregon. My classmate Alan Hamilton asked me to help him edit and produce the first issues of the new magazine of the Child Evangelism Fellowship, a work that was beginning to spread across the nation. I found it challenging and rewarding to edit the articles, help design and lay out each issue, work with the printer, and finally to hold the fresh, lovely, newly printed magazine in my hands. I glowed with pleasure at the help it would be to its readers.

Another periodical that began about the same time was the Inter-Varsity Christian Fellowship magazine, with the unusual name *HIS*. The title, which I felt could easily be misunderstood, was the only thing I did not like about the magazine. Its editor, Robert Walker, had done a superb job of putting together articles of interest to Christians on college campuses. He included insightful pieces on spiritual growth, encourage-

ment in evangelism, even short stories with spiritual significance. I was captivated by it. I remember a day when I was
walking along a sidewalk in Dallas, reading the new issue of
HIS that had just arrived in the mail. While waiting at a street
corner for the light to change, I became so absorbed in what
I was reading that I missed the next green light entirely!

Because of my interest in the magazine, I was delighted—in
fact, overwhelmed—when I received a letter that summer,
inviting me to move to Chicago and succeed Walker as the
editor of *HIS.* I didn't know how to answer. I still had another
year to go before getting the Th.M. degree. The dining hall
job entitled us to the best of the student apartments, and we
had many friends. Moreover, Margaret was, to our surprise,
pregnant again.

Nevertheless, the invitation to Chicago seemed to be the
opportunity of a lifetime, and I didn't have to pray about it long
before I was convinced it was time to stop preparing for my
life work and actually begin it. I took the train to Chicago,
leaving Margaret and little Becky behind until I could find a
place for us to live.

I had made arrangements to work only part-time on the
Inter-Varsity magazine at first, so that I could finish my seminary work at Northern Baptist Theological Seminary, then
located in a deteriorating section of Chicago's west side. I
found a three-room apartment a block from the school and a
block from the elevated train that would take me to downtown
Chicago, where the Inter-Varsity office was located. The
apartment house was very old and dingy, but our unit was on
the first floor, which would be convenient for my pregnant
wife and nine-month-old daughter. During those war years,
apartments were difficult to find; to get one so conveniently
located seemed a godsend.

I sent Margaret an airplane ticket, which was in itself an
event, as neither of us had ever flown. A neighbor drove me

to Midway Airport—the only commercial airport in Chicago at that time—and I soon had my family walking into their new "home." I was not prepared for Margaret's reaction. She took one look at the sooty walls of the dark rooms and the rusty springs of the sagging bed we had inherited—and burst into tears! I had been so happy just to find any kind of place to live that I had forgotten to look at it through her eyes. She would have to be there all the time, while I could get away to school and to work. She quickly composed herself, however. We scrubbed away the soot from the walls and floor, and Margaret made it as homelike as possible.

The year at Northern Baptist Seminary went smoothly. My thesis for the master's degree was entitled "Success Factors in Missions." It was an attempt to analyze why some overseas churches grow and some do not. If I were writing that thesis today, I would be much less sure of the answers, or that any really exist. Why the huge growth of the church in Latin America? Most of that growth is in the Pentecostal churches. But that is not the case in Africa, where church growth is equally explosive. And why the rapid growth in Korea, now claiming a Christian population of 15 percent? Why is there virtually no church growth in Japan, where 1 or 2 percent is the usual tally of Christians even after more than a century of faithful missionary work, including a large and vital literature ministry? And in China, deprived of missionaries for more than forty years, the church numbers 5 percent of the population, up from less than 1 percent only a few years ago.

The only factor common to all church growth seems to be the providence of the Holy Spirit, and He goes wherever He wills. Our calling, as I understand it, is just to be faithful in the proclamation of the gospel to the ends of the earth, regardless of whether or not we see a harvest.

The Rumor

I heard it,
So I told it to another,
And he told it too.

The facts were otherwise
(As I learned later),
And now,
With twenty years gone by,
I can't remember
What it was
He didn't do.

But this I know,
That when his name is spoken—
Distrust,
Suspicion
Fill my mind.

How far the rumor swept
I never heard.
But if a hundred persons heard it in the end,
I wonder if for them,
Like me,
It never stopped at all,
But stayed for all these years
To smut their souls?

K.N.T.

Chapter 13
A New Job and a
Growing Family

THREE DAYS AFTER Becky's first birthday, Paul Kaufman, a fellow student, took us to the hospital for the birth of our second child. The baby was a boy, and we named him John. Paul's wife, Freeda, took little Becky out to Wheaton, where Mary Lou Benson cared for her while Margaret was in the hospital. Right from the beginning little John had difficulties. He had colic and cried with pain after each feeding. Sometimes he became even more agitated, with his cries escalating into desperate screaming. Nothing we did could comfort him, and we could not find the cause of his distress. We were frightened as we held him in our arms for long periods, trying to bring him relief. We also held him up before the Lord for healing.

One day Freeda, who was a nurse, was visiting Margaret when John had one of his attacks of screaming. When his diaper was changed, Freeda's trained eye detected that John had an inguinal hernia, causing the intestine to protrude into the scrotum, making it bulge to twice its normal size. No wonder he screamed. The doctor confirmed this observation and fitted John with a tiny truss, which prevented further rupture. It did nothing for his colic, but eventually he outgrew that. We hoped the hernia would heal by itself, but this did not happen. The only permanent remedy was surgery, which was performed about two and a half years later.

When the time came for the surgery, a check for one hundred dollars arrived unexpectedly from our church to help with the medical expenses. I still remember the wave of gratitude and the heartwarming realization that someone was thinking about us and caring for our needs. That is one reason I now give generously to our church's Care and Share Fund that helps many individuals and families through financial emergencies.

John's hospital stay for the hernia operation was distressing for all of us. In those days hospital rules did not allow parents to stay with their children past the normal visiting hours, no matter how upset the child might be. I shall never forget the agony of having to walk away from little John as he stretched out his arms to me, crying to be comforted at bedtime. I had to leave him despite his broken-hearted screaming. I have always been resentful of that policy and have wondered what I might have done to protect John from the harmful effects of the fear and sense of abandonment he must have experienced.

Meanwhile, my work as editor of *HIS* was pure joy, just as fulfilling as I thought it would be. I also had my first experience as a book publisher when I helped prepare the first book Inter-Varsity ever published—*Hymns,* compiled by Paul Beckwith. I sent the manuscript to a music publishing house to be typeset and printed and was told the books would be ready in eight months. In my inexperience I assumed it would be so. A few weeks before I expected the books to come, I advertised their availability on the agreed-upon delivery date. When the books didn't arrive that day, or the next, I called to find out where they were. I was told that the work hadn't been started yet, but the books would be ready in another five months! That was one of my first object-lessons about "the wheel that squeaks."

Eventually the books arrived and fulfilled a useful ministry among campus groups, going into printing after printing for many years. This book was the forerunner of many books to come from InterVarsity Press, which has become one of the highly respected Christian publishing houses in America.

Margaret and I were anxious to leave the city and were quick to accept the invitation of Stacey Woods, general secretary of Inter-Varsity, to rent his house for the three summer months. It was in Wheaton, the Chicago suburb where I had gone to college. What a welcome relief from the noise and grime of Chicago! With Becky a toddler and John six months old, we appreciated the extra room inside and the green lawn outside.

We expected that during the summer we would have time and opportunity to hear of a permanent rental opportunity. The wartime scarcity of housing was so acute that houses for rent never appeared in the newspaper ads or at real estate offices. The only way to find one was to get advance information about someone who was planning to move and then rush over and apply.

But the summer went by and we heard of no houses for rent. We prayed fervently, but when summer was over and the Woods family was due to return, we had found nothing. We had no idea where to turn. Then, at the crucial moment, we received a telephone call. Evan Welsh, pastor of College Church of Christ, who had recently been left a widower with two small children, said his mother would be moving into the parsonage with him, and her house in Wheaton would be available to rent. What a glorious answer to our prayers! The completely furnished house was located directly across the street from the Wheaton College campus, a prime location for getting additional income by renting extra bedrooms to students. We rented three of the four bedrooms to five college girls, and we all shared the one bathroom. The move was a fairly simple process, as we only owned two cribs, two highchairs, a playpen, a baby buggy, and our clothing.

A minor event occurred in 1944 that had an important impact and lasting results. Loren Zorn, editor of *Power,* an adult Sunday school take-home paper published by Scripture Press, printed an editorial note inviting writers and would-be writers to submit stories or articles for possible publication. Margaret and I read the note with interest one Sunday afternoon, and it occurred to me to try to write a short story and send it in. But I needed a push, which came from Margaret. She suggested that we each sit down that afternoon with pencil and paper and see what happened. I agreed, and while the children had their naps, we began.

I thought of the college audience who read the Inter-Varsity magazine I edited, and I tried to think of a theme that might be helpful to college-age Christians. After a few false starts, I began writing about a Christian girl who fell in love with a fellow student who, though a good man, was not a Christian. Eventually her good sense and knowledge of biblical teaching prevailed, and she walked away from the romance. I think I called my story, "Love Is a Dangerous Road." It still is.

Margaret wrote a piece about how we should be looking forward to our Lord's return. Both her article and my story were eventually published. This experience set me thinking about doing some more writing. I owe a lot to Loren Zorn for getting me started on a hobby that eventually led to professional writing and publishing. And I owe much to Margaret for issuing that Sunday afternoon challenge.

During my years of visiting Christian student groups on campuses, I had felt their need for a better understanding of the reasonableness of Christianity and why their pagan professors didn't believe in Christianity. I spent several days drafting and rewriting material for a small booklet, which I called *Is Christianity Credible?*

The booklet began by pointing out that both the atheist and the Christian come to logical conclusions, all depending on their presuppositions. The atheist begins with the premise that there is no God. He doesn't come to that conclusion by proofs, but begins with that conclusion and then decides that, since there is no God, there can be no miracles or fulfilled prophecy, and conversion is only psychological. His position is all very logical but has nothing to do with knowing the truth of his assumption.

The agnostic, one who says he doesn't know whether God exists, has a better chance of finding the truth if he has an open mind. There is plenty of evidence all around, in both the microscopic and macroscopic universes, to help him decide.

The Christian believer begins with the assumption that there is a God and that miracles are, therefore, reasonable. We believe that God has given the Bible as His instruction book.

The attitude of the atheist and agnostic versus the believer is seen in differing opinions about the origin of human beings. The atheist usually believes that mankind evolved from chance molecules. The believer insists either that God guided evolution, or that God created man instantly in his present human form.

To me, the most pointed fallacy of Darwin and his modern successors is their assumption that male and female organs developed as marvelously crafted mutations in the same year and in the same place.

My booklet was published by InterVarsity Press in 1946. It was well accepted on the campuses, and I have been gratified that it is still in print after forty-five years. The long lifespan of that little volume is typical of many of the books I have written, and I am very grateful to God for giving me this writing ability.

Mrs. Welsh's house was only one block from College Church, which I had attended during college years. We now attended regularly as a family, and Margaret and I soon became members. Commuting to Chicago was easy for me because of our proximity to the College Avenue train station.

We were also only a block from our good friends Ted and Mary Lou Benson. Ted was director of the Wheaton Alumni Association, and I was elected president for the 1945–46 school year. Ted and I spent a lot of time discussing what alumni could do to make Wheaton College even more effective in fulfilling its motto, For Christ and His Kingdom.

With college girls living with us, baby-sitting was no problem, and our social life picked up. We were able to attend more events at the church and concerts at the college.

We did have one problem for which we found no easy solution. Who would care for Becky and John when Margaret went to the hospital for the birth of our third child, due in January? Margaret's mother could not come. In the end it was my mother who came by train from Oregon. We paid for her ticket. We couldn't afford to pay for a sleeping berth for her, but the ticket still depleted our meager savings—what was left of our wedding gift money. She assured us that she didn't mind sitting up on the coach, as she would see more of the country that way.

We had no telephone, for during the war years one could not easily get a phone installed; labor and materials were directed to war efforts. Our elderly neighbors gave us a key to their house so we could come in and call the doctor when it was necessary. About 2:00 A.M. on a bitterly cold night toward the end of January 1945, we found good use for that key. I went next door to notify the doctor that Margaret was in labor. Then I called the assistant pastor of our church, who had kindly volunteered to drive us, day or night, to the hospital in Aurora, twenty miles away. A few hours after checking into the hospital, Margaret gave birth to our second little girl, Martha.

When I reported the happy news at my office, my pleasure was enhanced when my boss, Stacey Woods, informed me that with a larger family my salary would be increased. He also gently suggested that Margaret and I, with three children, need not feel further obligated to fulfill the scriptural injunction to Noah and his wife to populate the earth! His advice went unheeded, however, for in the next eleven years we had seven more children—a total of ten.

While I was satisfied at Inter-Varsity, my vision kept turning to the mission field and to the needs of the masses for Christian literature. The leader of tract publication in America was young Clyde Dennis, a printer and publisher in Minneapolis. He was repulsed by the cheap, one-color tracts that were common at that time. He made a radical change by using good quality paper and printing tracts with full-color illustrations. Tract users gladly welcomed these attractive leaflets, and soon they became widely popular.

One day Clyde shared with me his vision of translating his tracts into other languages for use overseas. He had recently moved his business to Chicago, and he asked me if I would be interested in joining his newly founded company, Good News Publishers. Again I struggled with my inability to make decisions. I wanted to stay with Inter-Varsity, with its vital campus ministry, but I keenly felt the need overseas.

A few weeks after Clyde's offer I attended the Inter-Varsity staff conference near Toronto, Ontario. My job dilemma was uppermost in my thoughts, and one evening I slipped away for prayer. Alone with God, I finally felt peace of mind about leaving the editorship of *HIS*.

When I told Margaret about that decision, she was quite willing. She has always seemed to feel she should happily go along in whatever directions the Lord leads me, rather than being actively involved in the decisions. I realize now that on the whole we did not talk things over enough. We should have done so more often, because her judgment is frequently better than mine, or at least she gives me a different perspective.

Eventually Pastor Welsh remarried and took the pastorate of Ward Memorial Presbyterian Church in Detroit. This directly affected us, because Mother Welsh would be returning to her home, and we would have to move again.

Clyde and Muriel Dennis were living in Lake Geneva, Wisconsin, a city located beside a beautiful lake, sixty miles northwest of Chicago. Clyde commuted by train, an hour and a half each way. He said he did some of his best creative thinking and writing during those travel hours when others were reading the newspapers or napping.

The Dennises occupied one of several homes built for servants on the former summer estate of one of Chicago's wealthy families. With the war, conditions were very different, and families could no longer get hired help. The estate changed hands, and the auxiliary houses were now being rented out. Clyde told me that one of the houses was still available. During the winter months the rent was eighty dollars—steep for us, as my monthly salary was three hundred dollars. In June, with the beginning of the resort season, the rent would jump to one thousand dollars a month, and we would be on the move again.

Since no other option was available, we left the comforts and familiarity of Wheaton in the fall of 1946 for this house and community we had not seen, thankful for God's provision. The three-bedroom house stood among beautiful trees, and the spacious grounds were carpeted with autumn leaves—an ideal spot for the children. The half-hour walk to and from the train depot was good for my health. I left the house at six in the morning and returned home about seven in the evening, in time to help put the children to bed. The days were long for Margaret, alone with the children, who were now going on four, three, and two years of age, with another on the way. We had no car, but we attended the Baptist church when someone came to pick us up.

We expected the new baby to arrive in October. Again we arranged for my mother to come from Oregon. But after her arrival, week after week went by, and no baby! Apparently Margaret and the doctor had been a month off in their calculations. Eventually, a second son gladdened our hearts. We named him Peter.

For the first time, we had hospitalization insurance and had no worries about paying the bill. A sympathetic woman doctor saw to it that Margaret stayed in the hospital the full ten days allowed. She was discharged on December 5, Becky's fourth birthday, so I took Becky with me when I drove to the hospital in Clyde Dennis's car to bring Margaret and baby Peter home.

Having been away from home much longer than she had expected, Mother left for Oregon almost immediately. When I saw her off at the train station in Chicago, I had no idea it was the last time I would see her.

Five months later I learned of her death when my secretary brought me a telegram and quietly stepped out, closing my office door behind her. The telegram was from Doug, telling me Mother had died of a stroke. A wave of grief and regret overwhelmed me. Happy childhood and teenage memories mingled with self-condemnation that I had not been able to help Dad and Mother meet their financial needs. And what would Dad do now? He would be all alone after thirty-three years of marriage, as Lyman had enlisted and was with the occupation forces in Japan.

I left the office and walked the Chicago streets for a couple of hours, wandering disconsolately, grieving for so much Mother had missed in life, but also thanking God for my godly heritage.

We had no money for train fare to the funeral. Should we borrow it? Clyde Dennis offered to lend me money, but we were strongly opposed to going any further into debt. I still owed my parents six hundred dollars from college days. How Mother could have used that money, or even a fraction of it! How long since she had had a new dress, or even a dollar to call her own? I reasoned that going home for her funeral would not help her. I did not know then that funerals are for the survivors—to share their grief and to recount their blessings. My decision not to go was probably a mistake. Two years later a neighbor of my parents reprimanded me for what he perceived as my callousness.

Mother's spiritual influence in shaping my life was incalculable. I hope heaven will allow me an opportunity to tell her so.

Chapter 14
Housing Frustrations

MY WORK with Good News Publishers was challenging. How does one go about getting American tracts translated into African and European languages and distributed overseas? I know now what I didn't know then: it is foolish to try! The culture and point of view of the Frenchman, the Ethiopian, the Nigerian are vastly different from those of the American. Forcing these American tracts into other languages was impractical and the product often ineffective.

But I tried. I busily wrote to missionary friends, sending copies of our tracts for them to translate. Later on I found out that some of the missionaries who did the translating had more zeal than knowledge of the local languages, and the resulting product sounded to the native readers of that language as garbled as a tract written in Pidgin English would be to an American.

I suppose it was comparable to the instructions that sometimes come with products produced in Japan or Korea—for instance, "Point camera at facial feature"! We may smile at such translations, but it is not laughable when it involves communicating the truth of the gospel of Jesus Christ.

My negative experience with this tract translation program was valuable many years later when I organized Living Bibles International in order to develop Living Bibles in the major languages of the world. Translation must be done by nationals brought up in their language, not by missionaries.

On Memorial Day of 1947 we vacated our lakeside guest house, just before the rent skyrocketed for the resort season. We had arranged to rent "Doc" Paul Wright's house in Wheaton while he and his family made their annual summer move to South Dakota, where he was the supervisor of Wheaton College's summer campus in the Black Hills. Unfortunately, the house wasn't available until after the college commencement, another whole week. Our good friends Clarence and Gertrude Nystrom opened their home to the six of us during that interim. In their hospitality we saw a never-to-be-forgotten lesson in Christian love in action.

Over the months, I had gradually become aware that my grand plan at Good News Publishers of translating American tracts into other languages wasn't working, and I didn't know what to do about it. As I was facing this truth, Clyde Dennis found someone in Switzerland to start a missionary printing plant there. Most of my duties were transferred to that location, leaving me without much to do. This fact, combined with internal situations at Good News, made me question the wisdom of staying. After a few weeks of uncertainty, I resigned.

There I was, with no job, a growing family, and no idea what God wanted. I felt angry with Him for leading me to leave the work at Inter-Varsity and putting me in this predicament, so I went into a fit of spiritual sulking. I told God I wasn't even going to try to find other full-time Christian work. If that was what He wanted, He would have to send a bolt from the blue, for without guidance that dramatic I would never again believe I could discern His will.

My first day of job hunting in Wheaton was depressing, to say the least. I went to the manager of the local cab company, but he declared me overqualified and would not even take my application. I couldn't find any stores that needed clerks, either. That night, however, the local paper carried an ad for a carpenter in a factory in nearby West Chicago. Since I had had a few weeks of carpentry at the shipyards, I borrowed a car and went over first thing in the morning. The job turned out to be making chicken coops and hog houses, nailing together precut lumber.

I took the job, but even my very small carpentry skills were not challenged. I defiantly told God about my bitterness and complained about the way He was treating me. After a few hours the Lord graciously brought me to my senses, and I realized my foolishness in not trusting Him. Finally I was able to say that if He wanted me in carpentry or any other kind of secular work, it was His business to decide, not mine. In His grace He sent me release and relief of spirit.

When I wearily returned home after my third day on the job, Margaret said Russ Hitt had called. Russ was an Inter-Varsity friend who was now director of public relations at Moody Bible Institute in Chicago. Knowing of my need for a job, he had called to ask if I would come for an interview concerning a staff opening at Moody.

I'm sorry to say that in spite of my determination to follow God, made just three days earlier, I was hesitant about working at the Institute. I think I had been influenced during my Wheaton College days by the thinking of some Wheaton students that Moody, being a Bible school, was educationally inferior to our liberal arts college, and that some of its practices and rules were extreme. So it was with reluctance that I went into Chicago on Saturday afternoon to meet with J. D. Hall, director of the Moody Colportage Association (later called the Moody Literature Mission).

Mr. Hall was looking for an understudy before retiring in a year, after thirty-five years of faithful service. He explained that his department's main function was to mail thousands of sets of Christian books and Gospels of John to school rooms, especially in the South. This project was carried on with the cooperation of county school superintendents, whose offices sent the lists of schools and teachers. The response to the offer was huge. In this way scores of thousands of children were reached with storybooks about children whose lives were changed by Jesus.

I learned, too, that Mr. Hall was the author of the tract "Four Things God Wants You to Know," which has been translated into many languages around the world. Millions of copies have been used.

I was fascinated by Mr. Hall's description of his work. By the time he got through telling me what my part in this outreach could be in touching large numbers of children with the gospel, I began to be afraid I *wouldn't* get the job, instead of fearing I would, as had been my attitude when I came in for the interview. A few days later, to my delight and relief, the Moody personnel office called and offered me the job. Still, my old weakness asserted itself. On that summer day in 1947, as I headed for my new office in Crowell Hall, Moody's administration building, I found myself slipping into the familiar pattern of uncertainty. I hoped desperately that I wasn't making a disastrous mistake. What a way to begin what turned out to be sixteen of the happiest years of my life!

Now the job question was settled, but not our housing problem. Summer was ending, and the Wrights would soon return from the Black Hills. We had been so hopeful of finding a house to rent in Wheaton or in another suburb served by a commuter line that would take me to Chicago. We still did not have a car.

When nothing became available, we allowed ourselves to

think the unthinkable. Would Margaret and the four children have to go back to Oregon and live with her parents? In January our family would again increase with the arrival of our fifth child.

I cannot describe the turmoil of spirit in those anxious days. Would we never be able to settle down? Had I brought Margaret from her parents' luxurious home to a life of rootlessness and uncertainty? Despite shedding a few tears from time to time, Margaret was the stronger one during this dark and difficult time.

Again, in our extreme need, we found an "opportunity" of sorts. An acquaintance had just purchased an old, run-down hotel—the Garfield—at the edge of Winona Lake Conference Grounds near Warsaw, Indiana, about 120 miles southeast of Chicago. It was strictly a summer hotel, with no heating system and no insulation. However, four guest rooms at the end of the second-floor hall had been blocked off by adding a door in the hallway to make a poor semblance of an apartment. We could occupy those rooms but would have to buy a coal stove for heat. The unheated bathrooms were at the far end of the hall. Margaret would have to cook on an electric plate.

And so we moved to Winona Lake. I began taking the 5:00 A.M. New York Central train to Chicago on Monday mornings, arriving in time for work, and returning home Friday night. At first I spent the nights during the week in a sleeping bag at the Good News Publishers office, although I was no longer employed there, but later I found a room to rent from Ray Hill and his wife.

Margaret doesn't talk much about that year. I know it was extremely difficult for her. Again she was in an isolated place, alone with the children in that huge old building with the wind whistling down the long hallways. She had little opportunity to have contact with neighbors or acquaintances at the church we attended. The owner's idea of filling the building with tenants had been unrealistic from the start. A couple with no children occupied some rooms on the first floor for a few weeks but then were able to find quarters with heat.

We did become friends with Al and Verna Zahlout, who lived half a block from the hotel. Al was a violinist who supported his family by giving concerts at churches, and Verna accompanied him. They had five young girls. Because Al practiced his violin at home during the day, Margaret did not feel she should take the four children and visit Verna in their very small house. However, she did leave the children with Verna on the days when she went to the doctor for her monthly prenatal examinations. Other good and helpful friends to us were John and Sherry Benson, who lived nearby.

I was anxious to buy a car, not only so I could take the family for outings, but to make it easier for Margaret to do the weekly grocery shopping at the A&P in Warsaw. She took the bus at five cents a ride each Saturday morning while I watched the children. But the most important reason for wanting a car was to have immediate transportation home if Margaret went to the hospital during the week, while I was at work in Chicago.

One day we heard about a nearby farmer who had a twenty-year-old Dodge for sale. Since he used it only for occasional trips to town, the odometer showed just 28,000 miles. The price for this marvel was two hundred dollars. After seven years of marriage and four children, we finally had wheels!

With the onset of winter, and while I was in Chicago, the water pipes to the bathrooms froze. Margaret called a plumber, who, because of previous experience with the owner, would not come until assured that we were able to pay him. When he looked at the situation, he complained bitterly about the location of the shut-off valve, requiring a fifty-foot crawl beneath the hotel floor. He "wasn't paid to crawl through places like that!" But he did it.

We had no money to buy presents for the children at Christmas, but Frances Ferries, who had been our neighbor when we lived in Mother Welsh's house, sent a box of new winter clothing for the children. Margaret especially appreciated the Dr. Denton sleepers, as there was no heat in the bedrooms. Even after more than forty years, Margaret can get teary-eyed when she tells about the box of crayons and coloring books that came from another Wheaton friend, Betty Boardman, in time for the children's Christmas. Grandma West sent clothes and diapers for the coming baby.

A January thaw caused more plumbing problems. A fountain of water from a broken pipe cascaded down the stairs into the lobby below. Margaret felt she couldn't or shouldn't wait for a plumber, so she crawled the fifty feet on her hands and knees through the cobwebs under the hotel to find the water shut-off valve. After turning off the water, she called the plumber to make the necessary repairs. When he came and saw her condition—due to go to the hospital any day—he gave her a stern lecture. He told her never to go under there again. "Think of the children . . . what if something happened to you . . . if you have more broken pipes, just let the place float away!"

The Saturday before Margaret's due date, her sister Harriet came by train from Detroit to Fort Wayne to pick up Becky and baby Peter, returning home that same day on the next eastbound train. She and her husband, John, had four young children of their own, so that was no light undertaking. We counted on the Christian compassion of two families in the Free Methodist Church in Winona Lake to take John and Martha when the actual day came.

Since Margaret was feeling particularly uncomfortable one day, Verna Zahlout decided to spend the night with her, just in case. And indeed, that was the night Margaret went into labor. Verna wakened her husband to take Margaret to the hospital.

Then she called me in Chicago, and in the morning she took John and Martha to the homes where they would be staying.

I received Verna's call around 2:00 A.M. Fortunately, the ancient car started on that frigid January morning, and I arrived at the hospital about three hours later. It was a country hospital without the usual "no fathers permitted" rules of that period. When I arrived in the delivery room, Margaret was under heavy sedation. Almost immediately I saw the top of our baby's head begin to appear, but one of the nurses pushed it back and held it there while they waited for the doctor to arrive.

I had never seen a birth and knew very little about the process, but it seemed to me it would be safer to let my little one be born. The nurses said no, they had to wait until the doctor was present. When he hadn't arrived after fifteen minutes, I demanded that they let the baby out, but they still refused. The nurses were obviously much afraid of the doctor, who was also the owner of the hospital, but finally one of them hesitantly called him again and found he had gone back to sleep.

After another fifteen minutes he arrived, very grouchy and surly. Ignoring me, he walked over to Margaret and pushed roughly on her abdomen, and our baby girl popped out—white and silent. The nurses slapped her to try to get her to breathe, but nothing happened. I remember how panicky one of the nurses was.

"Get the oxygen! Get the oxygen!" she exclaimed.

"Fool!" the doctor snarled. "If it isn't breathing, what good would oxygen do?"

At this point I went into a side room and got down on my knees and prayed, "Lord, if this child is ever going to need you in her entire life, it is right now. Please let her live. Still, Lord, if for some reason—perhaps because of something in her life you don't want her to have to face, or if perhaps she would not receive the grace of Christ or would abandon Him—then your will be done. It would be better to take her now. But please, Lord, let her live."

I hurried back to the delivery room, and just then the baby began to breathe and to cry. A few moments later I went back to the little "prayer room" to thank the Lord for His kindness. And so baby Janet came into our lives as a special act of God.

One early spring weekend when I came home from visiting schools in the South, where I had not been accessible by telephone, Margaret had a frightening story to tell me about sixteen-month-old Peter. He had toddled out the back door onto the unprotected fire escape and had fallen the fifteen feet to the hard ground below. God mercifully protected him from landing on the wire clothesline or the clothesline pipe.

During the late winter we had put a down payment of one thousand dollars, given to us by Margaret's father, on a lot in Northlake, a new subdivision west of Chicago. The house was to be framed for us and I would do the inside finishing. The framing was to be ready in May, but when I went out to see it in May, it hadn't even been started! I asked for my down payment back, but was refused. I went through a very hard time emotionally, because that thousand dollars was all we had.

The salesman finally said that if I would be at his office at 4:30 on a certain afternoon, he would return my money to me. I was unfamiliar with the route to his office and had to travel by streetcar and bus, since Margaret had the car, so I didn't arrive until 5:00—and the office was closed.

I still vividly remember my sense of desolation. In fact, that was the only time I have ever thought in any serious way about committing suicide. As I was overwhelmed with despair, I thought I could finally understand why people might be driven to end their lives.

Eventually, we did get the money back. But when it came to caring for my family's fundamental housing needs, I felt like an utter failure.

Chapter 15
A House of Our Own

WE STAYED in the Garfield Hotel nine months, but when summer came we moved back to Doc Wright's house while he and his family were in the Black Hills. Again we renewed our search for a permanent home in Wheaton, but the rental possibilities had not improved.

We were not the only young family in desperate need of affordable housing at that time just after the end of World War II. One couple we knew who shared our dilemma were Doug and Virginia Muir. Doug had attended Wheaton College when I did; Virginia, soon afterwards. The Muirs were members of our church. They were living with their two children—a toddler and a new baby—in a small house-trailer in the country outside of Wheaton. They had lived through one very cold winter in that poorly insulated trailer and were eager to get better situated before another winter began. We got together to discuss our mutual problem and looked at some properties for sale that we thought we might be able to divide into a sort of duplex.

We settled on a large house facing the railroad tracks just east of Wheaton. It had been divided up so that five couples or families were renting rooms. In our desperate need it would do for our two families, but we were cautioned against signing any purchase agreement until all the renters were out.

September came too soon. The Wrights were due to return, and again we had no place to live. It was time for Becky and John to start school, but where? Our friends Ted and Mary Lou Benson graciously came to our rescue and said we could set up our beds in their basement. It was a small house for their family of eight, and for the seven of us to move in was an extreme imposition. There was only one bathroom. Since there were no cooking facilities in the basement, Mary Lou did most of the cooking for both families. Becky and John walked to nearby Holmes School with the three older Benson children, leaving Mary Lou and Margaret with six preschoolers.

Weeks went by and the house we were hoping to buy with the Muirs still was not completely vacated. I left on a trip to visit Indian missions in British Columbia with my associate Peter Gunther. When I returned, John Sawyer, a friend from church who was in the real estate and insurance business, had interesting news for us. A property on the northeastern outskirts of Wheaton was for sale. It had two houses on it—an old, two-story farmhouse with a smaller, newer house beside it. The newer house had been built from scrap lumber salvaged from tearing down buildings used in the 1933–34 Chicago World's Fair. The driveway ran between the two houses and led to a large, dilapidated garage with farm sheds attached in the back. There were also three separate chicken and turkey houses. The lot was 150 feet wide and 600 feet deep. The whole property was for sale as a package for fifteen thousand dollars and was available on contract with a relatively small down payment. We still had the thousand-dollar gift from Margaret's father that had been the down payment for the Northlake house deal that fell through.

Mr. Sawyer was of great help to us and to the Muirs as we worked out the purchase. But when the time for the closing came, the Muirs experienced unexpected trouble in raising their part of the down payment, and all seemed to be lost. Margaret's tears flowed freely as we drove desolately away from that failed closing. It was hard to face the Bensons and report "no house." Something would have to be done. The strain was showing after two and a half months of living on top of one another. Margaret prevailed on the mother of one of Becky's first-grade classmates to take her in so Becky could continue in school. Then she loaded the other four children into our old Dodge and went back to Winona Lake. I moved back to live with Ray Hill and his wife in Chicago.

But then God intervened. The Muirs' financial dilemma was solved, and a new closing date was set. We divided the property, the Taylors taking the larger, old house with its adjoining property, and the Muirs taking the smaller house. Our portion of the cost was $6,300.

I cannot adequately express what a great day that was when we finally took possession of the house at 1515 East Forest Avenue during Thanksgiving week of 1948. We have now lived at that same address for forty-three years, though not in the same house. After eighteen years we built a new home to replace the old one.

Our house had many shortcomings, but we were immensely thankful for it. The interior of the house had been freshly painted and papered, which was a bonus, as we did not have any money left for redecorating.

We had three bedrooms, all upstairs, with the only bathroom downstairs. There was no basement and no furnace. Heat was provided by a large pot-bellied coal/wood stove in the middle of the kitchen and an oil-burning stove in the living-dining room. Another oil stove was upstairs in the bedroom that Margaret and I occupied. The children's bedrooms were not heated. The kitchen had no cupboards or counters, but a narrow walk-in pantry next to the kitchen took care of our storage needs at first. Several years later we bought a kitchen-full of used birch cabinets at a rummage sale.

Another basic problem was that the house had no foundation. It rested on cement blocks at the four corners, and one corner had sunk so much that spilled milk ran across the kitchen linoleum to that corner of the house.

At about this time we had the opportunity to get reacquainted with my brother Lyman. He had graduated from high school and had spent two years in Japan with the U. S. occupation forces. He went to Westmont College in California for a while, then transferred to Wheaton College for the rest of his undergraduate work. It was a delight to spend time with him during those years—and to watch his developing romance with Jeanetta Mae, who became a great sister-in-law. Lyman went on to Stanford University for the master's degree in geology.

Lyman's godly life as a geologist and, later, doing mysterious (i.e., classified) work at Lockheed, has been an inspiration and help to me. His three children and their families are a warm and close-knit group all living for the Lord. I visit them in California once or twice a year, and we always enjoy our fellowship.

Mark was the first child born after we moved into that old farmhouse. We drove over icy roads in the middle of a January night in 1951 and got to the hospital in time, but the doctor didn't. A night nurse was the only attendant, and Margaret had no anesthetic. Mark was born on Janet's third birthday.

About a year and a half later, Margaret went to the hospital on an important Sunday in May, and Cynthia arrived in time to be a Mother's Day gift to us all. (These days when we get a call from Cynthia, now a wife and mother in Delaware, she is apt to announce, "This is number seven calling.")

Space in the house was another problem. We had already filled it when we moved in with five children, and now there were seven. Margaret and I had a large bedroom, with room for Margaret's sewing machine and a large desk for me, but the children's two bedrooms were small. The girls' bedroom had no closet, and they had to walk through a corner of the boys' bedroom to get to their room.

Without a basement or family room and with bedrooms too small to play in, the children's indoor activities all centered in the living room: reading, roughhousing, board games, ball throwing, gymnastics, studying, and practicing on the piano and violin.

After six years of stove heat I spent a summer vacation digging out a crawl space beneath the house to install a Sears gas furnace that hung from the floor joists. As I dug, the children crawled away with the buckets of dirt. The furnace had to go under the house because the only first floor closet already contained the water heater. It was a difficult summer because Margaret had no confidence in my ability to install it properly and gave me no encouragement at all. The hardest part of the furnace job was trying to put the duct work into the crawl space where the floor joists were only about eighteen inches above the ground, a space filled with cobwebs and, in my overactive imagination, with scorpions, tarantulas, and black widow spiders!

That gas furnace almost blew apart—or so it seemed to me—when I finally got it installed and tried to light it! The problem was that I misunderstood the instructions for lighting the pilot, and the chamber was half-filled with gas when I lit a match. Fortunately neither the furnace nor I was hurt.

Margaret's unhappiness with me about installing the furnace was symptomatic of a growing tension between us. She was hurt by my indifference to our need for a larger house, and I felt her exasperation. But I always thought my ideas were better than hers, and she quietly resented this arrogance. There were no harsh words between us, but I became very defensive and was easily offended by any critical comment she made or even by ordinary remarks that I interpreted as criticism.

I find it painful now to look back and remember how I would sulk in moody silence, sometimes for many hours. Margaret, unaware of having offended me, was perplexed. At times I would leave the house and walk for hours, seething, until my anger was spent. Perhaps even worse were mornings when I left for work without kissing her, saying only a stony good-bye as I left. Then I was in turmoil the rest of the day.

I knew I had no right to be resentful and angry, but I didn't know what to do. I knew the Scripture and deeply desired to obey it: "Husbands, love your wives, and be not bitter against them" (Col. 3:19, KJV). And as one who believed in and practiced prayer, I was deeply branded by the Apostle Peter's admonition to husbands to treat their wives properly, "That your prayers be not hindered" (1 Pet. 3:7, KJV).

But what I wanted and longed for—steady peace and joy with my wife—seemed beyond my ability.

I well remember taking a long walk the night I finally realized that this simply must not go on. There seemed to be two ways to respond to her criticism. One was to regard any criticism of me as a fault in her that I had to live with; it was unfortunate to have such a childish wife, but I would mentally pat her on the head and haughtily ignore this fault of hers. As soon as I said this to myself, however, I knew it was wrong and wouldn't work. That attitude would not expunge my bitterness. It would not qualify me as meeting the Apostle Paul's criteria for godly living, and it would not qualify me for getting my prayers answered.

The other solution was one I could not bear. That was simply to forgive Margaret for criticizing me. But I rebelled against this. It was unfair. Why should I forgive her for hurting me—and sometimes I was deeply hurt. But I was absolutely serious with God on that long walk that night, and I was serious with Margaret, though she was not there. The situation must end, and since Margaret would not solve the problem by no longer criticizing me, I would have to take the lead by acknowledging her criticism as valid, then trying to learn from her criticism, meanwhile forgiving her for hurting me.

As I came up the dark driveway to our home, I made my decision to acknowledge my fault. I rehearsed in my mind the remark she had made two hours before, acknowledged that she was right, and forgave her for hurting me. I entered the house quietly, but no longer in silent anger, and spoke to Margaret as though nothing had happened. It was one of the hardest actions of my life—to allow myself to admit the fault she had alleged, and concurrently to say in my heart, "I forgive you," and mean it. But God helped me.

The next time a criticism came—a few days later, I suppose—I flared up internally as before but rushed out and prayed for help to accept and forgive, then I came back quieted a few minutes later. Not many days went by before I realized that the flare-ups took a shorter and shorter time to deal with, and they could finally be handled immediately. A few weeks later, Margaret remarked to me, "You are different from the way you were," and I knew the Lord's grace had prevailed, the spiritual battle of many years was ended, and Satan, who had conquered for so long, was himself conquered.

And when the turmoil ended, the grass could become fresh and green and flowers could grow and bloom—and they did.

Gretchen was born in June 1954, the summer I was installing the furnace. Margaret's sixteen-year-old niece, Margaret Baden, came from Detroit to do the household chores and look after seven children while Margaret was in the hospital.

That same summer we converted the enclosed back porch into a dining room and the enclosed front porch into bedrooms for the three boys, who, being rapidly outnumbered by sisters, had been edged out of their upstairs room. Conversion of the front porch meant only putting up a partition, so that John could have a room of his own. Now the front door opened into Peter and Mark's bedroom! Since the porch was not heated, it was very cold in the winter. On the floor of the back porch/dining room we laid linoleum tile, put in a wall heater, and installed aluminum combination storms and screens on the *inside*. We left the original loose-fitting storm windows on the outside.

These make-do measures were my idea, not Margaret's. She was hoping that with the appreciated value of the property and of our equity we would have enough for a down payment on a larger house. My sincere (but probably wrong) conviction was that we should get by with inadequate housing and save any extra money for the children's college expenses and for increased contributions to the Lord's work.

We had to walk through the kitchen and living room to get to the narrow, steep stairs that led to the three bedrooms. I remember several occasions when Margaret had a Women's Missionary Fellowship meeting in our home. Rather than disrupt the meeting by walking through the living room to get to my "study" (the desk in our bedroom), I would climb up the apple tree that had branches overhanging the back porch roof and crawl through an upstairs window into the girls' bedroom!

Another summer Doug Muir and I dug a two-hundred-foot trench, six to eight feet deep, out to the street and laid copper tubing to replace the ancient, corroded iron water pipe. This finally put an end to flooding in the yard from frequent water leaks.

During the summer of 1955, Margaret stayed home with the four little children while I took the four oldest (eight to twelve years old at the time) to Washington, D.C., for the annual convention of the Christian Booksellers Association. We camped along the way. Still new to camping, I had not learned to find a campground and set up the tent before dusk. We pushed on until dark, and no campground signs appeared. Where would we spend the night? I suppose we could have survived in the car at the side of the highway, but to me it was a big crisis involving my poor judgment and failure to provide properly.

I stopped the car and we prayed for wisdom. As I started the car again, one of the children yelled, "There's a campground right over there!" And there, indeed, was a sign, partly hidden behind some brush. Soon we had the tent up and were safely bedded down for the night. I'm not sure whether the experience helped the children's faith, but it did mine. A small incident, but a lesson to remind me that God hears.

But I have an unhappy memory about that particular trip. Although I took Becky, John, Martha, and Peter, it seemed too difficult to take seven-year-old Janet too. She wanted to go, of course, but I promised that if she would help Mommy and feed the rabbits, I would bring her a Baby Ruth candy bar when I returned! Five-cent candy bars were not in our budget and were really an impressive treat. She reluctantly accepted the arrangement and bravely waved good-bye to us as we rolled down the long gravel driveway, headed for our three-day drive to Washington. All the time I was away, I kept wishing I had brought her; I could have managed that one small addition to our traveling tribe. True to my promise, I delivered the candy at the end of the trip, but I felt like a heel.

Gretchen's birth was followed quickly, in the next two years, by the arrival of Mary Lee in 1955 and Alison in 1956. Big sister Janet and some of her friends called them "the three littles" and lavished much motherly attention on them.

The "three littles" were almost like triplets in their playing together, and they took care of each other when school days came. Margaret remembers a time when Gretchen received a sucker as a treat for a kindergarten classmate's birthday.

Gretchen saved it and brought it home to be divided into three pieces so it could be shared with her younger sisters.

As our family grew to ten children, the Muirs' grew to five, and other families in the neighborhood had youngsters too, so the yard was often filled with laughter and fun as the children played baseball, hide and seek, touch football, kick the can, or red rover. Once when Dad West was visiting us, he put up a rope swing from a sturdy branch twenty feet above the ground. The children enjoyed being pushed higher and higher. Our children were content playing with one another and with their neighborhood friends, and the living room and front yard were always full of activity.

As they became teenagers, however, the older children became embarrassed about the condition of our old house. I was not aware of it at the time, but I learned much later that they would ask their friends to drop them off at the bottom of our long driveway. And they never volunteered our house for church youth meetings.

In our 1960 Christmas letter, after we had lived in the house twelve years, I wrote the following paragraph under the heading "Housing": "Uncertainty prevails. We are finding it very expensive to fix up this old one. We have just had the downstairs bath completely done over, put in a new rear entrance, converted the pantry to a coat closet, etc. A good bit of vacation time was spent jacking up the north side of the house. Many lessons in patience and piety."

Chapter 16
Traveling the World

MY WORK with Mr. Hall at Moody Bible Institute was as fulfilling as I could imagine. I was excited to have a part in his system of distributing Christian books and Gospels of John to schoolchildren in southern states.

Some of the favorite storybooks were *Jessica's First Prayer, Snow White and Little Dot, Rosa's Quest,* and *Aurie's Wooden Leg.* Later I added Bernard Palmer's great series of books about Danny Orlis.

Each fall Mr. Hall visited some of the schools where the Gospels and storybooks had been sent, to see how effectively they were being used. He invited me to go with him before he retired, and we drove to Kentucky, Tennessee, and Alabama, visiting several schools each day. The reception we received from teachers and students was heartwarming, especially at schools "in the rural," which I learned was a local idiom meaning out in the country. Sometimes "the rural" was pretty hard to get to, especially in Alabama, where we had to go through wet, slippery red clay or deep mud to reach some of the isolated schools.

When we arrived at the schools, the children pulled the

Gospels from their desks and held them high. The best readers took turns enthusiastically reading passages from the storybooks. Then Mr. Hall or I would give a little talk encouraging the children to read their Gospels every day and to use the storybooks for book reports.

Usually the rural white schools were reasonably well equipped with desks, blackboards, and a pot-bellied stove in the center or corner of the room. But some of the schools for black children were in pretty bad condition. Leaks in the roof, benches instead of desks, and faded or broken blackboards were not uncommon. In some areas, however, we saw new consolidated schools for blacks. These were first class throughout, in conformance to the "separate but equal" plan that prevailed in some parts of the South before integration was required.

Not long after I assumed these new responsibilities, I had my first contact with Peter Gunther, who became a lifelong friend. Peter applied to work with Moody Literature Mission. He had already had good experience elsewhere with a literature ministry in public schools and was exactly the right person to handle the day-to-day operations of the work with schools. Peter's integrity, hard work, ability, and love for God have been a deep inspiration to me through all the years since then.

In later trips to the schools, Peter Gunther accompanied me. I have a vivid memory of one of these visits to a school for white children at the top of a Kentucky mountain. We had written to a local pastor, telling him of our proposed visit, and he told us he thought it best to alert the teacher about our plan. She could tell the children, and they in turn could tell their parents. It seems this was a mountain bootlegging area, and there was a running battle with "the revenooers." Anyone from the outside was watched with deep suspicion, and it would not be wise to appear unannounced.

Since there was no road directly to the school, we had to

leave the car and hike along a stream through deep woods. We were alarmed (actually, I was scared!) when we passed a shack and saw a bearded, grim-faced mountaineer watching us with his shotgun ready beside him. My back prickled as we went along after calling out a friendly greeting to which he made no response.

But when we broke into a clearing where we were to take the trail on up the mountain to the one-room schoolhouse, the atmosphere changed remarkably. About twenty-five young-sters—the entire enrollment—were there waiting for us. Full of enthusiasm, they rushed ahead and behind and around us, all along the one-mile hike to the top of the hill. There the teacher greeted us, all smiles. We had a wonderful time.

Afterwards, two or three of the older students were designated to escort us down the hill again, where we said good-bye. We were happy and thrilled about our adventure but were glad to reach the car again and go on our way.

One year my son John accompanied Peter Gunther and me on one of these annual visits, and another time I took Peter. Still later, Mark and Cynthia had a turn. They were impressed at staying in motels—a first! They were also exposed to a part of the country and a segment of American culture they would otherwise have missed. They enjoyed the trips, and it was a good opportunity for me to get better acquainted with them individually.

One day a young student at Moody Bible Institute came to Peter Gunther and me to tell us his plan to go to Mexico during Christmas vacation to distribute Spanish Gospels of John. We arranged for Moody Literature Mission to sell him several thousand copies at a below-cost price. The young man was George Verwer, and this was the beginning of Operation Mobilization, which now has two thousand young missionar-ies scattered around the world. During high school George had become a Christian at a Billy Graham crusade. The

Gospel of John given to him at that time gave him an evangelistic zeal that has never left him. It is gratifying to remember having had even a small part in the early phase of his work. George and I have kept in touch through the years, and some years ago Tyndale House published his book *No Turning Back.* Tyndale House has also furnished Operation Mobilization's ships, *Logos* and *Doulos,* with many thousands of Living Bibles and other books.

One of my dreams for expanding the work of Moody Literature Mission was to develop Christian books in Third World nations, where there was (and still is) so little available. So I began writing to missionaries to ask them what books they would like to see published in the languages of the areas where they worked. We also made contacts with mission executives at home and abroad to find out which missions were already publishing and distributing Christian literature or wanted to do so.

The letters I received in reply made me realize how sparse and haphazard overseas Christian publishing was. I saw a need to meet the missionaries in person, to find those with special interest in cooperating with the Moody Literature Mission to translate, print, and sell books in local languages. As a result I began to travel overseas five or six weeks at a time every year or two, to see where Moody's financial assistance for publishing would be the most effective.

My first trip was to Europe in 1949. Paper was still scarce following the war, and I was able to provide much-needed paper to several Christian publishers—Eberhard Schroeder in Kassel, Germany; Mr. A. Biginelli in Italy; Samuel Vila in Barcelona, Spain. It was gratifying to be able to make such a concrete contribution.

On a later trip Moody Literature Mission was able to give significant help to Mr. and Mrs. Wilf Durham of Gospel Literature Service in Bombay. It continues to be one of the most effective publishers in India.

During the thirteen years that Peter Gunther and I were associated at Moody Literature Mission, we made many trips together. I particularly remember a trip we made with Gordon Fraser to the Supai Indians at the bottom of the Grand Canyon, and another to Vancouver Island, where we spent several days on the Shantymen's boat, *Messenger III,* to observe their use of literature among the Indians. Another trip took us to Alaska to check out what kind of literature work was being carried on in our forty-ninth state.

Something happened on an overseas trip that illustrates my lifelong sensitivity to the despair I see all around the world. One morning when I was staying in a Tokyo hotel, I awakened to the sound of the clomping of wooden clogs below my window as the crowds passed on the way to their day's work. As I looked out upon them, I realized that only 1 or 2 percent of them believed in Christ. As I thought of the lostness of all the others, I found myself almost hating the God who made them, and I cried out against Him. I think I was at the edge of a spiritual cliff, where the slightest further push could have toppled me into an abyss. I cried out to God for help and mercy, and in the end I grew quiet before His sovereignty, although hurting bitterly.

A few days later, when I was with my friend Jack Hywel-Davies in England, he told me that the previous week he had felt a great concern and the need to pray urgently for me. He mentioned the day and time. As I thought back and allowed for the time zones, I realized it was just the time when, halfway around the world, I had been undergoing my time of despair and horror.

I am just as interested now in overseas Christian publishing as I was then. The matter of literature distribution is even more important now than it was then, for the world's population has more than doubled. Reports from Africa say there are six million new Christians each year on that continent, but the Bibles and Christian books distributed there number at most a few hundred thousand. Six thousand new pastors are needed each year to minister to the new churches established for the converts. But the number actually being trained falls far short of the need. Radio messages are a vital help, but books and Bibles must be provided if new Christians are to grow strong and if pastors are to be trained. Otherwise, most of them will be virtually untaught. Many of them will be like the seeds told about in Christ's parable of the sower—they may grow quickly in the excitement of their new-found faith, but with little nourishment they soon fade.

The solution is hard to find. Bible societies do a valuable service, but they are underfunded to meet the great need. The church in prosperous nations seems to have its hands and hearts full with local needs, though many send out missionaries too. God's Spirit empowers gifted nationals to minister and preach the Word, but all too often the inadequately instructed inquirers are vulnerable to Satan's attacks.

I came across a striking example of this on the west coast of Africa. I had read about the Harris revivals and wanted to learn more. In 1912 a native Kroo African from Liberia named William Wade Harris (he had taken the name of an English sea captain he had served under) felt called in his old age to be God's prophet. He donned a white robe and turban, carried a staff with a cross on top, a Bible, and a calabash gourd to hold water for baptizing. Barefoot, he began itinerating from village to village, preferring to stay within sight or sound of the Atlantic Ocean. He was not particularly well received in Liberia. When he crossed the border into the French Ivory Coast, he could no longer be understood, and he resorted to Pidgin English, which was in turn translated into native dialects.

He may have baptized as many as 100,000 people in the next four years there and in the British Gold Coast before he was deported back to Liberia for political reasons following World War I.

His message was simple. He told his listeners to give up fetish worship, which they did, and he preached about a God who promised to protect them. He commanded his followers to wait for the white teachers God would send them. None of his converts could read French or English or their native dialects. They built churches, but no teachers or preachers were available to lead them.

I visited some missionaries in the Ivory Coast where Harris had preached, and I asked them to take me to one of the churches begun as a result of his work. The missionaries explained that none were left in that area. A few remnants of those groups remained, but their beliefs bore little resemblance to Harris's original message. Since the converts of Harris's day couldn't read, and they had no Bibles anyway, their early, eager faith was gradually adulterated with native religions. Within a couple of generations, little was left of the truth, and now it was entirely gone.

This is happening all over Africa, China, Latin America, and elsewhere. When believers do not have Bibles and Christian books to teach them and keep them growing, trouble lies ahead. A massive aid program of Bible and literature translation is needed. Instead, we are sending Christian soldiers out to war without ammunition.

While it is wonderful to see what God is doing even where no missionaries can go, as in mainland China, I am deeply concerned about the future of the churches of the Third World. Can they remain strong in the faith? I pray daily that we Christians in affluent countries will wake up to the situation and send not only our best young people as missionaries but also the Bibles and other literature they so desperately need to double the results of their work.

One of the benefits I gained from traveling overseas was the opportunity of getting acquainted with some of the finest people in the world: missionaries and their families and the leaders of the national churches. I have been surprised and pleased to learn, years later, that casual conversations—or so they seemed at the time—were helpful to missionaries with particular needs, often along spiritual lines. An example is a letter a young colleague of mine received recently from his father, who serves with Wycliffe Bible Translators in Guatemala. He said to his son, "If you should have opportunity to tell Ken Taylor hello for us, that would be nice. I still remember how much we benefited from his talking to us at Ixmiquilpan in 1969."

At the time of my early overseas trips, most of the literature projects and bookstores were controlled by missionaries. The nationals needed much training for those jobs, and often the missionaries did too. In Africa, national bookstore managers faced special problems. They had heavy obligations toward their extended families—parents, grandparents, uncles, children, and cousins. This created a serious tension between business responsibilities and home obligations. These managers often had difficulty in deciding between two irreconcilable courses: to make the store profitable, or to hire relatives whose services were not needed (or even to lend them money from the till, knowing it would probably never be repaid).

A missionary helped me understand the problem. He and a missionary colleague met me at an airport in Africa and drove me to my appointments. I was appalled by his colleague who did the driving. Many villages had grown up along the road to the airport, and the tarmac was crowded with women with baskets on their heads and babies on their backs. The driver sped along through the crowd, honking belligerently and sometimes yelling out the window at people getting in his way.

Later that day I was talking privately to the driver's companion about a problem in the mission bookstore. The African manager had been dismissed for stealing, only to be succeeded by another who exhibited the same problem. Now the missionary had temporarily taken over the management of the store. When he told me that the nationals who had been managers were devoted Christian men, I asked him how they could steal when they are well aware of the Bible's teaching about honesty. He gave me an interesting and wise answer.

"It seems to be a matter of culture and of degree," he explained. "In this part of Africa, it is extremely important to care for one's kinfolk. It is an absolute responsibility. Those managers tried to decide which scriptural injunction is more important—not to steal or to take care of those in their own household, for the Bible says that those who don't are worse than infidels. So they chose to steal."

Then he asked me if I remembered the drive from the airport that morning. Of course I did; how could I forget!

"Well, here in Africa," he told me, "patience is regarded as one of the highest virtues. My missionary brother does not have patience, but he is highly critical of the nationals for their dishonesty. Which is worse?" That conversation gave me a lot to think about.

The majority of the missionaries I visited were spiritually strong and mature, and I had many positive experiences. However, the less pleasant contacts reminded me of the importance of prayer for missionaries, who have great stresses and dark days just like the rest of us.

On one occasion, as I was planning to go to Brazil, a friend asked me to visit her missionary brother in northern Brazil, so I arranged my routing to accommodate this request. She wrote to tell him of my arrival, scheduled for nine o'clock in the evening. It was dark when the plane landed at the airport. No one was there to meet me, so I took a taxi the dozen miles out to his home, where I expected to spend the night.

He invited me in, rather indifferently, and after we had talked a few minutes he asked me where I would be staying, since his wife was away and it would not be convenient for me to use the guest room. He suggested that I try a house about a half mile down the road. So I left and walked along the road in pitch darkness to the other house. There my Portuguese-speaking host took me by lantern light to the basement stairs and indicated that there was a bed down there. For some reason, perhaps because they didn't have an extra lamp, I had to grope my way down through the thick darkness and find a cot. With my innate fear of snakes, spiders, bedbugs, and other vermin, I found it difficult to get comfortable, but I tried to get some sleep.

When my missionary "host" had learned that my flight would leave at 8:00 A.M., he told me it would be too early for him to serve me breakfast, but he did arrange for a taxi to pick me up. I never found out the reason for his lack of hospitality and his apparent hostility. I wondered if perhaps his mainline denominational background gave him some prejudice about Moody "fundamentalists," but I will probably never know.

On that same trip, as some missionary friends were seeing me off at an airport, they met a denominational official who was taking the same flight. The plane provided open seating, and they thought he and I could have good fellowship during the trip. We boarded together, but when he heard I was from Moody Bible Institute, he turned very cool and quickly disappeared toward the seats at the back of the plane. When we landed, he rushed off, passing me without a word or a glance, and disappeared.

Moody Bible Institute was not usually the object of disdain, however. Far from it! With thousands of Moody graduates on the world's mission fields doing some of the missionary enterprise's best work, I had the joy of visiting many of them and seeing their remarkable achievements under God.

One time in the Sudan I was staying at the same hotel with several businessmen from the United States. They invited me to go with them to a supper club, and naively I agreed. They were delighted and said their wives would be greatly reassured to hear they had spent the evening in the company of someone from Moody Bible Institute. However, the supper club turned out to be a nightclub filled with native prostitutes and bawdy performers. When I realized what was happening, I left and walked back through the dark streets toward my hotel. Along the way I found a restaurant still open. After I had eaten and paid my bill, the restaurant owner was quite concerned that I not walk to the hotel. He insisted on calling a taxi, saying it was not at all safe to walk. Doubtless the Lord's protection had surrounded me as I had earlier walked through the dark streets from the supper club.

Not all my experiences were distressing. Some funny things happened on those trips. I remember once in South America when a DC-3 commercial plane started to land but suddenly pulled up sharply. Looking down at the runway as we circled, I saw several cows. The pilot had been trying to scare them away from the landing strip by buzzing them!

On another occasion in South America, I was the only passenger on a DC-3 flight over the Andes mountains. The pilot and copilot asked if I would mind if they dropped down to get some pictures of a waterfall. I didn't, so they eased down a few thousand feet until we were traveling along a narrow gorge with steep cliffs on either side. Eventually we came to a very beautiful, high waterfall. They took their pictures and then climbed steeply up again over the cliffs and across a mountain pass.

Once when I was flying from Africa to Brazil, we started to descend for the landing, and the attendant made the usual announcements. I assumed we were being told to fasten our seat belts, but the message was entirely in Portuguese. The person who had planned to meet me was not at the airport, and I made fruitless attempts to telephone him. Finally, someone at the airport knew enough English to tell me the plane had landed at a different airport than scheduled, and the passengers were being taken by bus to the original destination. No doubt that had been the flight attendant's message I had not been able to understand.

I rushed out of the now deserted airport and found the buses gone. A taxi was there, however, and the driver said a Holiday Inn was only a few miles away and he could take me there for a certain price. He started out on the paved road, but suddenly turned onto a rutted road through what looked like a mile-long field, dimly edged by lights in the distance. My heart sank and my mind was flooded with all the stories I had read about bodies found lying in deserted spots with pocketbook gone.

The driver knew little English, and I didn't know Portuguese, so I kept saying, "Holiday Inn, Holiday Inn," and he seemed to be nonchalantly reassuring me that it was ahead of us. We bumped along, crossed the field, and finally came out onto a paved road again. Even after I was registered at the hotel and safe in my bed, my heart palpitated through the night. I don't know whether my driver intended any foul play, but I found out later that my junior-high-age neighbor was praying for me regularly while I was on this trip. I knew his prayers had been heard and my guardian angels had been busy.

In the 1970s, as our family's financial condition improved, I was able to take each of the three youngest girls—Gretchen, Mary Lee, and Alison—with me on extended trips while they were in high school. Gretchen and I went around the world, spending most of the time in India, visiting our Living Bibles International translators. Mary Lee went with me to Africa, which included going to see my brother Doug and his wife, Betty, at their mission hospital in Ingwavuma, Zululand. Alison accompanied me on a trip to Russia.

She Stood at the Window, Sobbing

Loneliness, divorce, and poverty
Have caught the world's throat with iron fangs.
I saw the woman crying.
Thy kingdom . . . where justice prevails . . .
Oh, come.

K.N.T.
San José, Costa Rica

Chapter 17
Moody Press

IN 1948, a year after my arrival at Moody, Bob Constable, the vice-president to whom I reported, asked if I would be interested in becoming director of Moody Press too, in addition to my duties with Moody Literature Mission. I wasn't sure. My work was fulfilling, and the department I was serving was useful. I feared it would suffer without my full-time attention. But Bill Moore, already an employee of Moody Press, was to be appointed as my assistant director, providing me with someone in whom I had great confidence to stand beside me. He could give me the experienced help and counsel I would need. So I accepted the offer and became director of both departments, Mr. Hall having retired by that time.

I remember the first day in the new office, getting down on my knees beside my desk and committing the work to the Lord, both in its outreach and in its business affairs. Thus began fourteen years of enthralling and absorbing work in trying to get Christian books published and distributed across the nation.

Soon after I added the Moody Press responsibilities, Howard Fischer inquired about the possibility of a production job.

Howard had been a classmate of mine at Wheaton College and was experienced in book production. I needed his help in reducing manufacturing costs. The department in charge of buying our printing was already busy buying printing for all the departments at Moody Bible Institute—bulletins, student catalogs, letters to donors, and hundreds of other printing jobs. But printing books is a huge production job all by itself and requires the constant attention of a specialist. Howard was of untold value to Moody Press for his many, many years of careful buying from paper mills, book printers, and binders.

Howard's first job was to negotiate a printing contract for the Moody Colportage Library, a series of 128-page paperbacks that we used at the rate of about one million copies a year. Lee Johnson, the Institute's comptroller, called my attention to the high price we had been paying for printing, and I asked Howard to investigate. He found that there were indeed huge savings to be made. He was able to reduce the manufacturing cost of those paperbacks from eleven cents a copy to eight cents. In these years of perpetual inflation, it is hard to remember that books could cost so little to print. Howard saved the Institute hundreds of thousands of dollars through his care in handling the Moody Press purchasing.

The combined efforts of my wonderful staff, along with guidance from the financial managers at the Institute, resulted in profitability for the first time in several years. We experienced the gradual growth of our book-publishing ministry during my fourteen years with Moody Press. We also opened three retail stores to add to the ministry of the main Moody Bookstore, located at the school. One of these new stores was in the business center of the city, one was in a black neighborhood, and one was in a northwest suburb.

An immediate problem I faced as the new director of Moody Press was a large stack of perhaps a hundred manuscripts piled in a corner of my office. Former editors had felt they should be published, but we didn't have the capital to carry out such an aggressive publication program. Anyway, I thought some of these manuscripts were not suitable for Moody to publish. I found it painful to notify many of those authors that we would not be able to go ahead with our intentions. Naturally this created a lot of disappointment and tension—and visits from some authors to plead the cause of their manuscripts.

Another problem I inherited was that the warehouse was filled with hundreds of thousands of dollars' worth of books that were not selling. Moody Press did not have salesmen to visit the bookstores, and there were far fewer bookstores in those days to sell to. Bookstore managers ordered books from the catalog we published periodically.

But God was working on both sides of this problem, because Van Kampen Press had just been organized and had salesmen but not very much product to sell. The solution to their problem and mine was for them to buy our books and have their salesmen sell them. We recovered some of our inventory costs to use in publishing new titles.

Knowing what to publish is one of the greatest challenges for any publisher. Each new title selected, no matter how valuable spiritually, is an experiment economically. It may or may not pay for itself. I know now, and soon learned then, that about half the books that are published don't make money. The low sales disappoint both the author and the publisher.

In my early years at Moody Press, all of us could see that the Christian bookstore industry was in a sorry state. Perhaps only a tenth as many Christian bookstores existed then as today and they were often in out-of-the-way or upstairs locations. Many were operated by people who had a desire for ministry but very little business experience. I began to discuss with Bill Moore whether anything could be done about this situation and specifically what Moody Press might do to strengthen this weak industry. We believed that the few strong stores should be giving counsel to those struggling for survival, but at that time no agency existed to bring them into communication with one another.

Eventually the solution—which now seems obvious—came to mind. The American Booksellers Association was a trade organization for general bookstores. Why not have a Christian Booksellers Association? And just as the American Booksellers Association held an annual meeting to discuss ways and means of increasing their business and their stability, so we could hold an annual meeting of the Christian Booksellers Association. The basement of Moody Church would be a good place for Christian publishers to set up their exhibit booths, and we could ask members of the church to entertain out-of-town bookstore managers in their homes.

I finally decided the day had come to move forward instead of just thinking and talking about the idea. I was always better at ideas than action, so I gave Bill Moore a memo proposing that he telephone the few Christian stores in the Chicago area and invite the managers to lunch to discuss the possibility of such an association.

Bill was a person of action. Two weeks later he told me he had met with a dozen store managers at lunch that day, that they had decided to incorporate under the name Christian Booksellers Association, that they had set dates for a national convention the following September (1950), and that the convention hall of the LaSalle Hotel in downtown Chicago had been reserved for the desired dates.

I was stunned! "But, Bill," I protested, "the convention hall is far too big and too expensive, and Christians can't afford to stay in a downtown hotel!"

But it was too late; the Christian Booksellers Association was launched. Thank God for Bill Moore, who turned a memo into a giant organization of three thousand member stores. He became its first executive director.

I have observed throughout my life that God mixes my abilities with those of others, so that we strengthen one another in the tasks God gives us. I am troubled that often I get the credit while others do the hard work. That's the way it was with Bill Moore and Peter Gunther and other associates God gave me.

As Christian bookstores increased in number across the country, Moody Press employed salesmen. Our first salesman was Sid Zullinger, who was on the road from east to west for weeks at a time without getting home, because of his deep concern for expense control. In my estimation he is one of the great men and unsung heroes of Moody Bible Institute. But I'm afraid I was callous in allowing him to volunteer far beyond the line of duty in this way. Thank you, Sid!

I began to learn more about human relations in exercising authority. I was puzzled by the huge accumulation of manuscripts and correspondence on the desk of our editor-in-chief, Elizabeth Thompson. I wondered if she needed additional help, or perhaps some better methods of filing or procedures. Rather than sitting down with her and asking her, I got the key to her office, which she always kept locked, and went in one evening after work to rummage through her desk. When she found out about it (apparently someone had observed me), she was furious with me—and rightly so. As I think over my administrative years, both at Moody Press and later when Tyndale House Publishers was formed, I realize that this has been a significant weakness of mine. It is important not only to have the right ideas, but also to be careful how to implement them with the cooperation of those involved.

One day Miss Thompson told me about William Norton, who had been director of Moody Press practically from its beginning, just before the turn of the century. He was then in his eighties, a bachelor all his life, and since his retirement several years earlier he had lived alone in a sparsely furnished apartment in one of the Institute buildings. Miss Thompson told me that Mr. Norton was still coming to work in a tiny office where he was engaged in some sort of research on the history of the Institute, though no one seemed quite sure what he was doing. He was long forgotten at Moody Press, except by two or three oldsters, and unknown at Moody Bible Institute except for a few people in the finance and personnel departments.

As the new director of Moody Press, thirty years old and very busy, I'm afraid I let several months go by before I took the trouble to go down to Mr. Norton's cubbyhole office and introduce myself. He was crippled and lonely, and his office was stacked with newspapers. I spent half an hour with him, asking him about the early days of Moody Press. He was glad to have someone to talk to, and he enjoyed reminiscing. I'm sorry to say I did not visit him again. One day not long afterwards he was found unconscious, and he died shortly afterwards.

Mr. Norton made a lasting impression on my life, and I began to realize that we Young Turks could learn a lot from our elders. We too would inevitably be pushed off the scene by others and soon forgotten. The corollary was that whatever God has for us to do, we should do without delay. It took me a lot longer to learn that doing is not as important as loving God and loving other people. Especially in my position as the new director of Moody Press, I ought to have befriended the old man who had once been in my position and had laid the foundation upon which I was building.

Because of my long-standing difficulty with Bible reading, I was pleased to have Moody Press republish *The New Testament in the Language of the People,* by Charles B. Williams, in 1952. The book had been published fifteen years earlier by another publisher, but had gone out of print. I think it was Bill Moore who somehow learned of its availability and called it to my attention. I was immediately interested and went to visit

Dr. Williams in his home in Florida. He was in his later years, and I found him to be a warmhearted scholar who was, of course, pleased to have his translation back in print. I was a bit alarmed, however, when he told me he was not a premillenialist, but a "promillenialist"! By this he meant that he was in favor of it! I have never been very clear about the final events, so I guess I am a promillenialist too! I'm all for it—the lion lying down with the lamb, and the swords being beaten into plowshares.

Dr. Williams's translation was a best-seller at Moody Press for many years.

I served as director of both Moody Press and Moody Literature Mission until the end of 1961. Although I enjoyed my work, I was being prepared for a change. While on a trip overseas for Moody Literature Mission in 1962, I kept a diary beginning with a backward look at recent events in my life:

> Concerning myself and Moody Press: For the past three or four summers, during vacation, I have prayed about whether this was the place for me to be. Each time the answer seemed to be, and was, "yes." Nevertheless, as a question of priority of time and opportunity and strategy, the question persisted. I was not questioning the enormous usefulness of the Moody Press output, but simply noting that other Christian publishers were also fully engaged, and the question of what still *needed* to be published was becoming very thought-provoking. I came to the conclusion that although there were probably places of more usefulness, this work as director of Moody Press was my gift and calling, and where I work in the Lord's vineyard is not determined by my own ideas of strategic importance, but by where God puts me. And I never failed to realize the joy and privilege of leading

this mighty ministry, and to recognize its continuing usefulness and potential.

During November 1961 I read the Psalms with interest and value for the first time, until then having read with boredom and some cynicism about King David, the psalm writer. Nevertheless, the Lord loved David—and the Lord loves me, too, despite faults. Anyway, I was struck by the promised blessings and assurances, which I was enabled to accept very personally. This prepared me spiritually for a sudden change in direction in God's guided tour of my life.

That sudden change came about when Bob Constable dropped into my office and asked me to spend all my time with Moody Literature Mission, leaving Moody Press in other hands, beginning January 1962. He also told me to feel free to go overseas as soon as I could get away—which I had been requesting for many months. At first I thought it was a suggestion, but it soon became apparent that it was a command. I was fired from Moody Press, I think, but it was done so graciously that I have never been sure! I moved out of my spacious office and into cramped but adequate quarters on another floor—and tried to find enough to keep me busy.

Going back to my diary:

Bob Constable's idea is that Moody Literature Mission should become the leading light of the world regarding Christian literature, reflecting to everyone the glories of Moody Bible Institute. Although I do not accept this point of view in the same way, I agree that it is likely that Moody Literature Mission will be much more useful if Pete Gunther and I can both spend full time with it, rather than 95 percent of my time being with Moody Press. So, after the first shock, I was and am content.

Moody Press made $1,000,000 profits during my administration, opened three stores (and Moody Literature Mission helped open seventeen last year), tripled our sales, published the Wycliffe Series of Christian Classics, and began the Moody Giants, Acorns, Compacts, Moody Pocket Books and Moody Diamonds. So I believe I have left a good heritage.

Chapter 18
Evangelical
Literature Overseas

IN 1952, while I was still at Moody Press, I was invited to speak to the mission executives of the Evangelical Foreign Missions Association. I still remember how nervous I was as I went to the platform to deliver my address. I was afraid they would not understand or accept the proposal I was going to make to them. I wanted them to disband their literature committee and, instead, allow the formation of a new literature committee with which they would cooperate, but which they would not control. As I began to speak, I was well aware that this powerful group of mission executives might not wish to yield that control to the new inter-mission literature organization I was about to propose.

Their own literature committee had not been able to function effectively. Although its members were concerned about the need and were willing to serve, in practice they could get together only once a year for an hour or two. Very little was actually being accomplished.

"I think the time has come," I told them, "to find people who can come together once a month to craft a significant literature outreach. We should not expect that those from various parts of the country can do this—it is obvious that they cannot."

I reminded them of the power of literature in supplementing the missionaries' teaching abilities, and as follow-up for new Christians, as well as for inadequately trained pastors.

"And," I pointed out, "the gifts of the Spirit go far beyond evangelism and church planting. The gift of teaching is another of the special abilities given by the Holy Spirit. The national pastor, and even the missionary, may not have this particular gift. But if we can find God-called people to whom He has entrusted the gift of teaching, that gift can be captured in print so that pastors and lay people alike will grow in grace much faster than if they were simply on their own. Teaching is as vital as preaching, and well-written Christian literature can be that teacher.

"But," I continued, "we have scarcely begun this aspect of the Great Commission of baptizing and teaching. We have been doing the baptizing, but not enough of the teaching, which literature can help to do."

It seemed to me on that autumn afternoon that a great deal hung in the balance. A negative vote on my proposal would mean the status quo and the probability of very little happening during the coming years. A positive vote, on the other hand, would give opportunity for some of us with special interest and a call to literature ministry to organize, independent of the assembled mission directors. This would also allow us to draw in the interest of the other major group of evangelical missions, the Interdenominational Foreign Missions Association. The proposed new organization could include any who were personally committed to the fundamental historic statements of the faith and also had a strong and impelling interest in the development of Christian literature.

I was so anxious for a positive vote that I was tempted not to restate clearly, in my concluding remarks, what I feared might be too much for some of my audience to accept. Fortunately, I put the temptation aside, and, trusting the Lord, reviewed the situation as clearly as I could. When the matter was put to a vote, the result was unanimously positive.

How thankful I was to God. Within the next year (1953), the mission leaders in the Chicago area, and others whom I knew to have vision for literature ministry, came together and formed Evangelical Literature Overseas (ELO) as a not-for-profit foundation whose objective was to develop and distribute Christian literature in Third World countries.

Almost immediately we saw a pickup in literature ministries overseas. ELO gained immediate financial support from Moody Literature Mission and began to assist in the development overseas of Christian magazines, Christian publishing houses, and individual book and tract projects. We also held literature conferences in this country to train missionaries on furlough.

Harold Street, a missionary for many years in Ethiopia, was the man we chose to head up the work. He was the ideal person for the job—a man of God and an excellent speaker. As an experienced missionary, he knew the ways of working with field leadership to get cooperation in designating missionary personnel for literature involvement. His organizing ability for the ELO literature conferences was outstanding.

When Harold Street retired, Jim Johnson, a prolific writer and one of the founders of the Wheaton College Graduate School of Communications, took the leadership for many years of development and growth.

The one flaw was that we were never able to convince the mission boards that literature production and distribution was as much a priority as medical and educational work. Sending doctors, nurses, and teachers to the mission field was assumed to be part of a mission's obligation, but literature was considered optional, to be undertaken only if there were funds, which was seldom. An outstanding exception was the Sudan Interior Mission with its huge investment in *African Challenge* magazine.

Nevertheless, the work of ELO went forward for many

years. Ultimately, ELO merged into Media Associates International, whose important contribution is in training national leaders to write and edit. But at this point, as throughout ELO's history, funding is still inadequate for training nationals and publishing the books they write.

I wonder how to evaluate this part of my life and ministry. I do not doubt that God was calling Harold, Jim, and me and our boards of directors to this work. I continue to consider it of great importance, now more than ever because of the fast-growing church in many parts of the world and the need for training materials for pastors and for new Christians. All the missionaries in the world—some sixty thousand of them for five billion people—cannot begin to accomplish the task without a strong literature ministry.

Yet I see no solution to the funding problem for the scattering of Christian publishing houses in various parts of the world. They have great potential for increased publishing and distribution, if and when their funding can be increased.

But who is sufficient for such a task as this? I am praying that God will raise up someone to take the leadership in raising millions of dollars as revolving funds for publishing across the world. I am confused about the ways of God. Here is a ministry God used me and others to begin with such high hopes and good results, and yet it moves forward so slowly. Why is the progress so slow when God has granted rapid progress in other works to which I have been called? Have I missed some part of His guidance? Are there further paths ahead for faster development? If so, I long and pray that I or others will find them.

I am grateful for the thousands of books that my colleagues and I, and other groups, have helped to produce—books that have helped hundreds of thousands grow in the grace of our Lord Jesus Christ. And I continue to pray that God will, in His own time and way, develop this ministry to a far greater extent than ever before.

The founding of Evangelical Literature Overseas was followed a year later by another idea I had for helping missionaries and making their ministries more effective.

On a trip through West Africa in early 1954, I stopped to see my Wheaton classmate Gordon Timyan, who was serving with the Christian and Missionary Alliance. My schedule had been disrupted a few days earlier, and with the irregular mail service I had no way to tell my friends of my changed arrival time, so no one met me when my plane landed late in the evening. I found a broken-down taxi to take me to a flea-bitten hotel at the edge of the city and got as much sleep as I could through the hot night.

The next morning I bought a couple of bananas and a warm bottle of Coke from a street stand. When the post office opened, I found someone who spoke enough English to direct me to the Timyan home a mile or two up in the nearby hills. I decided to walk, since I needed the exercise. And besides, I suspected that the taxi fare would probably be excessive, since I did not know the language and could not haggle over the price! I enjoyed the walk, as the sun was not yet too hot. I trudged along the dusty dirt road, and eventually their house came into view.

I started eagerly toward the door, passing an automobile on jacks in the weather-beaten yard. I was startled to hear a voice calling out, "Hello, there!" At first I couldn't see who was speaking, but then I noticed two legs protruding from under the car. They slowly emerged and my smiling missionary friend appeared. I had a wonderful day visiting with Gordon and his wife, Jan, discussing the project that was the purpose of my visit.

Back on the airplane the next day I thought about those legs sticking out from under the car, and the memory did not fade during the next few years as I made other trips overseas. Frequently the missionaries I visited were spending long hours of precious time working on their cars, generators, and anything else mechanical. Many of them didn't have mechanical ability, so they had to learn much patience as they made their trial-and-error repairs.

I thought how wonderful it would be if trained mechanics, agriculturists, medics, teachers, secretaries, and many other technical specialists could go overseas for a few months' break from their jobs and share their talents for awhile with the career missionaries. They would not have to learn the local language, and in some cases they could start work the day they arrived.

They would not be there to make converts or plant churches. Their role would be to help missionaries with the physical aspects of living in a culture or country where it took much longer to get things done because the specialized expertise and also tools and/or parts were unavailable. A combination of experience and ingenuity was essential. For instance, couldn't nurses volunteer to help in hospitals without making a lifetime commitment or learning the local language?

I wasn't in a position to make my voice heard on the subject, but I thought and prayed about it a lot. The general feeling of missionary executives with whom I discussed the idea was that it might be more trouble than it was worth.

Several years later, President Kennedy set the Peace Corps in motion, and thousands of eager people, aged eighteen to eighty, were volunteering to take their skills overseas. A friend casually mentioned to me that he wished there were such a thing as a Christian Peace Corps. He wished he himself could go to a mission field for a few months' work. Several weeks later someone else said almost the same thing to me. In consulting with mission leaders, I found their attitude had changed—they were now willing to send people overseas for just a year or two, provided they were committed Christians and had a particular skill.

Better yet, some of these mission executives were willing to serve on the board of Short Terms Abroad, an organization I wanted to start. Some who became board members at the inception of STA in 1965 were Dr. Clyde Taylor, executive secretary of the Evangelical Foreign Missions Association; the Rev. Edwin L. (Jack) Frizen, Jr., executive secretary of the Interdenominational Foreign Missions Association; Dr. Vernon Mortenson, general director of The Evangelical Alliance Mission; Dr. Malcolm Forsberg, candidate secretary for Sudan Interior Mission; businessman Dr. Wallace Erickson; and Peter Gunther, my successor as director of Moody Literature Mission and Moody Press.

Short Terms Abroad was not a new mission or even a sending agency, but served existing mission boards by recruiting personnel, screening applicants, and referring candidates for short-term service abroad. Tyndale House Foundation paid all the expenses of this recruitment service.

We named Richard Wolff as executive director of Short Terms Abroad. He was succeeded a few years later by Irving Philgreen.

Irv had a license for flying private aircraft and belonged to a flying club. The first time he flew on Short Terms Abroad business, he went to Canadian Keswick in 1967. He took his whole family along and made it a family vacation. Irv canvassed existing mission agencies and came up with 712 openings for short-term service. No one before had put them all together. He published a directory listing the opportunities and circulated it as widely as possible to Bible schools, Christian colleges, and mission conferences, updating it periodically.

At Inter-Varsity's midwinter Urbana conference, Short Terms Abroad was not permitted to have a booth, because it was not a sending agency, but Irv was there, and he saw to it that copies of the directory were prominently displayed at the booth of every mission that had listings in it. By the next

Urbana conference the rules had changed, and Short Terms Abroad had its own booth. At the following Urbana, STA was asked to provide a directory to be included in every registrant's packet—all 10,000 of them!

The 1972 directory, called *Opportunities,* included 1,664 personnel needs listed under 126 job titles with 177 mission agencies. Because some entries requested several people, there were openings for more than 3,800 workers. Even that was far from complete because, among others, Southern Baptists, Campus Crusade for Christ, and Operation Mobilization were not included. They were actively recruiting short-termers on their own.

Irv recalls that at the height of Short Terms Abroad's ministry the post office sent a truck daily to his home/office to pick up the outgoing mail. In addition to a full-time secretary, the Philgreens' two children were busily involved after school.

By this time the mission societies picked up the idea themselves and began to tell their constituents about short-term openings they had. How wonderful to see this happen. I hoped that Gordon Timyan and many like him no longer had to do their own car repairs but could give more hours to translation of Christian materials for local believers, as well as church planting and training of national leadership.

Meanwhile, God had given a similar vision to Phill Butler in Seattle, Washington, whose organization was called Intercristo. He was a step ahead of Short Terms Abroad in using a computer to cross-check all skills of applicants against needs presented by mission boards. Because of considerable overlap in our activities, our board members finally decided that Short Terms Abroad should combine with Intercristo. This was done in 1975. That may be one of the few instances in history when a parachurch organization voluntarily closed its doors! But it had served its purpose.

Short Terms Abroad was one of God's instruments in sowing the seeds of the movement that now sees thousands of Christian young people spending summers helping on mission fields in many parts of the world. This is in addition to the thousands of adults of all ages who are serving overseas for a year or two or more. I personally know several retirees who have put in rewarding years assisting at mission stations.

The Billy Graham Center in Wheaton, Illinois, has recognized the contribution that Short Terms Abroad made during its ten years of existence by including in its mission archives all the material that Irv Philgreen could furnish them.

The most recent directory of the Missions Advanced Research Center (known as MARC), with headquarters in Pasadena, California, listed 30,750 short-termers from the United States serving overseas. In 1985 the number was 21,200. So the trend continues to grow. I do not know whether anyone has made a complete study of how many short-termers eventually apply as career missionaries, but it is a significant number.

Chapter 19
Family Life

I AM SOMETIMES asked how we could afford such a large family. We were poor in comparison with the standards of most of our friends, but we always had enough good, simple food on the table. Moody Bible Institute paid its employees once a month, and Margaret used careful management to make the money come out even with the month. I had one suit with two pants, and Margaret made the rounds of church and charity rummage sales for clothes for herself and the children. Neighbors and church friends sometimes gave us their children's outgrown clothing.

So my biggest problem was not keeping bread and butter on the table—Margaret skimped and saved to accomplish that—but it was the realization that I was not giving adequate time to the children. Each had his or her individual needs, and I tried to accommodate those needs on a group basis, but this was inadequate, and I knew it.

My normal work day during the years I worked at Moody didn't allow me much time with the children. I would get up at 5:00 for a devotional time, leaving the house at 6:30 (before the children were up) for the three-quarter-mile walk to the commuter train. I would get home again at 6:00 in the evening.

I was frustrated about finding ways to give some individual attention to each child; in retrospect, I know I certainly was not meeting their needs. This has always been a source of regret, although I still do not know how I could have handled it differently.

One of our adult children has told us that when she was a child, she often longed to talk to her mother or me about life at school and many other things, but we were too busy to give her our undivided attention. I'm thankful to say that she has now forgiven us for these childhood hurts, but it pains us to look back and recognize this failure with all of our children. We still see some deep scars in our family.

One way I tried to relate better to our children was to take one or two of them at a time to my office at Moody when there was a school holiday. I wanted to give them at least an idea of what I did all day so that when they were asked, "What does your father do?" they could say more than, "He works in Chicago." Riding the train was a novelty for them, and thanks to the cooperation of my secretary, Elsie Pera, and other colleagues, they were kept occupied around the office, or riding the elevators and going to the Sweet Shop for ice cream cones.

Those secretaries were wonderful people, not only in character and work habits, but also in their kindness. On more than one occasion a couple of them teamed up to come to Wheaton and take over our lively household in order to give Margaret an overnight break as we went to a resort for a time of sleeping, walking, and reading.

The major family event each evening from my point of view was the family devotion time after dinner when we read from the Bible or a Bible storybook and had prayer all around. I think this was an important part of our family life. As time allowed, we also read aloud from other books, such as those by Patricia St. John.

A significant purchase I made during those years was a set

of fifty children's classics, which the kids read on their own. We could hardly afford the expenditure, but Margaret and I were anxious that the children read good books.

We also decided early in our marriage not to have television in our home, and we have never owned a set, even after we could have afforded it. We felt it was too difficult to raise our kids with exposure to the frequent depiction of immorality and violence. We are increasingly sure we made a good choice, for through the years, TV censorship standards have fallen lower and lower. The media, to whose tune we dance, are controlled by a few hundred men and women, almost all of whom, according to their own admission in respected polls, are libertarian and agnostic or atheistic. They are indifferent to, or even favor, all the things God has forbidden, so they are opening Satan's pollution valve wider and wider—releasing sewage into America's homes, defiling viewers' minds and hearts.

I recall my surprise in the early days of television when I was visiting a Christian friend and was treated to a comical TV rendering of "The Lady and the Ape." I was amazed at my friend's amusement as the ape attempted to undress the lady. The world was already taking possession of that home. That program would seem tame now, with graphic bedroom scenes so common.

The average American watches TV for several hours each day and is bombarded with scenes of seduction, fornication, rape, profanity, and criminal violence, including a dozen murders. Evil is presented as normal, exciting, and fun. And inevitably this results in a change in the viewers' own moral attitudes and standards. They become less and less sensitive to the sins that make God furious.

Margaret and I do not want to take that chance, so we continue to have no TV set in our home. We miss many good programs, but that is a sacrifice we are willing to make. Many parents try conscientiously to control the dangers of television with careful monitoring of programs, but they cannot anticipate what will appear in previews of coming "attractions."

I fear deeply for my nation. Younger people can hardly realize the incredible decline of morality in America during the last thirty years. I don't need to review here the statistics of divorce, unfaithfulness, homosexuality, and crime, or the deterioration of ethics in business and politics. We are controlled by television's version of ethics and morality.

Sunday school and Sunday morning church attendance were a regular part of the week's activities for our family. Margaret and I did not get to sit next to each other in church for years, as we always had at least a few children between us. Our family filled the second row on the left side of the center aisle!

Several of the long-term Sunday school teachers had each of our ten children in their classes. We thank God for their faithfulness in teaching the little ones about the life of Christ and about the heroes of the Old Testament. I had mixed feelings about "children's church," preferring that the children be with us for the adult worship service, even if it was over their heads. But we weren't consistent about this, as evidenced by the fact that Cynthia was left at children's church on two occasions when we drove home without realizing that only eleven of us were in the car. A teacher had to bring her home!

As they got older, most of the children were active in the high school youth group and sang in the youth choirs. Their social life was centered in the youth group activities. Gretchen and Mary Lee married young men they knew from church and had dated through high school.

I was Sunday school superintendent for one term, served on the missions committee, and had several three-year terms on the board of elders. Margaret has been a faithful member of the Women's Missionary Fellowship.

"Forsake not the assembling of yourselves together" applied when we were on vacation, too, even when we were camping. We drove to the nearest town and found an evangelical church where we could worship.

I wanted the children to learn the elements of business and the responsibilities of earning and saving money. Margaret read about a local family whose children had had an egg route, so she helped Peter start one. Each week Margaret drove out into the country to a chicken farm and bought eggs by the crate. The children put them into cartons and delivered them in their little red coaster wagon around several blocks. They had regular customers with standing orders, and they delivered as many as sixty dozen eggs per week. Their customers were happy to have fresh eggs delivered to the door. After Peter "graduated" from the egg route, the next six children in turn inherited it. The boys also had paper routes. John earned the money for an English racer bike when he was ten.

Another enterprise the youngsters had was the sale of cookies, which they made with Margaret's help. They found a ready market door-to-door for fresh, home-baked cookies and bars. Some customers placed a standing order to be delivered on any baking day. Becky and Martha earned their way to summer camp from cookie profits. Later the girls did baby-sitting and house cleaning.

In addition to the daily challenge of providing for my family, I was greatly concerned about their future. I was especially determined that they should all have college educations. With a salary in the mid-1950s of $400 a month, and college expenses of at least $60,000 looming ahead for my ten children, there was obviously no way for them to go to college without scholarships, working their way to whatever extent they could, and borrowing. It was borrowing for college that concerned me, because I hated for them to start their adult lives with huge debts.

To save $60,000 from my salary over a period of a few years

was obviously an impossibility, so I was left with the only option I could think of, which was to make a killing in the stock market. I did not put an exclamation point after the last sentence because I believed that God would use this means to solve the problem. Looking back, I can laugh a little about my investments, which usually left me twisting in the wind.

I used our savings of several hundred dollars to buy some stocks. It was all very exciting. A friend who had a lot of investments loaned me several stock advisory sheets, and all of the recommended stocks were so certain to shoot skyward in value that it was hard to decide among them. I prayed for wisdom, made my selection, called a broker to execute the order—and watched with chagrin as my stocks began to fall in value. Each evening as I scanned the prices in the daily newspaper, I became more and more depressed.

However, one of my purchases seemed to be rising, though unsteadily, and that gave me hope. So from day to day my spirits shot up and down; I was sometimes elated and sometimes in despair. I sold when one of the stocks was headed downward, and bought when a "hot tip" from my broker gave me fresh hope. Occasionally, I added to my original investment with royalty money from my children's books.

I realized at the time that these emotional highs and lows, paralleling the stock market, hardly constituted a fitting way for me to live, but it seemed to be a necessary part of achieving the college education goals.

I well remember the day when, after I had completed a new purchase with my broker, he remarked, "Of my hundreds of customers, you are the only one who lost money last year!" So I quit, and closed the account.

While I was still playing the stock market, I was introduced to a missionary who had purchased several hundred acres of land in Brazil to be cleared and planted in coffee. I bought eighty acres from him, which he and his team would plant and tend for me on a sharecrop basis. When the coffee trees grew enough to begin producing beans, his mission would get half of the profits, and half would come to me. Of course, I knew nothing about raising coffee beans in Brazil, and it did not occur to me that perhaps he didn't either. I didn't think of the possible hazards. I was only interested in the big picture, the huge profits that would accomplish my goals.

But all those unknown hazards happened! After we had waited three or four years for the first crop, a bitter freeze destroyed all the trees. We replanted, and when the trees were next ready for bearing, a forest fire raged through the coffee plantation. Meanwhile, a great deal of tension developed among the personnel of the mission, and a strong letter of denunciation went out from one of the missionaries to all the property owners, complaining bitterly about mismanagement. So I gave up and donated my land to the mission rather than face further expenses.

Another investment I made required only thirty dollars to get started. A friend told me about raising Christmas trees. One could buy tiny, eight-inch Scotch pines for three cents apiece from the Illinois reforestation program, with permission to cut and sell them after several years when they were the right size for Christmas trees. So I bought a thousand trees, dug a thousand holes in the acre lot behind our old farmhouse, and—with the entire family planting and watering—we were suddenly in the Christmas tree business. From my friend's experience I was confident that in a few years thousands of dollars would be deposited in that college fund.

No literature had come with the seedlings, and nobody told me that I should go to the public library and get some information on raising Christmas trees. I didn't know they had to be trimmed year by year to make them shapely. By the time I realized that my trees were very ungainly in appearance, it was too late to trim them, and another dream bit the dust.

Years later, when my small income had been replaced by a generous salary as president of Tyndale House Publishers, along came a wonderful opportunity from a friend to invest in a new business that had every prospect of success. My ten-thousand-dollar investment gave me an opportunity as a major shareholder to sit on the board of directors. This was a heady experience for me, as I fancied myself to be a capable businessman who could help steer this infant business into strong profitability. At long last I would have a successful investment! However, as sometimes happens, things did not fall into place as smoothly and quickly as projected in the budgets. I received a telegram while I was overseas, saying that a fifteen-thousand-dollar loan was essential to save the company. I had not learned that a gambler needs to know when to quit, so I made the loan. A few weeks later I sat in what turned out to be the final meeting of the board, when one of the other directors offered his shares at one-tenth of the price he had invested, but there were no takers. A few days later the company closed its doors.

At this point I decided that investing was not the way of success for me. When a friend told me that ServiceMaster company was going public and shares were available at four dollars, I declined. Since then ServiceMaster shares have gone up a hundred times in value! I should add, however, that God in His own way, and apart from my devising, scheming, and gambling, took care of all the childrens' college needs, which in the end totaled a lot more than $60,000!

John and Martha started college with state scholarship assistance. Then in 1964, when *Living Letters* really took off, I wrote to the state scholarship commission to say we no longer needed the scholarship. I guess they had never received such an announcement, because it took them a while to figure out how to un-grant a scholarship!

Although my motive for investing was probably pure at the

beginning, I realize now that I was looking for success and money, the love of which is "a root of all evil." No wonder that God, by sending abject failure in these ventures, destroyed all possibility of pride in my being a financial wizard!

Meanwhile, vacations were a highlight of our family's year. In the early 1950s it meant going to a lakeside cottage in Wisconsin for a week. We were still driving the old 1928 Dodge, so we were badly crowded. Margaret began praying for a larger car. The children did too. Kathy Niles, a neighbor girl, remembers coming over to play and finding Becky and Martha sitting on the front steps with their heads bowed.

"What are you doing?" Kathy wanted to know.

"We are praying that our family will get a new car."

Kathy knew about praying in church, but not about praying for new cars! But God answered the prayers. One day soon afterwards I was called to the personnel office of Moody Bible Institute and was told that a trustee of the Institute had a car he wanted to give to a deserving family. The personnel director lived in Wheaton, so he knew our transportation needs. What a thrill it was to drive home a good-as-new Dodge sedan. I sold the 1928 Dodge to a young car buff for one dollar!

For a few months we crowded into the new car for the drive to church, but with summer approaching we realized that even this roomier car would not be large enough for a family vacation trip. Finally we sold our "new" car to a Christian worker for a bargain price and bought a twelve-year-old Cadillac limousine for $250. I saved the balance of the sale money to purchase our next car when the Cadillac would give out. Our huge car created quite a sensation among our friends and neighbors! But eventually it was not worth the constant costly repairs, so we replaced the 1942 limousine with a 1948 model already ten years old. It had electric windows, and a sound-proof plate glass window between the front and back seats could be raised or lowered.

We started camping when we could no longer find vacation cottages large enough for our growing family. For eighty dollars I bought a large army tent that was roomy enough to sleep the whole family. I also bought a Coleman stove and wool sleeping bags from an army surplus store. The first year we camped, 1955, was with eight children. We stopped at various sites along Lake Michigan. Margaret was seven months pregnant, sleeping on the ground, learning to cook on a temperamental Coleman stove, and washing diapers by hand! At least the rest of the family enjoyed the trip, and she did not complain, even though it was not a restful time for her.

I worried constantly about the unexpected cost of repairs on our old car and about finding used tires the right size when tires blew out, which happened frequently on our long camping trips.

When Becky made a trip to the West Coast with friends after graduating from high school, she became aware for the first time that frequent stops for repairs or changing tires was not necessarily a part of vacation trips!

I know some people who could have made a joke out of the problem and thereby added to the vacation fun, but that was not my nature. On more than one occasion I listened gloomily to some unusual noise in the engine that kept growing louder, causing the day's journey to be aborted in favor of a closer campsite. Then there was an hour or two or three at a garage, correcting the evil that had been building up during the day. The result was that I spent time at the garage worrying, rather than with the family exploring the area around the campground.

Worry is one of my weaknesses. When I was young, I heard my father jovially declare himself to be a worrier, but he seemed to talk about it more than he really did it. I was just the opposite. Some people have optimistic temperaments. They can trust God and see the bright light beyond the dark places in life. I tend to focus on the dark spots and forget to lift my eyes and see the light ahead. Through the years I have made some progress in this regard, but I'm sorry my growth has been so slow. If I had realized much earlier how worry dishonors God and had committed my need to Him, He could have helped me sooner.

Chief among our good memories of camping trips are the evening campfires. As we sat in the light of the fire, I would tell stories I had read, or I would make them up. We sang choruses and fun songs, and I read Bible stories.

Once when we camped on the shores of Lake Michigan, we hiked up the beach in the afternoon and discovered an abandoned house. It was built on a sand dune, and the winter storms had washed away the sand. The house was ready to slide away and crash to the beach below. That night's campfire included Jesus' parable of the wise man who built his house on the rock and the foolish man who built his house on the sand. I applied the illustration to our lives, showing the children that God is the solid rock, and He invites us to base our lives on Him, so that the storms need not destroy us.

Our first major trip after we had all ten children was a camping expedition to Colorado. Margaret had to hold baby Alison all the way, and another child sat between us on the front seat. Four children sat on the jump seats and four children were in the back seat. We had to monitor a rotation system so everyone got a turn at a window seat. Sometimes we noticed people counting us when we piled out of the car at a rest stop! Finally the children made a hand-lettered sign they could hold against the window. It said "12 OF US!"

Ted and Mary Lou Benson had moved to Colorado Springs several years before, and their three-story home was our destination. Their family had grown to eleven children. We stayed with them for a week, making happy memories with trips to scenic spots every day in their station wagon and our limousine. We also made the local paper with a picture of all twenty-one children on the stairs of the Bensons' home!

On my way home from a trip to Japan in 1957, I stopped in Oregon to see Dad. He had been living alone in the family home for the ten years since Mother's death. He had a standing invitation to come live with us and had been to visit us two or three times, but he preferred to live in familiar surroundings within driving distance of friends. He kept up his newspaper evangelism in a number of county papers, thanks to several friends who paid for the ads.

Finally we began to hear from his neighbors that he had lost his driving skill and had had several near misses on the highway. When I visited him I found his car had finally broken down, and he was isolated without transportation. I persuaded him that it was time to join us in Wheaton, and he agreed to come. He had just turned eighty-three.

Our old house was more than filled with the ten children, ages one to fourteen, so we built a new room, attached to the dining room (formerly the back porch). I dug the trenches for the footings by hand, then watched one side cave in when the cement truck came too close as the driver prepared to dump his load! We installed a gas wall heater so Dad could keep the room as warm as he liked.

We were relieved to have Dad safe in our home, and I was more than pleased and grateful for Margaret's willingness and ability to add her father-in-law to her already very large list of responsibilities.

What surprised me was my own inability to adjust to his coming. Dad was a genial person who had always been the conversational leader in social situations, both as a pastor and as father in the home. As a commuter, I had very little time with my children, and I cherished the dinner hour as a time for open conversation around the table. Dad, however, tended to take over the table talk, asking me about my day at the office or telling us about people he had met on his daily walk, weather permitting, to downtown Wheaton or Glen Ellyn. I didn't know how to ask him to be quiet enough to let the children talk, without being disrespectful to him. So the situation continued, and I bottled up my frustration.

I became overly sensitive to everything he did—for instance his long "pastoral prayers" at church prayer meetings. Others remarked about their pleasure in hearing him pray, but I cringed with embarrassment, especially the time he publicly reminded the Lord about "that time Ken was hitchhiking down the Canyon Road." I wasn't sure what his point was, but he was probably thanking the Lord for my safety.

My sensitivity became even more acute as he became somewhat senile. He would forget where he had hidden his billfold and would think the children or a thief had stolen it during the night. It was usually hidden in a dresser drawer under his winter underwear, and we were able to recover the billfold quickly, much to his relief. Early one morning I came downstairs to find him fumbling with the telephone directory to find the number for the FBI, to report his loss. We were both relieved to find the billfold in its usual hiding place!

I knew very well I wasn't handling the situation with a proper attitude, and I looked upon my failure as a terrible spiritual defeat. I didn't know what to do about it and finally began asking the Lord to take him to heaven before he became any more confused. One morning when Dad was eighty-four years old and had been with us a year and a half, Margaret was out in the neighborhood for a little while, collecting for the Red Cross. As Dad was sipping his mid-morning cup of tea at the kitchen table, he put his head down on the table and was gone.

"Grandpa's asleep," the preschool children told their mother when she returned, but with one glance she knew otherwise.

Out of my despair about the poor relationship with my much-loved father grew a paranoia about my relationship with my own children. I feared they would be as irritated by me as I had been by my father in those last years. The result was an absence of the easy camaraderie that I have seen and envied in other homes. I am pleased now to see the good rapport between my children and their children, and I'm grateful that my failures are not being reenacted in the new generation. To some extent I have freedom with some of my grandchildren that I didn't feel with my own children when they were young.

Are All the Children In?

Are all the children in? The night is falling,
  And storm clouds gather in the threatening west;
The lowing cattle seek a friendly shelter;
  The bird hies to her nest;
The thunder crashes; wilder grows the tempest,
  And darkness settles o'er the fearful din;
Come, shut the door, and gather round the hearthstone—
  Are all the children in?

Are all the children in? The night is falling,
  When gilded sin doth walk about the street.
Oh, at last it biteth like a serpent!
  Poisoned are stolen sweets.
O mothers! guard the feet of inexperience,
  Too prone to wander in the paths of sin!
Oh, shut the door of love against temptation!
  Are all the children in?

Are all the children in? The night is falling,
  The night of death is hastening on apace;
The Lord is calling: "Enter thou thy chamber,
  And tarry there a space."
And when He comes, the King in all His glory,
  Who died the shameful death our hearts to win,
Oh, may the gates of heaven shut about us,
  With all the children in.

                                        Elizabeth Rosser

Chapter 20
A New Kind of Translation

WE HAD READ over and over again to our youngest children (different years, different children) all the available books of Bible stories geared to three- and four-year-olds. Some were on the life of Christ, others on Old Testament heroes such as Joseph or Daniel, but I could not find a book that covered the entire Bible for very young children.

Finally the thought occurred to me to try writing such a book myself. I experimented with the idea and wrote some half-page stories that could match pictures in the Sunday school papers the children brought home. I would hold a child on my lap, show the picture, and read the Bible story I had written about the picture. I asked a few questions and could tell whether the story was understood. My children's response to the experiment was good.

The material was handwritten, so I arranged with the typing pool at Moody Bible Institute to type as much as I had written. But partway through the Bible I became discouraged, and wondered whether to continue with the project. A few days later a young woman stopped me in the hallway and told me she had been typing my manuscript and was very enthusiastic about it. This greatly encouraged me, so I decided to finish writing the book. Since this was an important decision, I went the next day to the typing pool to thank the young woman for her enthusiasm. I didn't see her, so I asked the supervisor whether the person who typed my manuscript was away for the day.

The supervisor looked puzzled. "Katherine typed it," she said. "She's right over there." But the person she pointed to wasn't the one I had talked to in the hallway. I described her to the supervisor, but she said no, all her typists were there in the room. And certainly none of them was my encourager.

I believe it was an angel God had sent the previous day, to tell me to go ahead. That book is *The Bible in Pictures for Little Eyes,* published in 1956, and there are now more than a million copies in print. It is still a best-seller for Moody Press. In fact, *Publishers Weekly* recently placed it thirty-fourth on their list of all-time best-selling children's books. With the help of our good friend Angus Hudson in London, England, it has been printed in fifty-four languages, with the same pictures on each page that two generations of English-speaking children have looked at and learned from. I thank God for sending His angel that day in the hallway of the seventh floor of Moody Bible Institute.

An amazing story concerning one copy of *The Bible in Pictures for Little Eyes* was told me by my friend David Howard, international director of World Evangelical Fellowship.

In the early 1960s Dave was in the back country of Colombia, training lay pastors for evangelism and church planting. One of his students was Manuel Domeko.

Dave had no Spanish Bibles to distribute to that group of lay pastors, so he used copies of the Spanish edition of *The Bible in Pictures for Little Eyes* as his text. When Manuel went out into remote mountain areas to witness, he took with him his copy of the book.

When Dave Howard next met Manuel Domeko, seventeen years had passed. Manuel was still carrying that copy of *The*

Bible in Pictures for Little Eyes, carefully wrapped in a plastic bag. He had preached and witnessed from that one book during all those intervening years. The pages were tattered, the color pictures were faded, and the cover was falling off. Yet it remained Manuel's most prized possession—the number-one tool for his ministry.

Before writing *The Bible in Pictures for Little Eyes,* I had already completed *Stories for the Children's Hour* and *Devotions for the Children's Hour,* also published by Moody Press. These books too have had wide distribution, the latter now in its hundredth printing! It is a condensation at a young child's level of Dr. Chafer's excellent theology courses I had taken in seminary. The stories in *Stories for the Children's Hour* were those I told my children while on Sunday afternoon walks in the fields behind our house. Some of these stories were based on my own childhood experiences, some on situations the children knew about in our neighborhood, and some on my imagination. All of them end with a moral—a literary device not much in favor in today's children's literature, but one that I feel is very important.

Once at a Christian Booksellers convention a young woman told me good-naturedly, "I hate you! Your *Stories for the Children's Hour* has been the favorite book of each of my four children, and I am so sick and tired of those stories, especially the one about Mr. Bert, the cat! Why don't you write something else for them?"

When my book *Devotions for the Children's Hour* was published in 1954, we read it in our evening devotions. But that was not reading from the Bible itself, so the following year, when Becky and John were going on thirteen and twelve, I began to read from the New Testament Epistles. It was time for them, and for Martha and Peter, too, to study doctrine and learn how to live the Christian life. Since Romans was over the head of the younger children, Margaret took them to our bedroom and began over again with the simplest books.

But the transition from stories of heroes of faith in the Old Testament and miracles of Jesus in the New Testament to reading Romans and Galatians in the King James Version of the Bible was difficult. I found it hard to hold the children's attention even though I stopped the reading after every few verses to explain and ask a question or two. It was painful to live my life over again through my children; it brought back my own struggles with Bible reading not only at their age but in subsequent years as well.

I prayed about this problem and tried to think of ways of making Bible reading more attractive. And some of my ideas were fanciful indeed. Would it help if every page were a different color of paper? What about printing some sort of fragrance onto the page?

One Saturday afternoon in 1955 I sat at my desk in our bedroom, working on one of my storybooks. I became tired of the project and pushed it away, then began to ponder again my children's spiritual needs. I could hear in memory my father's voice as he said to my brother and me, "Unless you fellows get into the Word of God and get it into your lives, you'll never amount to much as Christians."

Again I prayed, "Lord, how can our family devotions become more interesting and valuable to my children, and how can I myself learn to read the Bible with more interest?"

As I prayed, I thought of a popular lecture my mother had frequently given to women's missionary societies, in which she summarized the entire Bible, from Genesis to Revelation. At my encouragement, she had once written out her talk. Now I wondered if her twenty-five-page outline could be expanded to a hundred pages. Would this strike the world's fancy and become widely used? Perhaps, but it wouldn't accomplish what I had in mind for the family.

Then I thought about summarizing each book of the Bible, and it seemed this might be of help to some people. But it would not serve to get people into the text of the Bible for themselves.

What about a chapter-by-chapter summary? Same problem! Then I considered this: What about restating each verse to make it more understandable? I didn't actually shout "Eureka!" but my mind and heart leaped up, and I wondered whether this might be the answer I'd been searching for during these many years. Why not explore the idea further? I would experiment.

I reached for my King James Version and took a fresh sheet of paper and my pencil. I opened the Bible at random and looked at 2 Timothy, chapter 2. I read the first several verses, thought about them, and carefully analyzed them word by word and phrase by phrase. Then I wrote down their meaning in everyday language.

Here is an example of the King James Version compared with what I rewrote for the children:

King James Version	*My rewrite*
No man that warreth entangleth himself with the affairs of this life; that he may please him who hath chosen him to be a soldier. (2 Tim. 2:4)	As Christ's soldier do not let yourself become tied up in worldly affairs, for then you cannot satisfy the one who has enlisted you in his army. (2 Tim. 2:4)

I went on this way through all the verses in the chapter. With great interest and satisfaction I read what I had written. That night after supper I read it to the family and, as usual, asked the older children some questions to see if they had understood the verses. I was elated to note that they were able to answer—they had understood! We went on to some discussion of what Paul had said and of how it applied to their lives at school and at home.

I was so encouraged by the family's response that from time

to time I prepared another chapter from the Epistles for family devotions. I usually received the same positive response, but when I used the King James Version, the result was often bafflement. I remember that after I had explained the meaning of one particular verse from the King James Version, Janet, then about eight, said, "But Daddy, if that's what it means, why doesn't it say so?"

More and more during the next few weeks I wondered if this was really and finally the answer to my prayers and concern of so many years, both for the family and for myself. I enjoyed reading my paraphrase too, and got much more out of it than from other Bible reading. Gradually I sensed a deepening of the conviction that I ought to paraphrase all of the Epistles—the letters of St. Paul to the Romans, the Corinthians, and other early churches, and the letters of James, Peter, John, Jude, and the writer of the book of Hebrews.

And so my thoughts began to crystallize. I began to believe that God wanted me to translate the New Testament Epistles into words that anyone could understand. At some point it occurred to me that other families might be similarly helped if they had this easier text to read. I decided to get to work seriously on the project.

But when could I do this writing? With a large and still increasing family, I obviously had a lot to do at home in the evenings. The answer was to do my writing while on the commuter train, so I began systematically working through Romans as I rode. It took me about a year to paraphrase all the Epistles. As the swaying train bumped along over the tracks, I sat with a Bible on one knee and a writing pad on the other. I tried to keep everything balanced and not let it fall over on my seatmate as he perused the morning paper.

I chose the American Standard Version of 1901 as the basic text, because it was, and still is, in my opinion, the most accurate of the word-for-word English translations. It was

Above: My older brother, Doug (right), and I were best of friends. This photo was taken in 1925.

Left: My parents, George and Charlotte Taylor, and my younger brother, Lyman, in 1937.

Above: Doug and I
attended Wheaton
College together.
This is in the col-
lege library, 1936.

Right: My wrestling
days at Wheaton
College, 1936.

My senior picture, Wheaton College, 1938.   Margaret in 1937, when she was a
student at Oregon State College. She and
I first met as freshmen in high school.

Top: Margaret and I were married on September 13, 1940.
Bottom: Our first apartment in Dallas, Texas, 1942.

Top: We had five children by 1950—Janet (2), Becky (7), John (6), Peter (3), Martha (5).

Middle: This family photo from 1957 includes all ten of the children. Seated, from left: Cynthia, Mark, Mary Lee on my lap, Alison on Margaret's lap, Gretchen. Standing: Martha, John, Becky, Peter, Janet.

Left: My father lived in Wheaton with us from 1957 till his death in 1959. Here Grandpa and Margaret (in driver's seat) and all ten children are in and around the 1942 Cadillac limousine that served as the family car.

This photo was taken in my study in 1970, as I was working on the translation of *The Living Bible*.

This photo of Margaret and me was taken in 1971.

I presented the first copy of *The Living Bible* to Billy Graham at Dr. Graham's Oakland-Alameda County crusade in 1971. When Dr. Graham first read *Living Letters* he said, "It reads like today's newspaper."

Margaret and I are talking with Tyndale House executives in 1972: Wendell Hawley, sales manager, and Harold Shaw, business manager.

Upper left: This photo was taken in a Wheaton park in 1972.

Upper right: I visited Papua New Guinea in 1978. I was exploring the need for modern translations of the Bible in that part of the world.

Left: With me are our good friends Joe and Mary Lou Bayly at the Christian Booksellers Association convention in 1976. Joe and Mary Lou's son Tim married our daughter Mary Lee that same year.

Top: I presented the 28 millionth copy of *The Living Bible* to President Ronald Reagan in 1983 in commemoration of the "Year of the Bible."

Bottom: I presented a copy of *The Living Bible* to Kenya's President Daniel arap Moi. Looking on are Lars Dunberg, international president of LBI, Professor George Kinote, Margaret, and Commodore Philemon Quaye.

Top: The mantle of leadership at Tyndale House Publishers is passed to the next generation. Mark became president of the company in 1984 in a ceremony held in the warehouse (which doubled as a chapel, due to space limitations). Looking on as I give Mark a challenge are Tyndale executives Doug Knox, Bob Bolinder, Wendell Hawley, and Margaret.

Middle: Tyndale House Publishers was named after William Tyndale, one of the early translators of the New Testament into English. He was burned at the stake in 1536 because of his translation. This portrait hangs in the Tyndale House office.

Bottom: A display of some of the translations prepared by Living Bibles International. LBI has completed modern-language translations of the New Testament in more than fifty languages.

Left: At a family reunion in 1990. The children are standing in order of age from the top of the slide: Becky Kraft, Marty Taylor, Peter Taylor, Janet Taylor, Mark Taylor, Cynthia Brown, Gretchen Worcester, Mary Lee Bayly, Alison Lingo, Margaret, Ken. John Taylor was unable to attend the reunion.

At the family reunion in 1990, 23 of the 27 Taylor grandchildren posed for this picture. Front row: Margaret Taylor, Rebecca Taylor. Second row: Stephen Taylor, Jordan Lingo, Michal Bayly, Lindsey Worcester, Tara Lingo, Alexi Taylor-Grosman, Nathan Brown, Kimberly Worcester, Joseph Bayly, Erin Lingo. Third row: Kyra Taylor-Grosman, Keri Worcester, Stephanie Worcester, Kristen Taylor, Katie Kraft, Heather Bayly holding Kenny Brown. Last row: Christopher Taylor, Jeremy Taylor, Joe Mason, Jonathon Taylor. Not pictured are Lee Mason, Ariele Taylor, Preston Taylor, and Hannah Bayly.

© Copyright, Chicago Tribune Company, 1990. All rights reserved, used with permission.

Above: Mark and I are standing in front of the new Tyndale House building, which was constructed in 1990.

Right: Even Bible translators have to relax occasionally! I went parasailing in Maui in 1988.

prepared by a large committee of scholars far more expert in Greek than I was. My study of seminary Greek had given me only a basic vocabulary and grammar.

In the evenings, after the younger children were in bed and the older ones were doing their homework, I would go over what I had done that day on the train. I had a copy of every English Bible translation on my desk, opened to the chapter I was working on, plus Greek word studies and commentaries. This was to help me check every nuance of meaning. For years my desk was covered with open books and sheets of manuscript on yellow tablet paper.

At the end of the year I was elated to finish the work, and I had the manuscript typed. The title I gave it was *Living Letters*. But before sending it to a publisher, I decided to reread it.

I was annoyed to find that the very first verse in the manuscript, Romans 1:1, needed a few words changed for greater clarity, and so did verse 2. Then, to my dismay, I could see that verse after verse needed some changes and that the manuscript was far from ready for publication. It had been a year since I had begun the writing, and when one comes back to a piece of writing after a year, one often sees things that were overlooked before. So I resigned myself to going through the entire manuscript again, and this took another year. Finally it was retyped and again ready for the printer.

But once again I went through the same agonizing experience—I kept seeing verses that needed improvement. So I edited the material carefully a third time, and thus another year went by.

One evening when reading to the family from the latest revision, I was brought up short when our daughter Martha, then a freshman in high school, asked me, "Dad, who are you writing this for?"

I replied, "For you and the rest of the family, and for other families."

"Well," she said, "I don't think it is for me or for other high school kids, because the language is insultingly simple."

As I looked over it again from her point of view, I could see she was correct. I faced the question of whether to go on with the translation at a level for young children or whether there was an even greater need to use vocabulary and construction that would be acceptable for the average reader at *Reader's Digest* level. So I revised *Living Letters* again. Perhaps later I would try for a Bible with a reduced vocabulary for children.

But it was no simple task to raise the reading age level. In fact, it took another year of hard work.

Once more the entire manuscript of the Epistles was complete and ready for retyping. Before submitting it to a publisher I decided to check it over one more time to be sure that everything was exactly right.

By this time I was aware that I needed to enlist the help of Greek scholars to resolve some problems in the Greek text where the meaning was not clear. These scholars made their suggestions and, though sometimes they disagreed among themselves, I made the necessary changes. It was a slow process, requiring great care to incorporate the increased accuracy while using my own technique of making the vocabulary contemporary and easy to read. All of this work took another year.

Then came a new realization, suggested by a friend who read the manuscript, that it needed some polishing in literary style. Luci Shaw, now famous for her books of Christian poetry, agreed to be my literary consultant. She spent many, many hours evaluating the text and making valuable suggestions. Often I was amazed at her skill at changing a word or phrase, and I wondered why I hadn't thought of it myself.

During these years, 1955–1960, as I wrote and rewrote the manuscript for *Living Letters,* it became my most precious possession. What if the house burned down while we were away? The unused chicken house was at a distance from the house; it wouldn't burn too. So when we went on vacations I hid my treasure in an old cupboard in the chicken house. I'm sorry to say I had more faith in the safety of the chicken house than I did in the efficacy of our children's prayers. Almost every night one of them would pray that our house wouldn't burn down. We were very fire conscious because the house was a firetrap.

In all, I made six complete revisions of the manuscript over a period of five years, in addition to the first year's basic work. Then, at last, I could read the manuscript all the way through without finding need for improvement. I could hardly believe the work was really done. On a scrap of paper I wrote, "Finished final revision of paraphrase, December 27, 1960, 3:30 P.M. with praise to the Lord," and signed it. Years later Margaret found that scrap of paper and framed it, and it hangs in my study.

I naively supposed that any publisher would be eager for the privilege of publishing this book and that I needed only to decide which one I should choose!

Naturally, my first thought was to have it published by Moody Press, but I had second thoughts when I heard one of Moody's vice-presidents wonder aloud if friends of the Institute might react negatively to it. They might be offended because of their high admiration for the King James Version and might even discontinue their financial support of Moody. As director of Moody Press I had the authority to make the decision, but I certainly had a primary obligation to the good name and welfare of Moody Bible Institute.

I went to Dr. William Culbertson, our president, to ask his advice, but he wasn't very helpful. "I trust your judgment," he said. "You must make the decision." I appreciated his expression of trust, but his attitude only made the weight of my responsibility heavier. Finally, after much thought and prayer, I decided it would be better not to risk involving the Institute, so I mailed the manuscript to the religious department of one of the well-known secular publishers. To my delight I received a kind letter of tentative acceptance. They would give me a final decision in about a month.

At the end of the month another letter came from them, and I eagerly tore it open. But my spirits sank as I read of their conclusion not to publish the manuscript. The theologically liberal scholars they had consulted liked it, but the evangelical scholars could not tolerate a paraphrase translation, insisting that any translation must be on a word-for-word basis, rather than expressing the *meaning* of the Greek text.

Discouraged, but still hopeful, I sent the manuscript to another publisher, who promptly declined it, and then to another and yet another. This was a setback I hadn't expected, since my own enthusiasm for the project had grown year by year and revision by revision.

I suppose it is not surprising, given my many years as director of Moody Press, that my next thought was to publish the book myself. The barrier, however, was the very practical matter of how to pay the printer. With a small salary and a large family, we had only two or three hundred dollars in the savings account, and no assets a bank could consider sufficient collateral for a loan.

Nevertheless, the first step was to find out how much it would cost to print the book. I took the manuscript to my friend Paul Benson at Lithocolor Press and asked him for a price on printing and binding two thousand copies. From my publishing experience I knew that would be the minimum cost-effective quantity.

A few days later Paul came to my office at Moody Press, not only to quote a price but to say he had read the manuscript and was extremely impressed with it! He was so enthusiastic about its potential that he offered to print the book and let me pay him as the books were sold. What a deal! Paul was certainly God's man to get *Living Letters* under way. He took the manuscript back with him and soon began the typesetting.

Chapter 21
Voice Problems

ABOUT THE TIME Lithocolor Press started type-setting *Living Letters*, I left on a four-month trip to Europe, the Middle East, and Africa. Before leaving, I told Margaret she would have to do the proofreading in my absence. She reminded me she had never proofread anything in her life, much less an entire book. I countered that I could trust her and she could find proofreader's marks in the front of a good dictionary!

Her letters to me in Europe were restrained, but I gathered she was having to stay up until one or two in the morning to keep up with the daily batches of galley proofs—the typeset pages—coming from the printer. We still had eight children at home—five in grade school, one in junior high, and two in high school. Her days were full.

I caught a cold on the plane between New York and Glasgow, Scotland. The propeller plane was cold and I was chilled. When I arrived, I went to bed with what felt like a high fever, but I awakened refreshed, though without my voice. Business appointments that day forced me to do some speaking, and I whispered as best I could. A day or two later I was able to speak almost clearly again. After another two days I was in balmy Portugal, addressing missionaries at a luncheon in my honor. Ten minutes into my talk my voice simply failed. The laryngitis had returned, and I had to stop and sit down.

No doubt if I could have rested my voice for a few days, all would have been well, but I had eleven weeks of travel and meetings ahead of me. My voice was a problem the whole time, but I kept going. I was carrying a portable Dictaphone for dictating my reports instead of writing them, and for some reason that effort always resulted in voice deterioration for a day or two.

Later I could report that I had a successful trip, because several publishing centers developed as a result. That trip was also full of general interest as I visited fourteen of the new nations that had been formed in Africa in the previous three or four years. However, my visit to Turkey was most distressing—thirty million Muslims with almost no Christian witness among them and perhaps only a dozen ex-Muslim believers in the whole nation.

The highlight of the trip was finding a package waiting for me in Jerusalem. It contained the galley proofs of *Living Letters*. To see the manuscript actually in type after those seven years of writing and rewriting, editing and revising, was a glorious experience.

I left my hotel and walked across the valley to the Mount of Olives and, with great excitement, read the entire manuscript, then began rejoicing before the Lord. I was especially touched to read in Margaret's letter that reading the proofs had helped her understand these Scriptures better, and she felt others would be helped too. I could not remember that she had ever made any comment, one way or the other, about the project during those seven long years. I had felt she was ambivalent about the value of the manuscript when she considered how much I had deprived our children of my time.

After I completed the reading, I sat there looking across to the city of Jerusalem and prayed that God would use this work for His glory. The thought came to mind that I was sitting in the very land where Jesus used five loaves and two fish to feed five thousand people. I had in my hands what was going to be two thousand copies of *Living Letters,* and I thought of those copies as two thousand loaves to feed God's people. Then I worked out on paper a simple mathematical equation. If five loaves fed five thousand people, how many people would two thousand loaves feed? The answer was two million! This was of course utterly impossible. Nevertheless, I bowed my head and prayed earnestly that some day two million copies of *Living Letters* would be in print!

As I am writing this book, twenty-eight years later, I can report that before we stopped printing *Living Letters* as a separate volume, the number had indeed reached two million. And now the complete Living Bible has reached nearly forty million copies.

Something else of great significance happened on the evening of that same day. In my small hotel room I began to consider whether there might be other parts of the Bible that needed to be given a thought-for-thought translation. Up to this time I had had no intention of going beyond the Epistles, which had been the hardest part of the Bible for me to understand. I felt the Gospels were comparatively easy, but the books of prophecy, especially the Minor Prophets (called minor because of their length, not their importance) seemed quite boring and uninteresting. I supposed this was partly because of the Hebrew poetry style in which they are written, many verses containing phrases duplicated by a similar thought. I wondered if it would be possible to combine the repetitions into one sentence and so make the reading move more rapidly and with greater interest.

So even as the galleys of *Living Letters* were being read, I began to see a whole new vision of paraphrasing sections of the Old Testament too. That very night I experimented with the book of Isaiah.

On that trip, I had an audience with Emperor Haile Selassie in Addis Ababa, the capital of Ethiopia. I was meeting with him to request that he allow the Bible to be translated into the various languages of Ethiopia. He had forbidden this, saying it could be printed only in the one official language, Amharic. But millions who did not know Amharic, or were only struggling with it in school, were without the benefits of the Scriptures.

It was a serious time, but it had its moments of humor too. An elderly Swedish evangelist who knew the emperor prepared me as to the proper protocol. Above all, one must never turn one's back to the emperor. Approaching him, it was proper to take three paces forward, bow, take another three paces, bow again, etc.

I walked up the pathway to the rather unprestigious-looking building, between two mangy lions chained to stakes on either side of the walkway. The lions were to emphasize his claim to the title "Lion of the Tribe of Judah." The belief of the Ethiopians was that they were descended from King Solomon and the Queen of Sheba, who was, according to Ethiopian legend, a temporary member of his harem when she came to visit him.

As the emperor stood at the end of the reception room to receive me, I bowed appropriately, took three steps, then sidestepped around a sofa, bowed again, and took another three steps. We shook hands and sat down to talk.

"Your majesty," I began with my carefully organized presentation, "the Word of God is very important to all your people, as I am sure you agree. I have come to petition you to allow its translation into Galla and the other languages spoken in your great empire. More than half of your people do not speak Amharic, or they use it only as a second language. That is why the Bible should be in their tribal languages."

His response was firm. "My country must have only one language," he declared. "Otherwise there will be disharmony, disunity, and tribalism."

The discussion went on at some length, but he did not change his opinion, although he suggested that I go to see his minister of education.

He then changed the subject and began to taunt me a bit about the American government's fear of communism. He seemed to be strongly pro-Russian, so I later sent him a book by Cameron Townsend of Wycliffe Bible Translators. In that book, Townsend told about the Russian policy of encouraging the publication of scores of newspapers in various local languages throughout the Soviet Union, in addition to teaching Russian in the schools. I hoped that because of his appreciation for all things Russian, he would follow their example and allow publication of newspapers (and Bibles!) in various languages of Ethiopia.

Eventually the emperor stood up to indicate that the interview was finished. Remembering my etiquette, I thanked him, bade him farewell, and began to back out toward the door— three paces backwards, a bow, then another three paces backwards. But I had forgotten the sofa between me and the door. I suddenly found myself sitting on it, and the emperor laughed!

He had invited me to return if I were in Ethiopia again, but I never had that opportunity. Later the Bible translation policy was changed, whether by Haile Selassie or by the new administration after he was deposed, I do not know. Bibles are now being printed in Ethiopia in other languages. Praise to God.

When I got home from that particular four-month trip, my family, friends, and coworkers were shocked to hear my voice, or lack of it. I could speak only in a hoarse whisper, or sometimes squeak. Speaking had become more and more difficult, and others were having a hard time understanding me.

In the following months and years I tried every kind of

remedy that anyone suggested: sprays, potent lozenges, chiro-
practic and osteopathic treatments, psychiatric consultations,
and hypnotism. I attended healing meetings at our local Epis-
copal church, and concerned friends in different settings laid
hands on me in prayer several times. I went to singing teachers
and voice therapists, some of them as far away as the West Coast.

On the recommendation of a friend who had received help
for a similar problem, I went to a well-known chiropractor in
a small Wisconsin town. After several treatments during the
course of a day, he predicted my voice would be better in two
weeks. And it was. What a relief! But my physician friend John
Frame said it wasn't from the treatments but the power of
suggestion. Perhaps his comment broke the spell, for a few
days later my voice deteriorated again.

A Jewish psychiatrist I consulted in Chicago was quite sure
my problem was that I subconsciously felt guilty for "tampering
with the Word of God," and that I felt God was punishing me.

After three years I had a treatment from my friend Dr. Gus
Hemwall that involved injections in my neck, and I recovered
enough voice to get along. But even so, for years I turned down
all invitations that required speaking before an audience.

I learned that others have the same affliction; the medical
name is spasmodic dysphonia, which simply means that the
vocal cords fail to work in harmony.

Not a few saw my affliction as a blessing in disguise, because it enabled me to concentrate on paraphrasing the rest
of the Bible during the next nine years. I continued to pray for
healing all of that time and hoped that with the completion of
The Living Bible the "blessing in disguise" would be removed.
It wasn't. A 1976 article in the *Mennonite Brethren Herald*
spoke about my problem. In reporting on an address I had
given, the editor wrote, "Taylor's voice has almost gone. It is
barely a whisper now. Even through a microphone it sounds
cracked and very tired."

Long before that, though, the problem with my voice changed my personality. Margaret has noticed it the most. I have become quiet and retiring. I used to be very vocal, sharp in repartee, and quick in making puns. Now, by the time I nerve myself to make a comment in group conversation, the opportune moment has passed.

Also, I am frequently misunderstood, and often it is easier to let the mistake stand than to take the trouble to correct it. It can be very frustrating, especially when it is Margaret who does not understand me!

But I have experienced humorous incidents too. A gentleman called me long distance and said he had read about my problem. "I can tell as we are talking now that you do have a lot of difficulty speaking," he said, "so I will speak to you very slowly and distinctly so you can understand me."

After twenty years of limping along with my gravelly voice and frequently being misunderstood, I considered the most drastic treatment of all. The procedure, which was being done by very few surgeons in the country, was to sever the nerve leading to one of the vocal cords, permanently paralyzing its activity. A friend had had this surgery, and while his voice wasn't strong, he no longer struggled to get words out. On the other hand, another friend had the surgery with no improvement.

I contacted the surgeon in San Francisco who was best known for his work in this field. Because the surgery would be done under general anesthesia, the doctor required that I have a cardiac examination that included a stress test. I failed the test. An angiogram indicated the apparent necessity of heart surgery to avoid the probability of an eventual heart attack. The diagnosis was confirmed by surgeons at a second hospital, and I had double bypass surgery a week later. While I was not particularly nervous concerning the outcome, it was a comfort to have Margaret and several of our children and their spouses at the hospital to pray with me just before I went into surgery. I was moved and blessed, too, when a resident assisting with the surgery leaned over the operating table and prayed for me just before the injection that put me to sleep.

Following my recovery I did not have the voice surgery that involved cutting the nerve to the vocal cord. By means of a second opinion I learned that by having an injection that only temporarily paralyzed the nerve, I could determine in advance what the results of the surgery would be. When I had that test done, my new voice sounded like Donald Duck's, so I quit thinking about the possibility of the irreversible surgery.

During the past two years I have experienced dramatic improvement in my voice by participating in an experimental program at the National Institutes of Health. I receive injections of botulin toxin, which paralyze the vocal cords on one side. After a few months the paralysis wears off and I need another treatment, but I thank God for the relief it has brought me.

In Thankfulness for Health

I woke at dawn
In a hotel in some far distant land
(And for one moment of uncertainty
I knew not where).

There was no pain,
But only vague discomfort,
And a sudden realization—
I wasn't well.

I wasn't really frightened (though alarmed),
But now I knew the barren walls
Of that bleak room
Would be my coffin for the day,
With all appointments cancelled
And my work undone.

Yesterday was full of joy
For all my God had wrought,
But I had never praised Him
For vitality and health.

So now, while lying here
Bereft of opportunity,
I humbly thank Him
For unnumbered past and future days
Of running, walking,
Climbing in and out of taxis,
And of leaping from my bed.

K.N.T.
Teheran, Feb. 14, 1976

Chapter 22
Living Letters

A DAY OR TWO after arriving home from my four-month trip I talked to the printer, eager to know whether *Living Letters* would be ready in time for the Christian Booksellers Association convention in July. He told me the job had taken longer than anticipated, due in part to my final corrections in the manuscript, which were illegible to the typesetters, and in part to the many changes Margaret had made in the galley proofs. She had taken out a bushel of unnecessary commas and changed most of the semicolons to periods. At that time typesetting was a slow process on the old hot-metal Linotype machines. I didn't have the heart to complain to Margaret about it, because she was working for quality, not speed.

In order to have books to display at that 1962 CBA convention in Chicago, we arranged for the printer to prepare several hand-bound copies. I felt much more emotion in finally holding a copy of *Living Letters* than there had been with my previous books. This was God's Word, but—by His grace and calling—my work too.

A flood of memories came: my own years of frustration and difficulty in understanding the letters of the New Testament, and the difficulties for the children when it came to reading this part of the Bible during the family devotions. I thought of the Saturday afternoon when God spoke to me, revealing His plan for a thought-for-thought translation, and I remembered the experimenting and the decision finally to try to fulfill the idea by paraphrasing all of the New Testament letters into contemporary language. I thought of the long hours during subsequent years, writing on the commuter train, and the evenings and weekends spent in rewriting as I worked through six revisions during the next five years.

I didn't know how to thank God adequately, but I thought of the offerings by fire made by the people of Israel as described in the Old Testament. There was a brush pile in our back field waiting to be burned, and I started a fire under the pile. I stood there in the presence of God with this first copy of *Living Letters* and prayed again the prayer I had prayed on the Mount of Olives, that God would use the little book mightily for His glory. Then I sank to my knees in thanks to God that the work was finished. When the fire was burning brightly, I took the precious copy and, with great emotion, threw it reverently into the midst of the flames as the offering of the firstfruits to my God. This was such a private act of worship that I told no one about it for twenty-five years.

Every company needs a name, even a company with only one product. I had always been fascinated by the story of the sixteenth-century Englishman William Tyndale. His lifetime goal was to translate the Bible into English, even though there was a death penalty for anyone who dared to do this. The Catholic church, which controlled the English government at that time, was afraid that people would read things in the Bible that contradicted teachings of the church. For safety, Tyndale left England and hid in Belgium as he worked on his translation. He finally finished the New Testament and found a printer to publish it. The copies were smuggled into England inside bales of cotton, or landed on lonely British shores at night and carried to London, where they were bought eagerly by people who all their lives had wondered what the Bible said.

William Tyndale's dream was accomplished, but in 1536 King Henry VIII arranged for Tyndale to be found, kidnapped, and burned at the stake for giving the Bible in English to the people of England.

I too had a dream of giving to America a Bible that was easy to understand. William Tyndale was my hero. So *Living Letters* was published under the name of Tyndale House Publishers.

I rented half of a ten-foot booth at the CBA convention, and there I sat with half a dozen green-jacketed copies of my one small book on a bare table.

As director of Moody Press I had enjoyed being around the action of the Moody Press booth during conventions. I had a chance to meet booksellers from around the country, and I enjoyed hearing in person how grateful they were for my children's books and how well the books were selling.

But sitting at our tiny little Tyndale House booth was lonely! Many booksellers stopped when they saw me at my little table, but I could scarcely talk because of my voice problem. I was given lots of advice about what I should do to get my voice back and every day I collected a pocketful of cough drops, donated by my well-wishers.

But nobody seemed to notice the little sign that said "Tyndale House Publishers" hanging at the back of the booth. If they did see the sign, it didn't register that it had anything to do with me. Since I am not a salesman by inclination, only a few sympathetic friends ordered copies of *Living Letters*.

I realized I needed to learn fast to be a salesman, so I went out into the aisle and pushed a copy of *Living Letters* into the hands of people passing by, explaining it was a new translation of the Epistles. I asked them to turn to a favorite passage and read a few verses. It worked! They were amazed and pleased at the way some of the profound passages from the Apostle Paul's writings had turned from hard, rocky wilderness into milk and honey. Almost everyone I talked to ordered a copy or two, and some even ordered five copies.

It was hard to get the attention of people I did not know as I constantly cleared my throat in a futile attempt to make my voice do what it was supposed to do. It was so exasperating! Margaret was with me, and she did her best to fill in and amplify when my balky voice couldn't be understood.

I had devised a contest in which I asked people to do their own paraphrase of a certain passage. The winner would get a free copy of *Living Letters* at the end of the convention. I did not get as many entries as I had hoped for. Years later at Tyndale House we received a package containing a copy of *Living Letters* that was literally falling apart. The owner wanted it replaced. It was the hand-bound copy he had received at the 1962 CBA convention when he was winner of the contest!

Each day just before the convention floor closed, I would try to find prospective customers to whom I could lend a copy overnight. "But be sure to bring it back first thing in the morning," I told them. "These are the only copies we have."

I was especially gratified that my friend Gordon Mitchell, who distributed books in Canada for Moody Press and many other Christian publishers, agreed to try to distribute my book too. He ordered two hundred copies. Including that order, the total sold at the convention was around eight hundred copies of the two thousand copies we had printed. I was immensely relieved that most of the printing bill could be paid when the books were shipped and paid for. I felt encouraged to believe that the entire two thousand copies would eventually be sold.

A couple of weeks later, Norm Wolf, Paul Benson's assistant, appeared at our back door with the first thousand copies. We had no garage or basement, so when I came home from work that night I found a huge pile of cartons in the middle of the living room. I don't think it had occurred to me to plan where to store books, but fortunately we had a lot of beds to put them under.

Margaret had already typed invoices and labels for the orders we had taken at the convention, as well as labels for family members and friends to whom I planned to send complimentary copies. The invoices and labels were from stock pads purchased at the stationery store. We rubber-stamped the Tyndale House name and address on them. Margaret was as careful with company money as she was with our own, and when she saw that the pads of parcel post labels cost two cents less at Woolworth's, they got our business!

I purchased Jiffy bags and unassembled shipping boxes from Moody Press and brought them home a bundle at a time on the train. With rolls of stamps, a tape dispenser, and a small postage scale, we were in business. The final step was to type up a four-by-six-inch index card for each store and enter the date, invoice number, number of books purchased, and the invoice amount. This constituted our order entry system for the next three years. I kept the cards in my desk drawer with a rubber band around them. When the stack grew, we kept them in a shoe box.

Our only typewriter was an ancient Royal we had inherited. Margaret's father had bought it used in the late twenties, when her older sisters were taking typing in high school.

The children worked right along with Margaret and me, and activity filled the dining room and living room. When enough packages were ready, we stacked them in the back of the old limousine and took them to the Wheaton post office. I waited with great anticipation for the stores to sell these books they had ordered at the convention and to reorder more.

I waited . . . and waited . . . and waited!

I had arranged for the manager of the Moody Bookstore to order five copies and place them on the counter by the cash register so customers couldn't miss seeing them. Every day I went downstairs from my seventh-floor office to the store to check on sales, and I was surprised and puzzled, day after day, to see all five copies still stacked on the counter. One day I found only four—but the lack of interest in the book was very discouraging.

When I got home each evening, I inquired eagerly whether any stores had reordered books, but the answer was always no. As a month went by, and then another, I concluded that all the publishers who had turned down the manuscript of *Living Letters* had shown good judgment and that the book was "dead in the water." It became clear that our new publishing house would not survive its infancy.

I wondered how to get rid of the rest of the books. Lithocolor Press was storing the second thousand, so that was not an immediate problem. I sent a copy to the American Bible Society and asked if they could give them away, but they declined on the basis that their bylaws required them to distribute only "standard" translations. I got the same response from the Gideons. Another possibility was to send the remaining copies to missionaries. I knew they would be helped by *Living Letters*, but I didn't have enough money for the postage.

Then one evening I came home from work and found a letter from a bookstore that had ordered five copies at the convention. I eagerly tore open the envelope. It was a reorder—for one copy! That was pretty faint encouragement, but during that same week Moody Bookstore sold the four copies that had been there so long. They reordered—as did four other stores. Gradually my spirits lifted.

I decided to send a sample copy to each store that had not attended the Christian Booksellers convention and to each store that attended but did not place an order. With the book I sent a letter of explanation, saying the store could have the copy free if they would send back the enclosed card ordering five copies. Or they could buy the single copy for a reduced price of two dollars. If they didn't want it at all, they could return it in the same mailing envelope; I enclosed a return address label and a stamp to cover the postage.

Of the several hundred stores that received that mailing, quite a few sent back the order card asking for five more copies. A fairly large number sent the two dollars, and some sent the book back. I received two or three letters of protest from stores who said they had not ordered the book and were not going to return it or pay for it! We received no answer at all from some stores, but almost ten years later one of them sent back the card with two dollars in payment!

During November, as the Christmas season approached—traditionally a heavy book-buying season—I began to think the two thousand copies would finally disappear. We now had to decide whether to be thankful that they might soon be gone, and consider the experiment concluded, or to gamble on another printing. We were receiving orders that totaled twenty-five or thirty copies a day, but would this continue after the Christmas rush or was it a temporary phenomenon? If we printed another two thousand copies, would we have them in our house forever?

I remember getting up early on Thanksgiving Day and spending a long time in prayer, trying to sort out the matter in my mind and asking for God's wisdom. I realize, in retrospect, that it was a very critical hour. If we had gone out of print, it would have been the end not only of *Living Letters* but of the entire Living Bible project.

I made the decision to go ahead with another printing . . .

but how many should we print? At twenty copies a day, we would sell five thousand copies during the next ten months, assuming that the pre-Christmas rate of sales continued. Then something happened that helped me make the decision. We received an order for fifty copies from the Berean Bookstore in Bakersfield, California. It was our largest single order from an individual store. I telephoned the manager and asked how he was selling so many. He told me that one customer in particular was buying most of them, but that he saw a growing interest among his other customers too.

That was what I needed to hear, so I called our friend the printer and in my new enthusiasm ordered five thousand copies. Within a few weeks I was glad I had done so, because the Bakersfield experience was duplicated in other parts of the country. Soon orders were coming in at the rate of a hundred copies a day, and that second printing began to melt away.

Our family's annual Christmas letter in 1962 contained this paragraph from Mark, age eleven.

> Daddy published his latest book this summer, *Living Letters*. The publishing house is called Tyndale House after one of the first translators of the Bible into English. *Living Letters* is a paraphrase of the New Testament Epistles. In a way it is sort of a family project. Becky and Martha helped type manuscript at various times. (It seems like Daddy has been working on this book for as long as I can remember.) Mother checked the proofs last spring when Daddy was in Africa, and now she helps him with the records. Cynthia and I help pack the books for mailing. Next week we will be busy because that's when the second edition will be ready and we have a stack of orders to fill.

We had started without any capital, and the growing business needed a line of credit. I visited a new bank in Wheaton that had just opened its doors. I hoped it was looking for customers to lend money to. I needed sixteen hundred dollars and wondered how many weeks would be required for the loan committee to decide. I filled out the loan application and gave it to the bank president, then asked hesitantly how long it would be before the loan committee would be meeting. He smiled and, to my amazement, wrote out a check for sixteen hundred dollars, handed it to me, and wished me good luck!

Chapter 23
Tyndale House Grows

INTEREST in *Living Letters* continued to pick up dramatically during the winter of 1962–63. The second printing of five thousand was gone in a few weeks, not in a year as I had calculated. I ordered another five thousand in February, and additional printings quickly followed in April and June.

One day that spring a representative from Billy Graham's headquarters came to my office at Moody with the incredibly exciting news that Billy Graham wanted to give a free copy of *Living Letters* to anyone in his television audience who asked for one. Would I be willing? Would I! Nothing could have pleased me more. The whole idea behind the long years of preparing the new translation was to reach out as widely as possible, and here was an obviously God-given opportunity. They estimated they would need fifty thousand copies!

There is an interesting story about God's guidance in connection with Billy Graham's decision to give away copies of *Living Letters*. About the time I started my first tentative efforts at paraphrasing, in the mid-1950s, I was returning from a Christian literature conference in Cuba. My seatmate was a businessman named Doug Judson. When I spoke to him about Christ, he showed me a tract someone had recently given him; he said it had helped him understand Christ's claim on his life. I think our conversation was helpful to him, and we continued to keep in touch after that trip.

When *Living Letters* was off the press, I sent Doug a copy, and he wrote to say he thought it was terrific. He had meanwhile become an assistant to the Billy Graham evangelistic team, helping wherever he could, so he frequently saw Dr. Graham. I also sent a copy to Billy Graham himself, and, in case not all his mail got through to him personally, I also sent a copy to Ruth Graham at their home.

Doug shared his enthusiasm for *Living Letters* with the Grahams and with anyone else who would listen. At about that time, Dr. Graham was hospitalized in Honolulu, and while he was recuperating, he read the book and was equally enthusiastic about it.

Dr. Graham's decision to use *Living Letters* as a TV giveaway was a bold step. He had never before given a book as a premium to viewers, so it must have been a step of faith for his organization to give away thousands of *Living Letters*.

They asked how much royalty I would require. The answer was easy: none! But Dr. Graham insisted that there be some royalty, so we agreed on five cents per copy.

The Billy Graham Evangelistic Association contracted with a large printing company in St. Paul to print the books. Bill Horton was the salesman handling the account, and we gained new friends in Bill and his wife, Doris.

The 1963 Christian Booksellers Association convention was in Washington, D.C., and again I rented half of a ten-foot booth. I hoped to get a lot of attention with a large poster hanging in the back of the booth.

25,000 COPIES IN PRINT
STOCK UP NOW
BILLY GRAHAM IS GOING TO GIVE
THIS BOOK AWAY ON HIS
TELECAST THIS FALL

The message backfired. The bookstore buyers placed routine orders, based simply on how many they had been selling in recent weeks. They did *not* stock up. They reasoned that if Billy Graham was going to give the book away, it was bound to cut into their market. They played it safe. But although sales were a bit disappointing, I was more than rewarded by the testimonials many store managers took time to share with me. Some confessed that previously they had not been able to get much out of reading Paul's letters, and now they were reading with understanding. And they passed on the testimonies of their customers who were coming back to buy more and more copies of *Living Letters* to give to family members and friends.

Margaret, Janet, and Mark went with me to the convention. (It was eight years since I had bribed Janet with a Baby Ruth candy bar to stay home when I took the four older children to D.C.!) We did a lot of sightseeing in the mornings, as the convention booths were open only in the afternoon. After the convention we drove to Fredericksburg, Virginia, to see our son Peter, sixteen, who was working on a restoration project run by Youth for Christ at the site of George Washington's boyhood home.

Bookstore representatives asked me at the convention whether I would be paraphrasing other parts of the Bible. I had, in fact, been using my commuting time on the train to begin paraphrasing the Minor Prophets. I felt they were often overlooked by Christians and little read, yet of great importance. But they seemed to me so dull in the King James Version. I tried to find ways to bring the text to life by expressing each thought in contemporary language.

Later that summer of 1963 we took the six younger children on a vacation trip to northern Saskatchewan, where our friends Bernie and Marge Palmer had begun a summer community on the shores of Dore Lake. Eighteen-year-old Martha stayed home and, with the help of a friend, managed Tyndale House, doing the invoicing and packing, and taking the books to the post office. Fishing for northern pike was excellent, and we kept Bernie busy as he helped us reel them in. It was a new experience for me as well as for the children. When we returned home, we brought a hamper full of frozen northern pike fillets.

On our way to Saskatchewan and again on our way home, we spent a night in Minneapolis with Doug and Virginia Muir, who had moved from the house next door to us four years before. We told them how our little company was flourishing and how we would soon be needing someone to help Margaret handle the orders. They told us they were moving back to Wheaton, and Virginia said she would be able to help Margaret part-time after they had moved and were settled.

That fall Billy Graham began his giveaway program. I remember one humorous sidelight. A few weeks after the 50,000 books were printed, I received a telephone call from George Wilson, business manager of the Billy Graham Evangelistic Association. He reminded me of my agreement that the Graham organization could print 50,000 copies. His call alarmed me for a moment; I wondered if they had overprinted and wanted to send some back. But the problem was just the opposite. They had reprinted the book several times, eventually reaching 600,000 copies and hadn't technically received permission for more than the first 50,000. So, could they have permission now? Naturally, I was delighted to give it!

What a wonderful experience it was for all of us to see how the response to Dr. Graham's offer literally sowed the nation with the paraphrased Epistles. But not to the saturation point. Readers who were being helped wanted more copies, or their friends who had not seen the telecast wanted copies. Christian bookstores were besieged. The hardcover copies they had in stock were soon sold out, but many people wanted a cheaper paperback edition. As a result Tyndale House began ordering paperback copies by the tens of thousands from the printer in St. Paul.

Only a few days after the Muirs moved back to Wheaton that fall, Virginia began working with Margaret. She worked flex time, before anyone had ever heard of that term. Our mail came midmorning. If there were enough orders, Margaret telephoned Virginia to come and help in the "office," which meant our dining room table! That is how Virginia Muir became the first employee of Tyndale House outside of our own family. Through the years she worked in many different capacities, typing, doing English styling on the various parts of *The Living Bible,* and, as the company grew, she was my secretary for three years. Later, when we branched out into the publishing of general Christian books, Virginia edited most of our manuscripts. She eventually became our first managing editor, then assistant editor-in-chief.

Margaret, with the aid of Virginia and the children, was doing a terrific job of keeping the little company running well, but I became more and more convinced that I ought to be spending more time doing further translation work.

I prayed for several weeks about this, filled with conflicting emotions and questions. Should I leave Moody Bible Institute? I loved the work; could I survive without its pleasant daily routine? Moody Literature Mission was going better than ever as my colleague Peter Gunther took more and more responsibility.

But without my salary from Moody Bible Institute, could I support my family? The answer was yes if I sold enough copies of *Living Letters.* Otherwise the answer was no. Would it be foolish to leave? What would happen to us if *Living Letters* died a sudden death?

So I continued to pray for guidance. During lunchtime I would climb up into one of the empty floors of the oldest building at Moody and there pace back and forth, praying aloud to God for wisdom.

At other times I would slip out of my office and down into the subbasement of the Moody Press warehouse. I would make my way carefully through the darkness to a window well that provided just a little bit of light as I prayed there alone. I didn't suppose that anyone else ever had occasion to go into that subbasement, so I was alarmed one morning as I heard voices. The door opened, and two men came in to check on something. I hid myself deeper in the shadows, hoping I would not be found there or have to step out to make myself known. I didn't want to startle them or have to explain to them that this was my "prayer closet"—a likely story! To my relief, they soon went away.

As the days went by and I continued to pray for God's help in deciding whether to leave Moody, I realized that I had already decided I should leave. I simply became aware that my heart was completely at peace; it was time to go.

I didn't find it easy to inform my boss, Bob Constable. We had been colleagues and friends for many years. He generously suggested, as an alternative, that I take two or three hours a day in the library for the translating, without reducing my salary. I tried this for a few days, but I became embarrassed and discouraged when one of my employees kept seeing me there. Perhaps I was overly sensitive, but I felt she was wondering why I was not upstairs at work in my office. I soon announced my date of departure, and we called it a two-year leave of absence.

The day I left, in October 1963, I had yet another reminder of my problem with decisive action, because I felt unsettled and unsure that I was doing the right thing. But a few days later I was near the Wheaton train station on an early morning errand. I stopped and watched the commuters as they piled aboard the train for the long trip to the city. I knew they would work hard all day, then make the tiring return trip, arriving home exhausted. And I was thankful—thankful for the job that had required sixteen years of commuting, but thankful that those years were now in the past.

Now my days were very different. I spent long hours shut away in my bedroom study, and the work was intense, hour after hour and day after day. But one becomes accustomed to new routines, and I don't remember ever coming to the end of a day with any dread of the next day's work before me. For the next several years I found the work a great challenge as I translated verse after verse, working my way through large sections of the Bible. Often I stopped to pray, asking the Lord for understanding in restating a verse. I constantly searched commentaries to find a meaning if it was unclear from the text.

It was a never-ending process of crossing out, rewriting, and rewriting yet again. I have included in the photo section of this book a sample of the thousands of sheets of manuscript paper used through those years of writing. It would be interesting to know how many times I wrote the entire Bible by hand, considering all the corrections and rewrites.

During those years of working in my upstairs room, I got into the habit of coming down to join Margaret and Virginia for a cup of coffee. I remember the afternoon our neighbor, Mrs. Black, ran over to tell us that President Kennedy had been assassinated. We stopped our work in the dining room/office and listened to the radio, along with most of the world, as the somber announcement of Mr. Kennedy's death was broadcast.

To keep up with the increasing flow of orders, I purchased an old garage for a hundred dollars from the defunct Chicago, Aurora, and Elgin Railroad and had it moved behind our house. We built a packing table in it, and the shipping operation moved from Mark's bedroom to the garage.

Now large trucks were coming down our quiet street with skids of books to be delivered. Invariably the truck stopped in the street and the driver came to the door to ask if this was the address of Tyndale House Publishers. He thought the address on the bill of lading must be wrong. Surely they weren't looking for thousands of books at that old farmhouse two hundred feet back from the street! But we were. We told the drivers to back the truck up the driveway and make a sharp turn around the corner of the house so the books could be unloaded. (On one memorable day, a truck driver miscalculated the turn and splintered a portion of the corner of the house!)

Of course we had no forklift to take the entire skid off the truck, so the cartons had to be unloaded one at a time. Unfortunately, union rules did not allow the drivers to unload the cartons from the back of the truck, so I did it. Several times when I was not at home, Margaret had to unload those thirty-pound cartons, carry them into the garage, and pile them up—as the driver sat by and waited.

At this point we published our second book—*La Cruz y al Puñel,* a Spanish translation of David Wilkerson's exciting book *The Cross and the Switchblade.* We printed 100,000 copies in 1965.

The orders from bookstores were getting larger and more frequent, and Mark, now in junior high school, was unable to keep up, even with help from other neighborhood boys he hired.

The solution was to get a full-time shipping clerk. We hired John Reeves as our first full-time "shipping room" employee. Hiring John was an act of faith for him and for me. Although there was too much work for Mark and his friends to do after school, I wasn't sure what we would do if *Living Letters* filled its market niche and sales dwindled away. John, who had a large family to support, would be out of a job. But he seemed willing to take the risk, and he was with Tyndale House as shipping manager for several years as the business grew and we moved on to larger warehouses and shipping rooms.

After many months of intense work on the Minor Prophets, the project was finally completed. I called the book, which included the New Testament book of Revelation, *Living Prophecies,* and it was published in the spring of 1965. Billy Graham said about the book, when offering free copies to TV viewers, "One of the needs of the church today is for the prophets to thunder forth, 'Thus saith the Lord.' In reading *Living Prophecies* my own soul has been stirred, my mind challenged, my conscience convicted, and I have rededicated my life to Jesus Christ. It is my prayer that this book will have the same effect on you." Within a year a million copies of *Living Prophecies* were in print.

In the spring of 1965 we moved the Tyndale House office to the basement of a building on Washington Street in Wheaton, next to the railroad tracks. Virginia Muir, Mark, and Margaret painted the rooms. The fresh paint smell helped to mask the chemical odors left over from the previous tenant, a photo lab.

The two years we were in that location were a period of rapid growth for Tyndale House. As the number of employees grew, we occupied more and more space until there was no more available. It was in our Washington Street offices that Bob Hawkins, Harold Shaw, Don Crawford, Donna Birkey, Donna McLean, Richard Wolff, Dwight Hooten, Odd Carlsen, Howard Smith, Harold Wonderling, Ted Miller, and others became a part of the Tyndale family. Margaret continued to do the accounting, banking, and payroll—all by hand. Eventually we splurged and bought a used, hand-cranked adding machine!

We now began to think about broadening our publishing efforts to include general Christian books. In 1966 Bob Hawkins, our sales manager, made arrangements for Tyndale House to publish *Spirit-Controlled Temperament,* by Dr. Tim LaHaye. This book shows how we can, with God's help, change the negative aspects of our temperament while enhancing and using our positive traits. In 1968 we published Dr. LaHaye's book *How to Be Happy Though Married.* For more than twenty years, both books have continued to be among our best-sellers.

Another early book (1966) was *Is God Dead?* by Richard Wolff, a fellow employee at Tyndale House and my chief advisor in business matters, which were going very smoothly at that time. He also wrote *Israel, Act III.* Richard is Jewish and naturally was fascinated, as we all were, by tiny Israel's six-day victory over vastly larger Arab forces in 1967. It seemed to be a clear act of God in helping his ancient race to whom the promise was given of repopulating the desert. With high interest by evangelicals in seeing prophecy being ful-filled right before their eyes, Tyndale House rushed Richard's book out a few weeks after the Six-Day War, and it had wide circulation.

I had not initially planned to paraphrase the Gospels because, despite the *thee*s and *thou*s used in the King James Version, the story of Jesus' life and death seemed fairly easy to understand. But something had happened at the 1964 Christian Booksellers convention that changed my mind. A young couple asked me when the paraphrased Gospels would be ready, and I re-sponded that I didn't plan to work on the Gospels, because they were reasonably understandable in the King James Version. They countered by quoting John 3:8: "The wind bloweth where it listeth, and thou hearest the sound thereof, but canst not tell whence it cometh, and whither it goeth: so is every one that is born of the Spirit." They asked, "Can't you say that more understandably?" I don't remember what I replied, but from that time on I began thinking of working on the Gospels and Acts, and eventually started the task.

When I was well along in the Gospels, George Wilson told me that Billy Graham would use *Living Gospels* as a TV giveaway if it could be ready in a few weeks. So I spent huge chunks of time finalizing it.

Living Gospels was published in 1966. Despite my original conclusion that it might not really be needed, the printing presses had to run overtime, and the book soon joined its companion volumes in the million-copy distribution league.

By now the decision seemed inevitable to proceed with paraphrasing the entire Bible. The decision to go ahead brought me both joy and fear—joy, because I felt as I labored day by day that this was indeed God's call to me, and that I had been chosen from among three hundred million English-speaking people for this task. But I feared the years of intense labor stretching on ahead, sitting hunched over a desk, pen in hand, prayerfully writing and rewriting. Then, after the scholars and stylists had finished their corrections and suggestions, the text would come back to me for final revisions. At the same time, I was spending half of each day at the office, managing our growing company.

One by one the new sections were published. *Living Psalms and Proverbs with the Major Prophets* appeared in the spring of 1967. These were the early days of the Jesus People movement and, concurrently, the modern charismatic movement. One leader of the charismatics gave me his opinion that *Living Psalms* was one of the chief sources of nurture within the movement. Certainly the charismatics' great emphasis on worship and praise has been a major contribution to the worldwide Church, and if *Living Psalms* has been helpful to this movement, I am very thankful to God.

Along with the books of Isaiah, Jeremiah, and Ezekiel, *Living Psalms and Proverbs* also included the book of Lamentations with its incredible pathos, as illustrated in these verses:

> Jerusalem's streets,
> Once thronged with people,
> Are silent now.
> Like a widow broken with grief,
> She sits alone in her mourning.
> She, once queen of nations, is now a slave.

She sobs through the night;
Tears run down her cheeks.
Among all her lovers,
There is none to help her.
All her friends are now her enemies.

Why is Judah led away, a slave?
Because of all the wrong she did to others,
Making them her slaves.
Now she sits in exile far away.
There is no rest,
For those she persecuted
Have turned and conquered her.

The roads to Zion mourn,
No longer filled with joyous throngs
Who come to celebrate the Temple feasts;
The city gates are silent, her priests groan,
Her virgins have been dragged away.
Bitterly she weeps.

Lamentations 1:1-4

Jeremiah, who wrote the book of Lamentations, should be given a posthumous Pulitzer Prize!

By 1967 we had again outgrown our office space and we had no warehouse or shipping area to call our own. In God's providence we were able to purchase a small office building at 336 Gundersen Drive in Carol Stream, just north of Wheaton. Over the next twenty-three years we were continually remodeling and expanding that building to make room for our rapidly increasing staff and our burgeoning product inventory.

Another important event in 1967 was the publication of *The Living New Testament,* in response to a great many requests to have the New Testament books in one volume, instead of spread among *Living Letters, Living Prophecies,* and *Living Gospels.* We were particularly amused by a letter from one reader who begged us to publish *The Living New Testament* so that she wouldn't have to carry the three little books to church. "The covers are slippery, and I keep dropping them on the floor during the service," she complained.

Next in the series came *Living Lessons of Life and Love* in 1968. This thin volume contained books of high drama and human interest—the stories of gentle Ruth and brave Esther, the tenderly romantic Song of Solomon, and the books of Job and Ecclesiastes.

Perhaps you can see now why fifteen years of hard labor translating the Bible could be so exciting—with something wonderful and fresh to feed on every day. I knew it was being used by the Spirit of God to make a positive change in millions of lives, and so it could change the life of the Church.

In the spring of 1968 Margaret and I learned that Ken and Jean Hansen were taking their whole family to England, Scotland, and several countries of Western Europe for a two-month vacation. It was something I would have liked to do with our five children who were still at home, but the logistics of transportation, what to see, and where to stay seemed beyond me. I had traveled in all those countries, but with the exception of one trip with Margaret in 1965, I had always been alone, so I doubted my ability as a tour guide for the family.

I must have expressed my feelings to Ken and Jean, because they impetuously responded, "Why don't you join us?" I was astounded. Were they serious? They were. So we decided to accept the invitation to travel with them.

They had mapped out their itinerary and Jean started to write to medium-priced hotels for reservations—for sixteen! For me, it was as simple as that. Both families have many happy memories of that summer.

In 1969 Wendell Hawley came to work with Bob Hawkins in the sales department. Wendell had been a pastor and, more recently, an Army chaplain. While he was serving in Vietnam, his life was miraculously spared during an enemy ambush that killed half of his contingent. He was of great help in developing the sales in our rapidly growing book division as well as in the Bible area. When Bob Hawkins left the company in 1973, Wendell became sales manager. In 1978 he moved into the editorial department and became vice-president and editor-in-chief. He is now senior vice-president. Through the years he faithfully kept up his Army Reserve commitment. He recently retired as a full colonel and received the Legion of Merit award, along with a commendation from President Bush.

As I worked on *Living Books of Moses,* which was published in 1969, the long sections describing the parts of the Tabernacle and their dimensions were a challenge, but somewhat boring. The priestly garments were interesting, but a mystery I left to pastors to apply today. I contented myself with making them as readable and accurate as possible.

A far greater problem to me personally came in writing *Living History of Israel,* the seventh and last of the separate volumes that later became *The Living Bible.* My problem can best be stated by the preface I wrote then and still feel deeply now:

> What then shall I say about the Scriptures in this volume, containing as they do so much of butchery of human life?
>
> If I state my personal reaction to these blood-filled books, will I harm the faith of others? Will I be unfaithful to my God? . . .
>
> [But] let me speak. I too am horrified at the God-ordained slaughter you will read about in the early pages of this book. As a pacifist, I am devastated that God is a God of war and judgment and vengeance. I wish He were only loving and kind—and how loving He always is to His people, and kind when they obey!

From reading these books I came very close, I fear, to a spiritual collapse, especially on one bright autumn afternoon that I shall never forget as I sat in the grandstand with my children at a high school football game and watched not the players but the doomed and happy people all around me. Why did God create mankind with godliness, only to destroy them again in hell? Why allow the Canaanites to be born at all, victims of sinful hearts that worshiped other gods, thus meriting slaughter upon slaughter, even of their little children and their cattle?

I regret that I have not yet found the answers to these questions. I only know I cannot live without God, and I worship Him alone, and I cannot testify enough of His personal kindness to me. I know that the world is sad and broken everywhere, and lonely, and I know that no one who comes to God is turned away. So I will spend my life helping them find the universal solution for all troubled hearts—the Lord Jesus Christ. And I shall weep for those who cannot find Him.

In 1970, the same year we published *Living History of Israel,* Bob Hawkins told me of a contact he had with Dr. James Kennedy of the Coral Ridge Presbyterian Church in Fort Lauderdale, Florida. Dr. Kennedy had developed an evangelism program for teams of his church members to use in visiting newcomers to the church and in door-to-door evangelism. The step-by-step presentation begins with two questions: "Have you come to a place in your spiritual life where you *know for certain* that if you were to die today, you would go to heaven?" Then, "Suppose that you were to die tonight and stand before God, and He were to say to you, 'Why should I let you into my heaven?' What would you say?"

A great many people have erroneous responses to those

questions. For instance, some say they have done enough good things to merit heaven—but the Bible says none of us is really good, and no one is good enough. Some simply have no answer or are so convinced of their unworthiness that they think they can never qualify. The Bible makes it clear that we can be saved only by our faith in Christ's sacrifice for our sins, and that salvation is available to all, regardless of what sins they have committed. Dr. Kennedy outlined this entire evangelism program in his book *Evangelism Explosion,* and Tyndale House became its publisher.

In that same year we published *Dare to Discipline,* the first of Dr. James Dobson's best-selling books, and it was soon followed by other books by Dr. Dobson, *What Wives Wish Their Husbands Knew about Women* and *The Strong-Willed Child.* We were really off and running, and Tyndale House soon became famous for having some of the industry's top sellers.

What Is in Your Bag?

"Yours is not my bag," he said,
And with a pleasant nod
Was off upon his lifelong way.

And what was in his bag?
I knew:
Uncertainties
Fears
And weakness
To fend against the monstrous
Years ahead.

And mine?
He could have had it
   for the asking:
Love
And peace
And Holy Spirit power.

K.N.T.

Chapter 24
The Living Bible

THE PREFACE to *Living History of Israel* was titled "At Last!" I went on to say, "This is the final volume in the Living series of paraphrased Scriptures, and I thank God for allowing me to finish the project."

The work of many years was finished, and the question in my mind was whether to publish the seven sections of the paraphrase in one volume, perhaps calling it *The Living Bible*. Looking back, that seems a strange question to have asked. But I wondered whether enough people would purchase a copy of the one-volume book when they already had a set of the individual books. However, pressure from my advisors to go ahead won out.

We scheduled the release of *The Living Bible* at the Christian Booksellers Association convention in July of 1971 and went into full swing to accomplish our goal. Our production manager, Edythe Draper, along with our sales manager, Bob Hawkins, and our finance vice-president, Harold Shaw, favored an initial printing of at least 100,000 copies. I was stunned, fearing that we would be left with thousands of unused copies and possibly unpaid bills. Edythe, meanwhile, began without my knowledge to negotiate with paper manufacturers and printers to be ready for reorders amounting to a million copies during the next six months! How thankful we soon were for her foresight! In the next few years we had increasing appreciation for Edythe's skill in dealing with our suppliers and in coping with the immense demand for copies of our Bibles.

In the editorial department, Virginia Muir made final editorial and stylistic changes and gathered a team of proofreaders. As the pace of the production schedule picked up and the convention drew ever closer, Virginia and Edythe had to make a June trip to Kingsport Press in Tennessee to finish proofreading the last several hundred pages—keeping just a jump ahead of the printers.

The sales department, meanwhile, was blanketing the country with advance promotion, for Bob Hawkins was sure *The Living Bible* would be a runaway best-seller. To my amazement, by June we had prepublication orders totaling more than 200,000 copies.

The first thousand copies from the first printing of *The Living Bible* were numbered and autographed. An especially gratifying promotional opportunity came in July when I gave Billy Graham copy number one of *The Living Bible* at his crusade in Oakland/Alameda County, California. It was awe-inspiring to sit on the platform and gaze out at the thousands and thousands who had come to hear Billy proclaim a simple message of God's grace, and to watch at the end of the service as streams of people flowed from their stadium seats to crowd deep around the platform. Hundreds made decisions for Christ that night, as in each of his crusades.

Copy number two went to Margaret (in a private ceremony!); numbers three through twelve went to our ten children. We also gave numbered and autographed copies to many friends and associates.

Billy Graham's public endorsement of *Living Letters,* and of *The Living Bible* when it was published as one volume, made an enormous contribution to the wide acceptance the books received in those early years. Obviously, I am very grateful that he saw their value so clearly, endorsed them so warmly, and distributed them so extensively.

I do not think it was just a coincidence that *Living Letters* was published during the time of Dr. Graham's great popularity and his use of television to reach millions of viewers worldwide. I think God personally and directly arranged this timing.

The Living Bible's timeliness upon the world scene is shown too by circumstances during the decades of the 1960s and 1970s. These years were marked by an explosion of youth unrest and rebellion throughout the United States. The Vietnam War and corruption at high levels of the government brought great disillusionment and cynicism to young people across the land. This youth rebellion took some destructive and damaging forms, but at the same time it produced a sort of counterrevolution called the Jesus People movement. Suddenly great numbers of young people in their late teens and twenties were turning to Christ for the answers they were so sincerely seeking. Many of them were alienated from traditional churches and were being won and discipled by a new and informal kind of evangelism, some of it with a strong emphasis on the charismatic gifts of the Holy Spirit.

The Jesus People were a receptive target audience for the fresh, up-to-date vocabulary and contemporary style of the Living version of the Bible. God was doing a new thing through the youth of America, and our new way of expressing God's Word was on hand at just the right time.

The same can be said of a wave of renewed vigor in some of the mainline denominations of Protestantism and in the Roman Catholic church. One of the most dramatic effects of Vatican II, a major contribution of Pope John XXIII, was a new emphasis upon the personal reading and study of the Bible by the laity. Because the time-honored Douay Version presented many of the same difficulties that the King James Version did, Catholics welcomed the Living translation.

Some have suggested that *The Living Bible* was a cause of the revival fires of those years. I do not think so. Rather, it was the oil from the Holy Spirit that helped make the fires burn brightly and brought millions to a fresh understanding of God and of His plan for their lives.

Gordon Mitchell, our distributor in Canada, has often reminded me of the story of Bob Hawkins's visit to him in Toronto just before the release of *The Living Bible*. Gordon wanted to order several hundred copies, but Bob declared that Gordon would sell ten thousand copies before Christmas, just six months away! Gordon was astounded. As the Canadian distributor for seven major United States publishers, he had never sold a tenth of the quantity Bob demanded that he order. But Gordon accepted the challenge.

Realizing that such a huge commitment required unusual effort, he personally visited all the major Christian bookstores in Canada, insisting that even the smallest take a hundred copies. By Christmas all were sold and Gordon was on the telephone to Bob, urgently requesting an additional supply.

Earle Fitz of Riverside Book and Bible Distributors in Iowa tells a similar story. He remembers when semitrailer trucks arriving at his warehouse were lined up, waiting to deliver Living Bibles, and still he did not have enough to supply the demand from across the nation.

Secular bookstores were also wildly enthusiastic about their sales, as was Doubleday, our copublisher, whose salesmen scoured the general bookstores for orders. The explosion in sales of *The Living Bible* was unprecedented in religious publishing and nearly so in secular publishing as well. In the well-known best-seller lists, such as *Publishers Weekly,* the *New York Times,* and the *Chicago Tribune,* a book can gain great status with the sale of a few hundred thousand copies. But *The Living Bible* zoomed quickly into millions of copies, capturing the attention and awe of the publishing and bookselling world. The result was that *Publishers Weekly* featured *The Living Bible* as the fastest-selling book in America during 1972 and 1973.

By the spring of 1972 *The Living Bible* had been on the best-seller list in Dallas/Ft. Worth for twenty-six weeks—number one for thirteen weeks and among the top three for thirteen. A survey indicated that 50 percent of the homes in Dallas owned Living Bibles.

How exciting and exhilarating it was to see millions of copies of God's Word rolling out of our distribution points. I could easily imagine the results of this new wave of Bible reading in the homes of America. Before long, many letters and telephone calls showed me that lives of readers were being dramatically changed to an extent that even my imagination had not pictured.

These large Bible sales, combined with the steady growth of our general book division, meant an increase in sales staff. In 1971 we had only five territorial salesmen, but over the next few years we added six more. They have been an enthusiastic and loyal group, some of them having been with our sales department now for more than fifteen years. In fact, this stability has been characteristic of our staff in general, for which I am extremely grateful.

With *The Living Bible* successfully launched, we soon became even more aware of the magnitude of the enterprise. In addition to the marketing efforts of our sales department, we needed help to deal with the great demand for publicity, both of *The Living Bible* and of me personally. Promoting myself certainly did not appeal to me, but all my advisors agreed that I must respond to the growing demand for personal appearances. So we saw it as a divine provision when Claude Cox and Ed Malone, from the Southern Baptist Radio and Television

Commission, offered to spearhead publicity. Claude and Ed were knowledgeable and experienced publicists. They felt called by God to help *The Living Bible* have the widest possible distribution, not only among Southern Baptists, but across the nation.

They proposed that they take me on a tour to visit religion editors of the nation's major newspapers and magazines and be interviewed by them. They arranged for radio and television interviews, too, and were successful in getting my picture and the story of *The Living Bible* on the front page of the *Wall Street Journal* and in the religion section of *Time, Newsweek,* and other widely circulated magazines. As a result, the entire English-speaking world became aware of this new version of the Bible and many were eager to see it. I will never forget the kindness and skill of Claude and Ed and their feeling (and mine) that God Himself had dedicated them to this particular task.

Another of their very successful ideas was to put 365 readings from *The Living Bible* on records to be aired daily over five hundred radio stations on free sustaining time. Each reading ended with a public endorsement by the huge Southern Baptist Convention.

Both Associated Press and United Press International carried the story of *The Living Bible.* Although dozens of newspaper articles and editorials appeared, referring to the great impact this new Bible version was making in the nation, I was particularly pleased with an outstanding article in the *New York Times,* written by the distinguished journalist McCandlish Phillips.

I had many interesting opportunities in connection with the promotion of *The Living Bible.* For instance, Astronaut James B. Irwin of the *Apollo 15* crew made arrangements for me to visit Cape Kennedy and meet more than forty of his fellow astronauts. They gave me their autographed photos and I gave each of them a copy of *The Living Bible.* I also wriggled into a space capsule, just to get the feel of it! Later Jim Irwin took leather-bound copies of *The Living Bible* to the heads of state of the USSR and other Communist countries.

I received an invitation to visit the cast of the musical *Godspell* while it was playing off-Broadway. They received me warmly and graciously accepted the copies of *The Living Bible* I offered them. Naturally, I hoped and prayed that the truth and significance of the "godspell" (an old-fashioned word for gospel) that they were portraying on stage would take root in each of their lives.

These were not the only people in show business to receive Bibles. In England the Salvation Army gave many copies of *The Living New Testament* to entertainers, a practice that had been started in the 1800s when William Booth and his staff gave Bibles as an evangelistic outreach to circus performers.

Ferdinand Marcos, then president of the Philippines, was given a first-edition copy of *The Living Bible* by the crew of the Operation Mobilization ship *Logos*. They also gave Marcos's young daughter a copy of *Taylor's Bible Story Book*.

Before long, we began to hear of interesting and unusual ways our readers were using the Living Bible text. One woman, teacher of a speed-reading course in the state of Washington, put verses on film strips for her students to use to test speed and comprehension. Later, after we began to market audiotapes containing the Bible text, a woman who had been plagued by obscene telephone calls kept her tape recorder by the phone and started the Living Bible tape running whenever she got such a call!

We were pleased when we got a request from the Hallmark Company to use Living Bible verses on some of their greeting cards. We also heard from a manufacturer who wanted permission to put Living Bible verses inside fortune cookies. And soon Living Bible verses began to appear in the lyrics of Christian songs. Perhaps the best known of these is Ralph

Carmichael's "The New 23rd," which is based on the text of Psalm 23. In 1973 Scott Foresman Publishing Company requested permission to use *The Living Bible* as the version to be studied in a new college text on the Bible as literature.

Television performer Art Linkletter agreed to be emcee in a videotape on which he interviewed famous Christians who especially enjoy using *The Living Bible*. This tape was used in bookstores with great effectiveness because Linkletter was widely admired as a personable and wholesome entertainer with strong Christian values.

Our office staff can tell many amusing anecdotes about those early years of distributing *The Living Bible*. One of our favorite letters came from a reader who said, "My puppy pulled my Living Bible off the table and chewed it while we were sleeping. Can you take the cover off, run it through the machine again, and put a new cover on it?" We sent a new Bible!

In the early 1970s we often received letters strangely addressed, and we felt gratified that Tyndale House was becoming well enough known that the post office could figure out where they belonged. "Miss Alice Tyndale," "Tyndale Noise Publishers," "Mrs. House P. Tyndale," and "Living Bible, Wheaton, Illinois" all found their way to the right address. We especially enjoyed the letters that began "Dear Mr. Tyndale: . . ."

Once at a literature conference at Wheaton College I met another man named Kenneth Taylor. But under his name on his name tag he had written, "Not THE Ken Taylor." He told me I was a constant problem to him. "Sometimes," he said, "when people ask me to autograph their Living Bibles, instead of going through the hassle of an explanation, I just sign them!"

The summer of 1974 brought a heavy advertising campaign, with television commercials aired on popular shows: the "Today" show, "Dinah's Place," "Hollywood Squares," and others. We also had full-page ads for *The Living Bible* in the June issues of *Good Housekeeping, Family Circle, Woman's*

Day, Parents, and *American Home*—with a combined circulation of more than 27 million and a total estimated readership of more than 60 million.

The World Home Bible League, under the direction of William Ackerman, embarked on a distribution of *The Living New Testament* to hotel rooms. Their copies had colorful covers to attract readers, and they used the startling approach of labeling the New Testaments, "Free! You may take this book with you when you leave the hotel. If you wish to do so, you may send us a dollar to help cover the cost." In 1974 alone, they distributed about 1.25 million copies in this way.

People often ask me if I had ever expected *Living Letters* and later the complete Living Bible to be so widely accepted. The answer is both yes and no. In an earlier chapter I told about my prayer on the Mount of Olives that my vision of distributing two million copies of *Living Letters* would become a fact. My faith was partial, yet God gave me the privilege of seeing this goal accomplished in answer to my prayer.

My hopes and fears are expressed in my diary of the months before that modest first printing of two thousand copies of *Living Letters.* I find entries such as these:

> *April 11, 1962 [three months before publication]:*
> It seems like people usually don't enjoy the Epistles much; they find them hard going—hard to understand without digging through the wording. I hope the paraphrase will help them, at least as an introduction to what the Apostles were saying. How lives would be radically changed if people could read the Epistles with ease and understanding! Well, I fear this "apologia" is useless. Some will praise the Lord for blessings received and some will think a paraphrase foolish, unnecessary, etc.
> Every author has great hopes for his book, and I am

the same. If it turns out to be a dud, I will know that here, as in other things, I sometimes react with a minority and that just because it has helped me, that doesn't mean others are helped. We shall soon see.

May 8, 1962 [my forty-fifth birthday, and two months before publication]:
I must add these thoughts of the future, as I have been reviewing them this morning.

1. That I must continue to grow in grace as husband and father.

2. That I must keep praying that *Living Letters* will help multitudes of people and that God will do a miracle of circulation for His own glory as His people understand what the Epistles are talking about, as I feel so many don't now. And that the unsaved will read Romans and Galatians as well as the Gospel of John. How clearly Paul brings out the way of salvation by faith, not works or law. Oh, that all people could read and freshly understand this, that they may sit down and read with understanding and great profit instead of fighting their way through the underbrush of verbiage. But it may be that I have not reached this goal, and God will gift others and qualify them better. Yet, even if this is but a link in the chain, it is worthwhile. . . .

3. If it has wide distribution, probably an effort should be made to set up a not-for-profit corporation to own it, using the profits to start a Christian digest magazine.

October 14, 1963 [after about seventy-five thousand copies were in print]:
Regarding Living Letters, I am praying for others to be roused up and gifted for paraphrasing of their own languages.

I am praying that as we enter this new era of tremendous sales (even millions) God will guide all the way and that we will be pliable and completely at His mercy all the way. And that we will know how to pray and praise as we should, with no limitation on what God is willing to do, by our own inadequate praying.

Chapter 25
Commendation
and Criticism

I SOON SAW that God was abundantly answering my prayer for large numbers of people to be helped in their reading and understanding of the Bible. Letters began to pour in from hundreds of readers of *The Living Bible,* saying that they, like me, had once found the Bible difficult to understand, but that now God was speaking clearly through their daily reading of His Word as expressed in the paraphrase. Many readers shared with me the fact that at last they were able to read the Bible with real interest. Testimonies about the impact of *The Living Bible* came from people of all ages, all levels of society, and all walks of life.

Hundreds of thousands of Scripture-starved men, women, and youth were finally reading a Bible they could understand. It was as though a great vacuum in their hearts suddenly sucked in the Word of God, and it filled and satisfied their lives.

A businessman wrote enthusiastically, "*The Living Bible* is the greatest invention since the wheel!"

A Bible study leader: "I cried when I realized I could finally understand the Bible."

A student at a Christian school told me, "We meet in our dorm lounge every night, fifty or sixty of us, and listen while we take turns reading aloud from the letters of Paul. I don't think any of us ever realized before what it was all about. Thank God for *The Living Bible.*"

One reader said, "Your Living Bible has become an intimate part of my life and is directly responsible for my spiritual growth over the past six years."

Another wrote, "Not long ago you made *The Living Bible* available through Campus Crusade for Christ for an extraordinarily low cost. The results at our church have been absolutely wonderful! The total impact has contributed as much as anything to the movement of evangelism and discipleship God has begun in our midst."

One of the testimonies that came surprised me. Dr. Jerry Falwell, chancellor of Liberty University and pastor of Thomas Road Baptist Church in Lynchburg, Virginia, told me that he never preaches from anything but the King James Version, so I had assumed he would not appreciate *The Living Bible.* But not so. He told me of the blessing it was in his home, where it was the preferred text for family devotions. "*The Living Bible* has ministered to me personally every morning for many years," he said. "There is no way I can measure the spiritual contribution *The Living Bible* has been to my ministry."

Dr. Bill Bright, founder and president of Campus Crusade for Christ, wrote to me to say, "*The Living Bible* has made the holy, inspired, inerrant Word of God understandable to the twentieth century. I believe it is one of God's greatest gifts to our generation. I read and study it daily with great personal benefit and blessing." On another occasion he wrote, "I want to express to you personally my deep and profound gratitude for the contribution you have made to the spiritual lives of multitudes of people around the world."

Charles Swindoll, beloved author of many life-changing books, and pastor of the large First Evangelical Free Church of Fullerton, California, says, "I like *The Living Bible* because it's like a stream of sparkling water wandering across life's arid landscape: intriguing, refreshing, nourishing, comforting. My thirsty soul is often satisfied by the invigorating wellspring."

A United Church of Christ pastor wrote me, "In the fullness of time, now, your paraphrase is the greatest Christian event since the Reformation."

A dedicated member of an interdenominational ministry said, "We no longer fight to stay awake while we read the Bible! Now we find we read more than we intended, and even then don't want to stop. . . . *The Living Bible* in our opinion should be ranked with electricity, radio, and TV as one of the *great* services for mankind in this modern age."

Another pastor wrote, "Before receiving my copy of *The Living Bible* I had never before read the entire Bible through (not at all to my credit!). At first I wasn't sure how I felt towards *The Living Bible* . . . but now I can say that of the translations I am familiar with, *The Living Bible* has done more for my attitude and interest in God's Word than all the others combined."

A brief sentence from a letter of another pastor says much: "*The Living Bible* is the simplest, most pleasant reading of the Bible in my experience, which goes back more than forty years." A similar statement from another pastor says, "I have read the Bible through every year for the last forty-five years, but this year, when I used *The Living Bible*, it is the first time I have read it with interest."

A Catholic homemaker wrote to me:

Dear Mr. Kenneth Taylor,

I've been wanting to write you a thank-you note ever since I realized how much of a treasure God's Word is in your Living Bible. Since I was saved thirteen years ago I've worn out several copies of *The Living Bible,* dragging them to church, to the cellar when I do my washing, soaking in the tub, camping, in bed, or wherever. My first Bible given to me was a King James. I loved to memorize verses or to use it with my concordance or sing songs to Jesus from it—Oh! but *The Living Bible*—THAT'S SOMETHING ELSE—I can just drink it all in with ease and apply it to my life—weep with it, and laugh, be convicted with, grow with, fall deeper in love with my Savior.

I make sure all my new spiritual babies get copies of *The Living Bible,* and have been discovering formulas within its endless Treasure Chest for happiness, marriage, kids, and you name it—and that it's not difficult but thrilling to read.

Another note addressed to Tyndale House says:

Dear Friends,

Would you see to it that Dr. Taylor reads this note? About ten years ago I left my wife (she was pregnant) and plunged deeply into a life of drugs in San Francisco. I used them copiously myself and sold large quantities to others.

In 1970, while hitchhiking, a young fellow gave me a copy of the *Reach Out* edition of *The Living New Testament.* Jesus became real to me through that book. I accepted Christ five years ago and am now enjoying life with my wife and nine-year-old son and a new baby girl.

I thank you for your devotion to Jesus, but He gets all the credit for accomplishing the change in my life.

My prayers are with all of you in your work.

And here is another:

TO WHOM IT MAY CONCERN:

My name is ———; you do not know me. Please make sure this letter is read by someone with authority. I began reading your book *The Living Bible* paraphrased. I've never been able to understand the King James Version of the Bible, so after thirty-six years of not knowing what the Bible was about, I finally was able to *fully* understand through your writings what the Bible and the world is all about. (I'm now thirty-six years old.)

Your book, *The Living Bible,* is a fantastic way to bring the truth to people like me. If I sound excited, I am! I've been reading your book day and night. Also, I've gotten many friends and relatives to read your book. It has changed my life from a Jewish religion I knew nothing about, to the glory and beautiful life that goes with the believers of Jesus Christ.

This one is from a third-grade public school teacher:

Although I have read hundreds of Christian books, dozens and dozens of which I own, I had never been able to sustain enough interest to force myself through the Old Testament. In August I began rising at 6:00 A.M. and having a forty-five-minute Bible reading, meditation, and prayer time, using *The Living Bible.* I'll have you know I'm now in Jeremiah and I haven't missed a single morning! I can't tell you what a delightful experience it is to read the Bible and feel you are understanding much of what you are reading, and eagerly looking forward to the next reading.

Although I have thirty-three third graders in my class every day, I find I am less tired this year in spite of my hour less sleep!

The Living Bible was warmly received in many Roman Catholic circles. We heard this from a nun: "I know it was the Holy Spirit's inspiration for you to translate the Bible, because He speaks to me all the time through *The Living Bible.* I am a Catholic sister, but I never understood the traditional translations. But, oh, *The Living Bible* makes my heart break out in praise and thanksgiving."

While many Catholics welcomed *The Living Bible,* others held back, fearing the disapproval of their church. The solution was to find a Catholic bishop authorized to give the official imprimatur and *nihil obstat* (a Latin phrase that means, in essence, "nothing here is damaging to faith or morals"). This we did, and later on we added the Apocrypha, paraphrased to my satisfaction by a Catholic priest. No changes were made in the text of *The Living Bible* itself.

Publication of the Apocrypha brought some protests from the evangelical community, but I felt it was good to add this material if it would help Catholics accept *The Living Bible.* I wanted them to have an alternative to reading (or not reading) from their old and difficult Catholic translation. The result of this decision was that we were thrilled to see wide acceptance of *The Catholic Living Bible* by many in the priesthood and in parochial education, as well as by Catholic laity.

The deputy head of Catholic publications in Dublin requested copies to be considered for use in catechetical programs. He wrote, "I cannot stop reading *The Living Bible,* and I hope our six catechists will use this instead of other versions."

A Canadian friend told us about his efforts to encourage his son to make a daily habit of Bible reading:

> While he always did well in school, he was not
> interested in reading more than he had to; and while
> he tried to do as I asked about Bible reading, it was
> obvious he wasn't getting very far. He told me he just

couldn't read the King James Version because of the language—but if I bought a Living Bible for him, he would read this.

I've come to love the language of the KJV—other versions don't seem to command my respect as much—so I was a little disappointed; nevertheless, I bought him a Living Bible for Christmas. My son kept his promise and read this Bible daily and made up his mind to read it through during the next year.

The youth group at our church had practically disappeared, but our son began to be burdened for some of his friends. Three or four kids began meeting at school. One of the boys accepted the Lord. This was like a breath of fresh air to all of us, but especially to the young people. They began to pray and witness to their friends, and we don't really know how many have accepted the Lord. There are now over a hundred names on our young people's roster and more than sixty usually attend the services. Most of these kids are using *The Living Bible* in their daily reading and in their Bible studies, and we are praising the Lord for the moving of his Spirit. I'm especially grateful for the way He has used *The Living Bible*.

Imagine how this letter thrilled me:

Doctor Taylor:

I have never ever in my life wanted to write to another human as much as I wanted to write to you. I knew of your work and often wanted to thank the man who opened the Word of God to me. I finally had a prayer answered. Tonight I was watching the "Good News" telecast and for the first time, I have been able to find a way to say thank you—after seven and a half years of waiting.

Bear with me because I'm not a highly educated woman. But in my own modest way I must tell you the feelings in my heart. How do you thank a man who was instrumental in removing darkness out of a blind soul? How do you thank a man who made it possible for a husband and wife to do Bible study together? My husband never has read through a book of any kind for the five years that we have been married. Now he spends hours every day studying the Word.

I love you, Mr. Taylor. I'll never get an opportunity to thank you in person in this world. God has used you to reach so many sinners. So many people hunger for the love of Jesus Christ. Through your work we begin to see the truth. Through your work many of us have seen love (for those of us who never felt love). You have made it possible for the hopeless to learn hope when before there has been no hope.

The uneducated finally have a way to understand what was closed off to them before.

You made it possible for me to give a priceless gift to my father. My father is much like you. He is a good humble man. He was in the hospital awaiting results of extensive heart tests. I was able to scrape up enough money to purchase him *The Living Bible.* His gratitude shone in his eyes because he never was able to understand the Bible before. I thank you for my father also. The Word was opened up to him at a time he needed reassurance of God's love.

I cannot really express my feelings in the way that I wish I could. But you'll be in my prayers. May God bless you for making it possible for Him to bless us.

Since *Living Letters* had initially been written for my own children, I enjoyed letters like this one:

Dear Sir:
I just wanted you to know that *The Living Bible* is
easy for a girl my age to understand. I am ten years old.

This letter was sent to a church that had participated with
World Home Bible League in placing Living New Testaments
in motels:

To my brothers and sisters in Christ:
Greetings in the name of our Lord. Some ten months
ago as I travelled en route to Toronto I stayed
overnight in a small motel in your city. When I found
your Living New Testament in my room I was curious
enough to want to explore it. That was the beginning of
a new awakening within me. I want you to know that
since then I gave my life to the Lord. Also my
brother-in-law and his wife and three kids are saved,
my wife gave her life to the Lord, and my two kids are
getting there fast (ages five and nine). My sister
(twenty-nine) gave her life to the Lord last month and
her husband appears to be on his way. Her children
will also respond soon I'm sure.
As a result of the changes in my life I am now
looking into outreach ministry within our church. With
God's help many more will be saved.
Grace and joy be with you all.

But along with these letters of thanks and appreciation of
The Living Bible, we received at first an occasional letter of
protest, and later quite a steady stream from some who objected to the idea of translating thoughts rather than the exact
Greek and Hebrew words. But the reason for a thought-for-
thought translation, or paraphrase, is to make the Scriptures
more understandable. All modern translations do this, some

more than others, and *The Living Bible* most of all. That is why it is the easiest of all to read and understand.

For instance, in 2 Corinthians 6:11, the Greek words literally say,

"The mouth of us has opened to you, Corinthians, the heart of us has been enlarged."

The Living Bible says,

"O, my dear Corinthian friends! I have told you all my feelings; I love you with all my heart."

The thought is exactly the same as a literal translation of the Greek words, but the readability and understanding are vastly increased.

One of the dangers of a thought-for-thought translation, however, is that the translators may not understand the thought correctly or completely. This gives the option of leaving the translation unclear, or else using the context to see whether the probable meaning can be determined. This probable meaning is then clearly translated.

I received many letters that questioned certain verses or phrases. These were carefully answered, and in some cases where I agreed that changes should be made, the next printing of *The Living Bible* contained the correction.

One pastor wrote a careful study of *The Living New Testament,* showing for three hundred pages how it differed from the King James Version, which he declared to be the only inspired translation. He titled his book *The Paraphrased Perversion.*

Another pastor with considerable influence in fundamentalist circles announced, "I believe Taylor to be a Christian, but so was King David when he committed adultery with Bathsheba." I felt that was an unkind remark!

Another man was very shrill in his monthly publication. Issue after issue was filled with invective against *The Living Bible*. This man had come to me soon after *Living Letters* was published to ask if I would let him take over the publishing and distribution, but I declined. After that, he obviously changed his mind as to its value.

I wrote to two of these three men and asked them to desist. I was bold enough to suggest that those attacking the Bible, even if the translation was imperfect as they felt it to be, might fall under God's discipline for discouraging people from reading the Word of God. Soon afterwards two of them died and the other went into bankruptcy. I do not know whether or not my suspicion was true that the Lord needed to remove these attacks. I simply state the facts.

I have had some interesting experiences with scholars who thoughtlessly condemned *The Living Bible* without ever reading it. I guess peer pressure is great, even in seminaries!

I had been told that one of these men, the president of a fine evangelical seminary, was very much opposed to *The Living Bible*. When I had occasion to meet him, however, I found he was not unfavorable. In fact, he was enthusiastic about *The Living Bible*. I told him I had heard about his previous attitude, and he said he had been negative but had changed his mind. Then he told me this interesting story. His teenage son had not been particularly interested or able to get much out of the Bible. One evening he didn't come down to dinner and his dad went up to his room to investigate. He found his son deeply absorbed in reading *The Living Bible!* His dad told me that this experience alerted him to the fact that he ought not to condemn it without reading it, so he began to read it himself and found that it was substantially accurate and very interesting.

The scholars are, in fact, divided over the issue of the accuracy of *The Living Bible,* although there is general agreement that it is without a peer for private devotional and family reading. And that was, after all, my primary purpose. Many professors who criticize its syntax have told me of the help it has been to them in their own personal lives.

An Old Testament scholar and member of the translation committee for Today's English Version noted in his review of *The Living Bible* that "examination of *The Living Bible* indicates that it was based on an informed and scholarly evaluation of textual problems, and is much more than a paraphrase of an earlier English edition. This is welcome news to the translator who may be consulting his work."

Another scholar declared, "A paraphrase is capable of far greater (not less) accuracy than a translation forced to be literal."

One scholar wrote, "There is no denying the fact that *The Living New Testament* is a faithful, clear, idiomatic, and expressive representation of the meaning of the original. But in many places it is so dominated by fixed theological presuppositions that it should not serve as a model for translators. . . ."

Meanwhile, as a friendly reviewer said, "No doubt the scholars may curl their lips and say the translators took too many liberties, but no doubt the common people will read it gladly." This proved true on both counts.

The negative comments about *The Living Bible* clearly reflected the strong, almost fanatical loyalty some Christians (usually older ones) have to the King James Version of the Bible. We learned that a large number of Bible readers (or, at least, Bible owners) thought that the King James Version was "the original" Word of God and that anything else was an untrustworthy counterfeit. Some pastors really believe that only the King James Version is the inspired Word of God. A pastor from Texas, however, was a bit extreme when he declared that since the King James Version was good enough for Abraham and Noah, it was certainly good enough for him.

Many, many times in my travels I meet men, women, even

teenagers, who come up—sometimes a bit shyly—to tell, with variations, what has become a wonderfully familiar story: "I can trace my conversion . . . my personal surrender to Christ . . . my love for God's Word . . . my call to Christian service . . . the mending of my broken home . . . better relationship with my children or parents . . . to understanding the Bible for the first time through reading *The Living Bible*."

When I receive that kind of confirmation of my early hopes and dreams, I thank God for His faithful blessing on the work He assigned me back in the 1950s.

I have been asked many times how the high degree of interest in *The Living Bible* by millions of people affected my outlook on life. Did it cause pride? My answer, as far as I can honestly tell, is that this did not happen. From the beginning I was clearly aware that God had chosen me from several billion people to do this work for Him, and day by day and sentence by sentence, the power came from above. I had very little to do with it except to sit there and write in the most understandable way I could, using the ability He had given me. I am very grateful that I completely understand and fully feel this, for if there is one thing God hates it is pride. God gives to some people the gift of preaching; to some, hospitality; to some, the ability to do quality work at a factory bench; and to me, the ability to paraphrase. We are each at the same level—His servants worthy of praise or blame depending on whether we properly use the abilities He gives us.

With the passage of time, and as *The Living Bible* took its place in the 1970s as the leading translation next to the King James Version, the letters of protest diminished and almost stopped. Nevertheless, I was concerned by the fact that some of those letters made valid points. I wanted *The Living Bible* to be completely accurate. I began the slow and laborious task of working it over. In some ways it was as difficult and as challenging as the original paraphrasing. Month after month, in all spare moments, weekends, and vacations, I labored to improve it.

I was working at this time only on the New Testament letters. But when the revision was completed, it still needed more work on it, and when that revision was completed, further work was required. Over a period of nine years, several revisions were completed, and at last the final product went to a group of Greek specialists who diligently compared it with the original Living Bible text. When they completed their work, I had before me many further changes they were suggesting. In many instances they thought the original Living Bible was more accurate than my revision! And so I realized that my many years of labor on the revision had been wasted.

In the final chapter of this book I tell what God did to solve this problem in a fantastic way. Why didn't God tell me about it nine years earlier when I began my revisions? Isn't my life, after all, a guided tour? There are still some mysteries!

Street Scene in Iran

They stood along the road—
A motley workman crew
With picks and shovels in their hands—
Illiterate and underpaid.

Across the road, a young, attractive peasant woman
Edged her way
Beside the open sewer to
Join the older women with the weathered hands.

Among that workman crew
Stood one I did not know.
He had a brain like mine,
And great ability—
Enough to be an emperor
Or keen-edged businessman,
A doctor, lawyer, or to work for IBM.

But such was not his lot.
His father's home was poor,
And he was not the one (as here and there one does)
To force his way
Against the odds
Of fate.

And so the youthful dreams
And fires
Burned out.
And he was left, a brawny carcass
Of a former man,
With pick and shovel in his hand

To beat against the brainless clods.

And she across the road,
Who could have graced the finest table in the land,
Moved on beside the gutter—
In passing phase
Between her childhood peace
And anguish of the coming days
Of drudgery to man and beast alike.

K.N.T.
Teheran, Feb. 15, 1976

Chapter 26
Tyndale House Foundation

BACK IN 1963, when Billy Graham decided to give away copies of *Living Letters* to his television audience—free to as many as might write in to request a copy—he thought there might be fifty thousand people who would respond. I was overwhelmed with joy that such a huge number of people would be reading God's Word in this easy-to-read form, and I knew they would probably grow in the Lord as a result.

That joy was all the payment I needed or expected, but the Graham organization felt that a royalty should be paid, and five cents a copy was the amount agreed upon. The fifty thousand copies at five cents a copy would come to a royalty of twenty-five hundred dollars! This was an amazing amount to me at that time when I had more children than salary!

Nevertheless, I had a strong conviction that the ability to write *Living Letters* was a special gift from God, and, because it was His word, He should get all the royalties. So we called on our attorney friend Paul Leetz to set up a foundation with a board of directors who would be responsible to give the money away to properly qualified charitable causes. We called the new organization Tyndale House Foundation. When the

Graham Association used 600,000 copies instead of the expected 50,000, the Foundation suddenly found itself with thirty thousand dollars, a vast sum at that time almost thirty years ago, when the purchasing power of a dollar was several times its present value.

In addition, Tyndale House Publishers paid the Foundation a royalty of seventy cents for every copy of *Living Letters* sold to stores. Two million copies were distributed in this way, with an amazing total of royalties. The same system of paying royalties to God (i.e., using the money for missionary projects and other Christian work) was used for all the books in the Living series, and for the 37 million copies of the complete Living Bible that are now in print. These royalties are paid to the Tyndale House Foundation, and from there they go to hundreds of Christian organizations all over the world.

Interestingly, even before *Living Letters* was published, I had asked a lawyer friend how to set up a foundation to receive its royalties—just in case it sold well. I felt foolish in even raising the question, since there was no way of knowing whether even those first two thousand copies would sell or ever be reprinted. I made my inquiry by writing a memo to one of the men in the legal department of the Moody Bible Institute. I hesitantly explained that I was in the process of writing *Living Letters* and wanted the royalties to go to a foundation—and how does one set up a foundation? My embarrassed question never received a reply, and I realized afresh how foolish my question seemed to him. We were friends, but I never asked him about it again.

But when the Billy Graham royalties were actually ready to be paid, the logic of my decision to set up a foundation to receive them was revived, and this was done.

Following the publication of the complete Living Bible in one volume in 1971, the royalties were huge—several million dollars each year. Selecting which worthy projects to give money to was an immense task. All of the letters of request from hundreds of organizations came across my desk. I was in a dilemma. How could I give them careful attention while being president of a fast-growing publishing company, deciding which books we would publish, and making long trips overseas to supervise the translation of Bibles in several dozen languages? I needed help! If I could turn over to someone else the responsibility for the Foundation, it would lighten my load considerably. I could think of no one more qualified than my son Mark. He had grown up with the company and had seen it in action from the beginning. He was now a senior at Duke University and demonstrated a good mind. During his campus days he had organized and led a Christian singing group and had shown spiritual maturity and administrative ability.

Mark was fully sympathetic to my goals for the Foundation. He had shown his concern for missions by spending a college summer vacation helping to build a hospital in Jordan. Well respected by his peers and adult associates alike, he remained respectful to his parents in the late 1960s and early 1970s, when this was difficult for many young men and women his age.

As Mark approached graduation in 1973, I asked him for his help. It was not an easy decision for him. He wanted to "make it" on his own and not be accused of taking an easy path that might be considered nepotism. But he finally agreed and became executive director of Tyndale House Foundation following his graduation. He and Carol Rogers were married that May and spent the summer in Africa, investigating the worthiness and appropriateness of various mission projects that had applied to Tyndale House Foundation for funding.

Years later, when interviewed by a business magazine, Mark described his initial reluctance to accept the position. He was frustrated, he said, by not having my creative abilities (though I seriously question this assessment of himself).

"But now," he said, "I recognize that I have different

strengths from my father's. I know I can complement his skills. I finally recognized that he didn't need creativity from me. He needed someone to help him sort the good ideas from the bad ones. That was liberating, knowing I had a unique contribution to make. It allowed me to make peace with myself" (Ellen Wojahn, "Fathers and Sons," *Inc.,* April 1990, 81).

After four years as executive director of Tyndale House Foundation, Mark acceded to my request that he become part of the management team of Tyndale House Publishers, and Mary Kleine Yehling, his assistant, stepped into his shoes as executive director of the Foundation.

More than $30 million has now been paid to the Foundation and distributed by the board of directors. Not all of these grants were specifically for evangelism. Many of them were to assist in book publishing around the world, and some were for social service work of various kinds, such as famine relief. In one case we donated $100,000 for the purchase of an airplane to transport food from a port city in Africa to famine-stricken regions that could not be reached by overland transit.

I enjoy looking back through the files of the hundreds of grants that have been made. Here are some, chosen at random to give an idea of the variety:

$30,000 to a training program for secondary school teachers in southern Sudan

$5,000 for the publishing program of Africa Christian Press

$9,000 for two literature distribution vans in the Philippines

$1,000 for a food program in schools in East Africa

$4,000 for equipment for a missionary printing plant in East Africa

$750 for air fare for a man going as a technical specialist to assist missionaries in a building program

$35,000 to help build a dormitory for Daystar Communications, a research and training center in Nairobi, Kenya

$1,000 for a children's service mission in Alaska

$5,000 for a literacy program in the U.S.

$500 to the American Cancer Society

$11,000 for the purchase of a Land Rover for use by a leprosy mission in Nepal

$10,000 to the American Scientific Affiliation for developing a program regarding science and Christian faith

$250,000 to the Billy Graham Evangelistic Association

$500 to help renovate an overseas office of a mission society

$35,000 to cover the first year's cost of putting Dr. James Dobson's radio program, "Focus on the Family," on the air (What a giant tree sometimes grows from a small acorn when it is nourished by God and his gifted people!)

$2,500 for Spanish evangelism in the Chicago area

$5,000 for a gospel mission in Chicago

$19,000 for child evangelism work

$100 for library books for a seminary

A friend in another literature ministry wrote to me after a worldwide trip: "After visiting literature leaders in several countries, I felt duty bound to write you and commend you and your Foundation on its work, which is a great blessing on so many fields. What a thrill to see the Word of Life Bookstore in Seoul, Korea, well located downtown and full of customers. [The Foundation had helped in the purchase of this store.] Then in Indonesia, Bud Rudes told me of his association with you in that great land. And people in other places as well mentioned your significant help in their literature programs."

God used a 1973 gift from the Foundation in a remarkable way. Chaplain (Col.) Jim Ammerman, with the U. S. Army V Corps, had been buying Living Bibles, but he and his fellow chaplains needed many more than they had funds to pay for. Loren Cunningham of Youth With A Mission contacted me. Could Tyndale House Foundation help? The need was for 100,000 copies, and we had 100,000 copies of *The Way,* an illustrated youth edition of *The Living Bible,* which we were able to send.

When the chaplains distributed these copies among the 500,000 U. S. military personnel in Europe, the Holy Spirit stirred hearts. Even men and women with no previous religious interest began openly reading the Bible. The changed lives became too numerous to count. The chaplain in charge described it as the greatest, farthest-reaching revival he had ever seen. Even some chaplains found the Lord. Much of the drug abuse came under control, and racial tension among the military virtually stopped. The chaplain in charge reported years later that he was still meeting people who came to know the Lord through that mass distribution of *The Living Bible.*

When Tyndale House Foundation was incorporated, one of the first questions to be decided was whether the royalty income should be invested, and only the interest given away, or whether the capital should be used as it came in. The latter course of action was decided on. As a result, the Foundation has distributed all of the millions of dollars it has received through the years, setting the money to work. It keeps no money in the bank except a small reserve.

I have jokingly said that if I had known at the time the Foundation began that it would receive more than $25 million instead of the original $2,500 from the Billy Graham Association, perhaps I would not have been so ready to give it away! However, I hope that is not true. In fact, I'm sure it isn't!

I receive a good salary for my work at Tyndale House Publishers (but no salary from the Foundation). So the Lord has cared for us well through the years.

Moving the Hands of God

Doors of motel rooms
Swing outward.
Perhaps it is a symbol of their rejecting nature.
They welcome me a night or two,
And then—
The checkout counter.

Yet always,
When I turn the key for that last time
And leave and fly away,
There is a sense
Of vague distress—
Like leaving an old friend!

Perhaps this shows a fear
Of less familiar doors ahead.
But I would like to think
It's something much more positive
Than that.

For here within my room in this motel,
Some great events occurred—
I moved the hands of God through prayer,
To change the world.

No wonder
That I leave this place
Of victory
With lingering
Regrets!

K.N.T.

Chapter 27
Magazines, Racks of Books, and Church Bulletins

NOT LONG AFTER the publication of *Living Letters* in 1962, Margaret and I were having a picnic with our children at Northside Park in Wheaton. At a table near us we saw our friends Ted and Jeanne Miller and their young sons. Ted was an editor at Scripture Press, publishers of Sunday school curriculum, and we naturally got to talking about our mutual involvement in publishing. To our surprise, we discovered that each of us had been dreaming the same dream about a Christian digest magazine.

For many years I had wanted to publish a Christian magazine that would be similar to *Reader's Digest* except that its content would be digests of articles from a wide range of Christian magazines.

I told Ted that if I ever had enough money to finance getting a magazine started, we should get together. He would be the editor.

The following spring as we published successive printings of *Living Letters,* there was more and more profit left over, and I informed Ted that we could proceed. He could continue to work at Scripture Press and do the editorial work for our new magazine in the evenings and weekends. I had decided to call it *The Christian Reader.*

We would publish the magazine bimonthly and sell it through Christian bookstores. The stores could put our special display near the cash register, where customers would see the magazine and pick up a copy to add to their other purchases.

Fortunately we still had time to rent a small booth (separate from our tiny Tyndale House half-booth) at the 1963 CBA convention in Washington, D.C., where we proudly displayed the first issue. It was dated October–November 1963, and it contained sixteen brief articles, each one a digest of a longer article that had appeared in a major Christian periodical. We wanted the magazine to appeal to a variety of readers, so we chose articles for that first issue from periodicals as widely diverse as *Christianity Today, Decision, Eternity, Alliance Witness, Sunday School Times,* and *Bibliotheca Sacra.*

Now we needed more help at our home/office for record keeping, typing labels, and helping with mailing *The Christian Reader.* Cynthia Rodgers, daughter of our friends Bill and Emily Rodgers, was a high-school senior. She was available to come after school every day.

How shall I ever forget the last afternoon Cynthia and I were working together, packing magazines into cartons to mail to bookstores? For at two o'clock the next morning—a bitterly cold January predawn—the phone rang. It was Emily Rodgers to tell us that their house was in flames and they couldn't find Cynthia or her ten-year-old brother, Bobby. Later we learned from the fire inspectors that Cynthia had stayed in the house to try to rescue one of her brothers. Neither she nor Bobby made it through the smoke.

As *The Christian Reader* grew, other friends came to help us, and soon our dining room/office was crowded with wonderful people—Grace Braker, Fran Kawano, Jeanne Burton, and others who worked with us from time to time.

At first we sold our new magazine only to Christian book-

stores, but we gradually developed a list of individual subscribers, soon reaching a circulation of twenty thousand copies per issue. Ted and I were excited to think of that many
copies going out regularly into homes, with surveys indicating that each copy was read by more than one person.

We had expected that the circulation would continue to
grow steadily, so it was discouraging when we found we had
hit a plateau. New subscribers just about balanced those who
dropped out. I longed for the magazine to bring spiritual
growth and encouragement to many, many more readers and
their families and friends. One cold Sunday afternoon in January 1965 I felt so deeply troubled and burdened about this
that I put on a heavy coat and went out to the garage/shipping
room where I could be alone to pray and even talk aloud to
God about it. I lit the heater and spent an hour with God,
telling Him in detail all the reasons why I thought He should
give us 100,000 subscribers within one year. As usual, I was
not conscious of any direct reply, but I returned to the house,
hopeful that He had been listening sympathetically. Remembering the many miracles He had done in behalf of *Living
Letters,* I was encouraged to expect the same for *The Christian
Reader.*

An hour later the phone rang. The caller was Bob Hawkins,
who was then a bookstore owner in Portland, Oregon. I had
met him at the Christian Booksellers convention the previous
summer. I recalled that he had expressed interest in *The
Christian Reader* and had ordered a few copies for his store.

"How's it going, Bob?" I asked. I expected some general
shop talk, but he had a specific reason for calling and got right
to the point.

"You know that little digest magazine you publish?" he
started enthusiastically. "Well, it's terrific, and it ought to have
twice the circulation—and I know how to do it! Send me a
thousand extra copies!"

I was amazed but gladly sent him the copies. Two weeks later he called again, asking for another thousand.

"Bob!" I exclaimed, "whatever are you doing with them?"

"I'll tell you later," he replied. "Let me test my idea a little more, and then I'll call you again."

In due time he called me with his report. He had given sample copies to local pastors; he urged them to take a regular supply of the magazines and to encourage their congregations to pick up copies in the foyer after the service. The price at that time was thirty-five cents a copy. The church would pay the store, which would then pay us.

I said, "Bob, I think it's time for you to come to Wheaton and tell me just how you are doing this. Can it be done elsewhere than in Portland? Can it be done across the nation?"

He came, and we spent a lot of time together working out a plan to implement his idea in many more churches. One of the most successful methods was pastors' breakfasts. We would set up a breakfast meeting for all the pastors in a community, give them copies of the magazine, and sign up as many as possible to institute this distribution in their churches. Of course these church copies led in many cases to individual subscriptions as well. Within a year the circulation had climbed rapidly from our 20,000 plateau to 100,000 copies each issue—the very number for which I had prayed on that cold Sunday afternoon.

I invited Bob Hawkins to join me at Tyndale House as sales manager, and he accepted, bringing his wife, Shirley, and their three children from the beautiful Pacific Northwest. He was with us for eight years, leading Tyndale House to very high sales records in Bibles and magazine distribution. He also started us on publishing books, something I had not originally planned for Tyndale House to do. Bob brought us some outstanding authors whose books are still top sellers after many years. Eventually Bob left us to begin his own company, Harvest House, where he is just as successful as he was in steering Tyndale House to major publishing status.

But not all of my projects were successful. We were selling huge numbers of *Living Letters, Living Prophecies,* and *Living Gospels,* with more money flowing in than we needed to pay salaries and bills. We had a healthy balance in the bank, and I felt it should not stay there, but be put to work. With some of that money we launched a new periodical in 1967 entitled *Christian Times.* It was a weekly newspaper for adult Sunday school classes. It reported on Christian events and movements around the world—and I thought it was one of the most terrific ideas I had ever had!

A weekly Christian newspaper seemed to me a good way to make Christians more aware of the Lord's work all over the world. I supposed this would make them more prayerful and would increase their giving. Whether or not those results could be confirmed by research, I don't know. I didn't even think of research or of analyzing the costs of editing, printing, promoting, and circulating. We had enough money to support it until it got going, and we had skillful staff available in the form of editor Don Crawford and his assistants, Donna Birkey and Donna McLean.

Unfortunately, budgets and cash flow projections were not attempted. Sometimes that casual approach may work, but in this case it didn't. Two and a half years later, having lost $250,000 on *Christian Times,* I surrendered to reality, and that excellent weekly sent out its final issue.

The story doesn't end there, however, because God did not let my dream come to an end. A year later, in 1970, while I was still nursing my personal pain and the financial disaster caused by the failure of the weekly news publication, God gave us a new and practical way to achieve the original goal. We prepared a monthly news sheet called *The Church Around the World,* designed to fit into church bulletins. We sent sample copies with order cards to many thousands of pastors, who responded warmly. The monthly circulation grew, and by Christmas of 1976 we were mailing out more than a million copies of the little news sheet each month, and this circulation has continued ever since.

So out of disaster came great usefulness. Why did the disaster have to come first? I think it was to destroy any pride and teach me valuable lessons in business. I had begun to think of myself as a successful businessman, something I had always wanted to be, but I needed to discover the truth about my shortcomings in that area. I had been impetuous about starting my pet project, assuming that anything I perceived as a need was obviously God's plan as well. Nor had I counted the cost, as the New Testament counsels us to do—and as a truly successful businessman would have remembered!

In 1968, while *Christian Times* was still being published, another project began. It was a monthly tract called *Have a Good Day.* It is not an ordinary gospel tract, for the first three of its four pages are filled with items of human interest, heroism, inspiration, and trivia, plus humorous cartoons. The back page has an interesting, solid presentation of the good news of Christ. We think of it as a "nontract tract"—a tract in its purpose and result, but not in its format. As a result even timid Christians can give it away. No one is offended by being handed an attractive pamphlet called *Have a Good Day.* It is used not only by individuals and churches, but by businesses owned by Christians who send it out with their invoices and statements.

The idea was mine, but the genius who chose the material and designed the leaflet is Leslie Tarr, a Christian journalist in Toronto, Ontario. For twenty-three years, until his recent retirement, Les edited *Have a Good Day* from his wheelchair. Les is a paraplegic, living with pain but trusting in God. Surely much credit for *Have a Good Day* must also go to his wife,

Catherine, and I pay tribute to her faithful support of Les through all these years.

The other major genius behind *Have a Good Day* is Dwight Hooten. Shortly after *The Christian Reader* began its rapid circulation growth, I had a visit from Dwight, an advertising executive and personnel director of a national advertising agency in Chicago. He and his wife, Jean, had a God-given desire to be involved in a direct, full-time Christian enterprise. This was not the first contact I had had with Dwight. Several years earlier he had visited me at Moody Press with the same interest in joining a Christian organization, but there had been no openings at Moody. Now the way was open for him to join Tyndale House.

Dwight took quite a cut in salary to make this change, but he was extremely happy in his new work as business and circulation manager of *The Christian Reader* and *Have a Good Day*. Later, as we added other periodicals to our list, he became director of the periodicals division of the company, a position from which he has only recently retired.

Have a Good Day has reached a circulation of close to a million copies a month, sending the Word of God out to both nonbelievers and believers all across America.

One Saturday morning in 1971, I was alone in my office at Tyndale House, busily engaged in all the paperwork that didn't get done during the week. At first I did not notice a tall young man standing hesitantly in the doorway. When I greeted him, he introduced himself as Ed Elliott, and I invited him to sit down. He seemed reluctant to take my time but had two messages to deliver. One was his deep appreciation for *The Living Bible* and what it had meant to him and his family. The other was to tell me about a friend of his who was between jobs and who he thought would fit into Tyndale House in our sales department.

I was not able to find a place in the company for Ed's friend, but within a few weeks we asked Ed to join the Tyndale House sales department, with the special assignment of developing the distribution of *The Living Bible* into drugstores, grocery stores, and all manner of outlets other than Christian bookstores.

One of my highest goals has always been to distribute Bibles and Christian books to the 80 percent or more of church families who never go into a Christian bookstore. This means our books must be sold in general bookstores such as Waldenbooks and B. Dalton, and also in grocery stores, drugstores, and the many other stores where people shop.

It was an amazing situation that confronted us in 1971 and 1972—hundreds of secular stores clamoring for *The Living Bible* because of its immense popularity. A great many stores were happy to display and sell it along with their other merchandise. When in all publishing history has there been such an opportunity for Bible distribution?

So Ed stepped into a huge network of unforeseen distribution opportunities. One day he came in to tell me that he had just been talking with the manager of a J. C. Penney store in a small midwest city, who was selling many Living Bibles but wondered how he could get a rack full of other Christian best-sellers such as *The Late Great Planet Earth* by Hal Lindsey, *Dare to Discipline* by Dr. James Dobson, and others. Since the books he mentioned were published by numerous companies, the manager did not have time to try to contact them all, and his orders for a few copies would not merit the discount he would need.

Ed neatly solved the problem by buying the books from our local retail store, half a dozen copies of each, and shipping them to the J. C. Penney manager, who displayed them on the racks in his store. A week or two later Ed came into my office with the encouraging report that the store was selling fifty Christian books a week. So Ed went to New York to see the book buyer for the J. C. Penney chain, who was already buying *The Living Bible.* Ed came away with an order to supply twenty-six of the major Penney stores across the nation with racks of Christian books! All Ed needed to do now was sell the idea to the twenty Christian publishers whose books were involved. They were as eager as we were to get their books into secular outlets. Thus Unirack was born, a name meaning that one rack contained books from many publishers. Eventually our racks were in five hundred Penney stores. Then three hundred K mart stores joined the program, along with Gibson's, Montgomery Ward, and several other major chains.

In 1975, when Ed Elliott was given new responsibilities, Jim Lofton, and later Paul Mouw, provided Unirack with excellent leadership and developed the program even further. For many years I have had the joy of seeing my dream in action, of reaching beyond the Christian bookstores. It was a wonderful experience, and very much an answer to earnest prayer. It was also the result of hard work and expert selling of the program to chain-store headquarters.

I have never calculated the totals, but hundreds of thousands, if not millions, of books went out across America in this unique way and found their way into many, many homes and lives. Meanwhile, other Christian "rackers," such as Successful Living, were doing the same kind of good distribution, and we eventually merged this part of our work into theirs.

In 1977 we added another new magazine to our periodicals division, but it proved to be a disappointment. We called it *Bookshorts.* It was similar to *The Christian Reader* in format, and it contained condensations of several new Christian books in each issue. It was, naturally, of interest to book readers and was an excellent platform from which to promote wider reading of worthwhile books. We issued it to churches every other month, alternating with the bimonthly copies of

The Christian Reader. We developed an excellent staff and began to publish (again with no research, since its potential success seemed so obvious).

We notified the churches that subscribed to *The Christian Reader* about this new product, and several thousand churches sent in orders. Unfortunately, they discovered that their people divided their interest and purchases, some continuing to choose *The Christian Reader* and some switching their allegiance to *Bookshorts*. Few chose to buy both magazines. The result was that while the new magazine quickly climbed to a circulation of 100,000 copies, *The Christian Reader* plummeted to 200,000 copies from its previous peak of more than 300,000. We were selling the same total number of magazines, but we had the much higher costs of publishing two magazines instead of one—more editors, double art costs, double promotion costs, and so on.

After three years we tried to solve this problem by discontinuing *Bookshorts,* so that those 100,000 customers would come back to *The Christian Reader.* We even added a couple of book condensations to each issue of *The Christian Reader* to keep everyone happy. But for some reason the *Bookshorts* subscribers never came back in great numbers. Thus another of my "brilliant" ideas bit the dust! Meanwhile, *The Christian Reader* continues to maintain its high quality and has one of the highest circulations among Christian magazines today. It frequently wins awards for journalistic and artistic excellence.

In 1988 we launched our next periodical. And it was a big one! Called *Dr. James Dobson's Focus on the Family Bulletin,* it is a church bulletin insert edited by Dr. Dobson's staff at Focus on the Family. I wasn't enthusiastic at first about the idea (which came from Bob Screen and from my son Mark), because I was afraid it would cut into the circulation of *The Church Around the World.* I was remembering how *Bookshorts* hurt the distribution of *The Christian Reader.* But when Mark persisted with the idea of the new periodical, I jumped on board and pasted together a sample issue. I was challenged by what I read and felt sure that many parents would be helped by reading it. It quickly became our periodical with the largest circulation, 3 million copies a month, without substantially reducing the circulation of the other periodicals.

And now, as I write, we are beginning to publish a similar monthly bulletin insert edited by Charles Colson, founder of Prison Fellowship. We feel there is room for all of these, for our combined circulation is reaching only a quarter of the 150,000 churches in America. We still have a long way to go.

Chapter 28
Financial Crises

WHEN *LIVING LETTERS* first became so popular all across America, I wondered if people in the United Kingdom could have a similar interest in it.

I arranged with an evangelical publisher there to take one hundred copies on consignment. A year later most of them were still unsold. But this was not God's final plan. The books needed to be publicized and promoted. God sent just the right person at the right time. His name was Jack Hywel-Davies, a Welshman with many contacts and a deep interest in the paraphrase because of his years of service as national youth director for his denomination. He knew from experience how few young people were reading the King James Version.

My associate Richard Wolff had met Jack during a visit to England in 1967. Jack developed a British branch of Tyndale House under the name of Coverdale House Publishers. Miles Coverdale was an Englishman who, a few years after William Tyndale was burned at the stake, was allowed and even encouraged by King Henry VIII to revise Tyndale's New Testament translation and complete the Old Testament.

Jack contacted Edward England, at that time the religion editor of Hodder and Stoughton, one of the major British publishers, who agreed to copublish *The Living New Testament* with Coverdale House. Edward is a splendid Christian brother and one of England's finest editors. In this way *The Living New Testament* was given exposure to the general bookstores throughout the British Isles, including the extensive W. H. Smith book chain. When *The Living New Testament* was first introduced, I had the pleasure of being in London and listening as it was read on one of the British Broadcasting Corporation programs.

Later, when the entire Living Bible was ready, it too was copublished by Coverdale House and Hodder and Stoughton. First, however, we had to Anglicize the text. Not only does the American edition use American spellings and punctuation, but it is colloquial and idiomatic, as is fitting for its style. Jack Hywel-Davies did most of the adaptation, with help from a Coverdale editor. Jack told me that one of the changes they had to make was to remove a great many exclamation points, which my own personal style and American informality had allowed, but which seemed inappropriate to the more reserved British reader. The British edition was released in the spring of 1974, with an initial printing of 200,000 copies—all presold—followed immediately by reprints.

Eventually, Coverdale House Publishers merged with Victory Press, whose managing director was Hugh Fuller, a man of great business acumen. He became managing director of the combined operation, while Jack Hywel-Davies served as chairman of the board and headed up the editorial operations. They were a marvelous team and the company grew rapidly, eventually changing its name to Kingsway Publications, Ltd.

Another major project at Tyndale House was in 1972— opening a Christian bookstore in a small shopping mall near our office building. This idea originated with Bob Hawkins, who had owned and managed such a store in Portland before joining me at Tyndale House. Under his skilled direction the lease was arranged and the stock and fixtures purchased. The store was an immediate success.

I had been concerned at first because Scripture Press had a Christian bookstore a couple of miles away, although it had been my experience and observation, having been responsible for four stores at the Moody Bible Institute, that new stores draw new customers rather than taking away from other stores. This is a mystery to me and seems to indicate that there is a latent population of potential book buyers who won't go out of their way to purchase books, but if the store is conveniently near, they will come in and become regular book buyers. In this situation I was reassured when I asked the president of Scripture Press, after our first year of operation, what our business had done to theirs. He replied that their store had never had a better year!

Buoyed by this success, I immediately began plans to open a chain of Christian bookstores in the Chicago suburbs, feeling that we should go where the people are—in the major regional shopping malls.

I soon realized that putting bookstores in major shopping malls with their incredibly high rents was beyond my expertise in being profitable, but it was too late, and I had signed leases in two other malls. Fortunately, by paying a stiff penalty, we were able to cancel the contract on one of them, but we opened the other store. These stores were a heavy drain on us financially, but I comforted myself with the realization that thousands of lives were helped by the books and Bibles we distributed through them.

My hat is off to Bill Zondervan, who started the Zondervan Family Bookstore chain, opening seventy-five or eighty of them, all in major shopping malls and almost all of them very successful.

Another costly and almost fatal event occurred in 1972, when an opportunity came to buy a Christian book distribution company owned by Multnomah School of the Bible in Portland. The business had been initiated and was being managed very successfully by Gordon Mohr. Since cash was readily available in those days—*The Living Bible* was selling at the rate of about 10,000 copies every day—I was able to buy the operation by paying Multnomah a generous price that allowed them to build a gymnasium. So I became the proud owner of West Coast Distributors.

We changed the name to Unilit, meaning "united literature," for our function was to buy books in carton lots from a hundred or more publishers, store them in our Portland warehouse, and ship them to stores that ordered one or two or a dozen copies of any of the thousands of titles we carried. We shipped immediately, so stores could have their orders within two or three days from one source, instead of having to write a hundred purchase orders, mail them to a hundred publishers, and have the books trickle in over the next several weeks or months. So it was a wonderful service to the stores.

I said that "I became the proud owner" of this business, and in all honesty I need to emphasize this point. As in all my activities and decisions, I prayed, but in this case I look back with shame to realize that I was asking the Lord to approve my decision rather than asking Him for His decision. For some reason this aspect of the publishing business was extremely tantalizing to me, and I knew this desire was influencing my decision. To use a football term, flags were down all over the field, but I went ahead anyway.

Within a few months of purchasing the business, I opened another Unilit warehouse in southern California, then in Ohio, Georgia, and Texas, with huge duplicate costs in inventory, warehouse space, and overhead. As a result, the profitable operation I bought soon became a millstone around my neck and around the neck of Tyndale House.

Next Tyndale House was offered a small publishing house

in Sweden that needed fresh capital for growth. Sweden, like England, is a nation essentially without God, with only about 4 percent of the population attending church. The only time most people attend is to be baptized, married, or buried. InterSkrift—that was the name of our company in Sweden— prospered but was always in need of additional capital for expansion.

Meanwhile, we decided to discontinue our inexpensive semiautomated invoicing system at Tyndale House. We transferred our order processing and invoicing to the computer of a service bureau operated by a neighboring Christian organization. But their charges proved to be far more than we (or anyone else) could afford, and financial clouds began forming over Tyndale House.

We decided to bring our computer work in-house, so we purchased (on credit) a huge computer for $500,000—but no software with it! So additional hundreds of thousands of dollars went to software experts who first had to learn the publishing business in order to know what we needed the computer to do. We also bought a huge computer for Unilit and made the same mistake there. Furthermore, the computer, when it was finally programmed, was so slow that bookstores who wanted to order twenty items would sometimes be asked to wait a minute or more on the phone between items, which of course they wouldn't do. The software vendor had guaranteed a two-second maximum wait, but there was no way to enforce the guarantee.

I well remember the day when a new consultant came in and suggested that we send back Tyndale House's $500,000 computer, paying whatever penalty we must, and abandon all the hundreds of thousands of dollars that had gone into the programming. He recommended that we bring in a minicomputer along with software that had been specifically designed for publishers. Never in my business experience have we had such a huge write-off with such wonderful success! The annual computer expense of hundreds of thousands of dollars dropped 80 percent at Tyndale House, though we were still trying to get Unilit's computer to work.

A final blow to Unilit occurred when we extended unlimited credit to a friend who had developed a business of selling books in churches. The experiment didn't work, and before we knew it, we were owed several hundred thousand dollars that could never be repaid.

All through this period, *The Living Bible* was selling at a tremendous rate, and Tyndale House was paying huge royalties into Tyndale House Foundation. In my zeal to get money into the Foundation, however, I had written a royalty contract that was not economically feasible—and that could not be altered for ten years. I remember that Harold Shaw, our vice-president and business manager, who had watched over the growth of Tyndale House through the years, had pleaded with me to reduce the royalty rates before signing the royalty agreement and assigning it to the Foundation. Harold was a dear friend, a wise counselor, and a spiritual giant. He saw more clearly than I did that the royalties were unrealistic. So Tyndale House could not keep up with its royalty obligations to the Foundation. At one point the publishing company owed the Foundation $6 million in Bible royalties.

Not surprisingly, the consortium of banks who had loaned us $2.8 million became concerned and demanded repayment. I remember so vividly the day their vice-presidents and loan officers gathered at Tyndale House to tell me of their decision to call in our loan. I still hadn't realized the seriousness of our plight until that morning. Now it was plain and stark. I told them we had no way to meet the demand, and we would be forced to declare bankruptcy. They said they knew that but felt it was the safest course for them to go.

But God and Gary-Wheaton Bank intervened. Its president,

Jerry Bradshaw, convinced the other banks in the consortium that, given time, we could repay them. To monitor our progress they set up an account for us that they would control. All of our cash receipts went daily to that account, and we began slowly to repay the consortium. Part of this daily income, after the payment to the banks, was returned to Tyndale House to pay our salaries, our printers, and all of our other costs of doing business.

It took eighteen months to complete the payments to the banks. But by the time the bank claims had finally been met, I had led us into more trouble. I had opened two more bookstores in expensive shopping malls, purchased the publishing house in Sweden with its need for expansion capital, and opened a warehouse in Miami to export books to Latin America. This operation, called Spanish House, was under the excellent direction of David Ecklebarger. We invested hundreds of thousands of dollars—money we didn't really have—to buy the Spanish language books to put in the warehouse.

To complicate our financial matters further, I had been in Norway two or three years before and had discovered a multi-volume Christian encyclopedia that captured my interest because of its huge sales success in Norway and Sweden. Looking back, I think dollar signs were dancing in my eyes, and worst of all in my heart, where the love of money takes root and brings forth all manner of evil. So I greedily bought the U. S. publication rights. Upon closer scrutiny we found the Norwegian material to be unsatisfactory, so we started over. We assembled a highly qualified group of scholars to contribute articles to an entirely new encyclopedia. The project was costing twenty thousand dollars per month—a quarter of a million dollars a year!

I remember so well a conversation with Dr. Victor Oliver, who had become Tyndale House's first editor-in-chief in June 1973. When I began our encyclopedia project, he asked me a simple question, "Do we have the million dollars or more that this will cost?"

With all confidence I told him, "Yes, we do." How right he was to ask, and how wrong I was in my answer! Vic's business judgment was excellent, but I thought of him only as our editor and, unfortunately, failed to accept his business counsel.

So the money flowed out into my many projects, never to return. Nevertheless, I came to the end of our 1977 fiscal year hoping that in spite of it all, we would at least break even. But then the roof caved in. When we counted the books in the warehouses and calculated their value, they were worth one million dollars less than we had earlier estimated. The manufacturing costs had not been entered into the computer correctly, and the financial reports and projections generated each month were all wrong. We were in great trouble.

I realized that I needed a board of directors to advise me and help direct the work. I turned to my friend Ken Hansen, who had built ServiceMaster into a large and very successful company. He was unable to serve on our new board, but he recommended several other people who could advise us. So our Tyndale House board of directors was established, with seven "outsiders" serving along with Margaret, Mark, and me. The board members were fully aware that they were in a potentially awkward position. They were elected by the shareholders (Margaret and me) to oversee the affairs of the company. As Paul Leetz, one of the directors, put it, a board's job is to hire and fire the president. But I was the president—so if they tried to fire me, I could fire them! But I assured them that in my role as president of the company, I would abide by their policy decisions.

Several months after Vic Oliver left in 1977, Wendell Hawley moved from his position in sales and marketing to the role of editor-in-chief. This left a big gap in the sales department, and we were pleased when Bob Bolinder agreed to join us as vice-president for sales and marketing. His experience and counsel helped us navigate the difficult waters ahead.

By paying close attention to overhead expenses and by raising prices of our Bibles and books, we were able to achieve a small profit in our publishing operation in 1978, but Unilit and the encyclopedia project continued to drain the company. Our financial problems were far from over. In fact, they were rapidly getting worse.

I recall the evening in the spring of 1979 when Margaret gave up. She was in charge of paying the bills at Tyndale House and knew how deep our trouble was as she handled the calls from vendors who were demanding payments. She is by nature an optimist, but now the approaching collapse of Tyndale House became deadly clear. She pointed out to me that no one was facing the facts—especially me—and that the company officers were obviously confused, helpless, or careless.

That night as the financial darkness deepened and I saw the bitter end in sight, I went over to the Tyndale House offices and poured out my heart to the living God, who alone could bring life from death if it were His good plan and purpose. I tried my best to be open to the possibility that God was willing for Tyndale House to end in failure. This was doubly hard because of my awareness that we would not be facing this darkness if God had given the privilege to others wiser and more capable than I.

Led, I believe, by God, I stood in the middle of my office and prayed God's blessing on every part of it. Then I went through the empty building from office to office, praying specifically for God's blessing upon that particular office or work area. I walked around each one, claiming it as Joshua did as he went around the walls of Jericho. I claimed God's power against Satan, the Destroyer, and asked God's blessing upon the inhabitants of Tyndale House. I spoke to the Lord about each person by name, and about his or her respective duties.

Slowly I made my way through the order entry department, the sales department, periodicals, editorial, customer service, the credit department, the computer department, the production department, and on and on. Then I went to our warehouse and put my head down on a carton of books and cried bitter tears. I suppose it was thirty minutes later that I had completed my tour, spiritually exhausted, hoping against hope, grasping for faith to move mountains, and feeling that there was nothing more I could do.

One evening soon after this, Margaret went over to Mark's house to tell him just how serious she felt the situation was. He was a vice-president of the company at that time and also helped us with various aspects of our personal financial plans. Margaret told Mark he had to take some drastic steps if the company were to be saved. I was glad for her to do this, and her analysis of the company's problems was reinforced a few days later when Ken Hansen, with whom I had been sharing our monthly financial statements, called Mark to give him the name of a bankruptcy lawyer.

At this point Mark, in effect, took charge. Soon afterwards, while I was in Europe on business, Mark made a decision I hadn't been able to bring myself to make. He shut down the encyclopedia project with its quarter-of-a-million-dollar annual expense, even though the project was more than half completed.

Then came the sale of our profitable, well-managed company in England. In a way it was good for it to be on its own instead of under the control of Americans. With a British board of directors, Kingsway was able to develop in its own British way without American ideas, which were sometimes less than acceptable but forced upon our British management.

But it was a sore blow to me to give up involvement with a nation of 55 million people, largely unchurched. The dream was always there of helping to see England, Scotland, Wales, and Ireland conformed to the image of Christ, just as in the days of John Wesley.

One of Mark's next actions was to promote Paul Mathews into a vacancy as controller and head of the finance department. Paul was certainly God's man, and he and Mark, under God's guidance, have helped the company to right itself and become strong and stable. Mark and Paul began with the financial disaster facing us. They spent time with our bankers and set up rigid budgets. (One department alone had overrun its budget by $200,000 the previous year, but I hadn't complained, feeling that the money was well spent!)

Mark's perspective—entirely logical, too—was that if we didn't have the money, we shouldn't spend it, no matter how worthwhile the purpose. Long discussions with our major bank gave us an extension of time and a payment schedule that the new austerity budget indicated we could meet.

Next we gave away InterSkrift, our subsidiary in Sweden. The Swedish company required capital to grow—capital we didn't have and couldn't provide. We gave InterSkrift to a Christian organization in Sweden who operated it successfully for seven years before it was merged with another Christian publisher to continue its good work.

Next went the stores, which had been a severe cash drain on the company. We sold them to the Zondervan Corporation.

Four of the Unilit warehouses had been closed in 1975, leaving only the one in Portland. Finally Unilit itself, my pride and joy, was sold in 1982 to Spring Arbor Distribution Company.

And so within a few years the growing cash-hungry divisions and the unprofitable divisions were gone from Tyndale House into stronger hands. The only remaining loss operation was Spanish House, our Spanish-language wholesaling division in Miami. This too was later sold.

Despite the successful efforts to save Tyndale House, we

went through another financial crisis in 1982 when a different bank with whom we had a million-dollar line of credit suddenly canceled it, with sixty days' notice. Once again we were in trouble.

During this time Wendell Hawley and I were traveling together on a business trip. That afternoon we had been discussing Tyndale's imminent financial danger and had prayed for God's intervention in finding another bank to replace the canceled loan. We turned on the television in our hotel room and found ourselves watching Pat Robertson hosting "The 700 Club." As we watched and listened, Pat was praying for various people with problems or diseases, declaring they had been touched by God and would recover. Suddenly we were all attention as he stated, "A businessman is watching who needs a loan of one million dollars from a bank, and he will get it!" We didn't know what to make of it, but we hoped Pat was talking about Tyndale House. Sure enough, a few days later we were able to negotiate a one-million-dollar loan from another lending institution!

I think I have felt a kinship with Job, the Bible character who lost everything he owned. But afterwards, because Job was righteous and had pure motives, God doubly blessed him, giving him more than he had lost. I cannot say that my motives have always been pure, but God knows I long to honor Him, and so He did not let Tyndale House collapse in disgrace. How grateful I am for His help and care.

Hymn of Going Home

Glory to God!
The work is done,
And I am going home.
Farewell to Afric's sunny climes
And Greenland's icy shores.

This time it's not to Beulah Land,
Where aged Paul resides.
For me not yet the Golden Shores,
But Illinois instead.

The world will little notice
Nor remember very long
What these six weeks accomplished,
But my God has said, "Well done."
He gave a task too heavy,
And now the task is done.

Homeward bound I joyous go
To loved ones far away—
A foretaste of my Heavenly Home
Where I'll forever stay.

Why then this icy feeling that clutches at my chest?
What fears are these I'm feeling that catch away my breath?
The fears are simply these, my friend,
And fully merit fright—
A hundred ogre problems
Await the touchdown of my flight.

Then comes this glorious knowledge
That sweeps away the gloom:
My God is there awaiting me
To slay the Dragon's brood.

As He has blest in every port—
Solved all Satanic plots—
He'll do the same with equal ease
When I get back.

        K.N.T.
        Accra, Ghana
        Feb. 27, 1976

Chapter 29
Living Bibles
around the World

ONE DAY in the mid-1960s, a missionary from Bolivia said to me almost wistfully, "I wish we had *Living Letters* in the Spanish language. My whole life has been changed since I began reading it in English. I struggled with my Bible reading for many years until someone gave me a copy of *Living Letters.* Suddenly the words from God became clear and plain to me. Scripture passages I had never understood came to life. How wonderful it would be if my people in Latin America could have the same experience."

I thought and prayed about this. *Living Letters* was changing lives all across America, but what about the billions of people in the world who cannot read English?

Something very unexpected happened one morning soon after I began thinking these thoughts. The strange event made me believe God was going to use *Living Letters* in a special way in other languages. God gave me a vision—a real vision such as he gave to Isaiah and Ezekiel in Old Testament times.

This was a great surprise, for I was brought up in a Presbyterian home, and Presbyterians aren't supposed to have visions. Moreover, I was educated at Dallas Theological Seminary, where I was taught that God does not speak in visions today. And all my life I had belonged to churches that rejected the idea of visions.

As I wakened on this particular morning and lay in bed a few moments before rising, I found myself walking through a woods. Suddenly, a furrow was there in the ground ahead of me, the fresh earth turned over by a plow. Curious, I followed the furrow and soon a second furrow was beside the first, and then another on the other side, so now there were three. But that was not all. More and more furrows were added to each side as I walked farther, and as I came to the edge of the woods and looked at the field beyond, I saw more and more furrows that spread out and covered the whole earth. Then the vision ended. Puzzled, I lay there trying to think what this strange event could mean. Then I realized that God had shown me the future of *Living Letters,* and that it was His plan for readable versions of the Bible to cover the earth.

But how could the world be covered by the English edition of *Living Letters* when fewer than one person in fifteen around the world speaks English? This question led me to feel sure that *Living Letters* would be developed in all the major languages of the world. African countries came to mind, then Japan, Russia, and many of the other lands I had visited through the years.

As I thought and prayed about this idea of translating *Living Letters* into other languages, I consulted an almanac that listed the major languages of the world and the number of people who speak each language. I discovered that although some five thousand languages are spoken throughout the earth, almost 90 percent of the world's population spoke in only one hundred of those languages. In my enthusiasm, I felt that one hundred translations of *Living Letters* was a practical goal.

One of my missionary friends from Latin America, with whom I shared this idea, saw its importance.

"Do you want me to try translating Living Letters into Spanish?" he asked.

"Dear brother," I replied, "if you will do that, I will be eternally grateful." I was elated and prayed for him diligently as he used whatever time he could spare to translate *Living Letters* from English into Spanish.

Many months later he completed the task, and the manuscript for the Spanish edition of *Living Letters* arrived. How eagerly I opened the package, and how I wished I could read it to find out whether it read smoothly and well.

I sent copies to other missionaries and national friends for their examination, hoping to receive enthusiastic responses. After a few weeks I began to receive their replies.

"It is a good translation," they wrote, "but it does not have the vividness or clarity of the English *Living Letters.*"

Another said, "This work needs to be done by someone born and brought up in the Spanish language. Only such a person can truly speak and write emotive Spanish."

And so, with many apologies to my friend who had done the translating, I abandoned the idea, and my dream ended in failure. Translating *Living Letters* into other languages would not be possible unless the Lord laid His hand on a "native" writer to make the Word of God as alive in Spanish as in English. But if there was such a person somewhere in Latin America, I did not know how or where to find him or her.

Yet, as the weeks went by, the dream and hope would not go away. In God's good time my thoughts turned to Juan Rojas, a friend who was born and raised in Cuba. Juan was a journalist and publisher. He had been in America for several years and was fully acquainted with *Living Letters* and the profound effect it was having throughout America.

"Yes, I think I can create a Spanish translation like *Living Letters,*" he said when I talked to him about trying out a few chapters in Spanish.

A few weeks later his manuscript arrived. I sent it out for comments, and it received enthusiastic approval. We were on our way into a worldwide ministry of new translations.

A new foundation was incorporated in 1968 with the name Living Letters Overseas. (Later, when the entire Living Bible was published in English, the name was changed to Living Bibles International.) I was the executive director, and Richard Wolff was my assistant. He began going overseas to look for translators in the major languages I had pinpointed, languages spoken by 90 percent of the world's population.

In God's providence I knew key mission leaders on many continents—Ken McVety in Tokyo, John Ferwerda in Beirut, Don Smith in Rhodesia, and others. I asked them to find and train teams of nationals to develop thought-for-thought translations of the New Testament (and, later, of the entire Bible) in the major languages of their areas of the world. They agreed.

This is a good place to explain an important translation principle. We do not translate *The Living Bible* itself directly into other languages. Rather, it is used as a model of readability and understandability. *The Living Bible* in English is a thought-for-thought translation, not a word-for-word translation from the Greek and Hebrew. A translation of the English Living Bible into another language would run the risk of straying too far from the meaning of the original texts. Instead, our goal in each language is to create a new thought-for-thought translation that is as fresh and readable in its language as *The Living Bible* is in English. The English Living Bible is our model, not our source.

From my travels I knew first-hand how much these new translations are needed. But do not these vast populations of the world have Bibles in their own languages? Yes, the Bible has been translated into hundreds of languages—but often these translations are very difficult to read. Many of them were translated by missionaries who did not know the native language very well, and in the hundred or more years since those translations were made, the languages have changed in many ways, so the Bible can be read only with difficulty. In some cases even university-educated people cannot understand the Bible written in their own language. Many words have become archaic and are no longer used in everyday speech. These friends often testify that reading even a few verses from the translation in their own language is a chore.

Lydia Benjamin, a highly educated woman in Sri Lanka, told me of her despair because the Bible in her language was so difficult to read and understand. "Usually," she said, "after battling through a few verses of the old vocabulary and strange syntax of my Bible, I give up and turn to my English Living Bible."

I pricked up my ears. "Lydia," I said, "why don't you try your hand at producing a Living New Testament in your Tamil language?" Of course she was startled, and she became very thoughtful. A few days later she told me she had begun experimenting and was hopeful that with the help of others she might succeed.

It was a long process, for Lydia was often sick. At one point she lost most of her household goods, and her life was in serious danger because of ethnic riots and mass murders of Tamils in her area. But with Lydia's dedication and God's grace, the work was finally finished.

I heard the same story from Marianne Lovrec in Zagreb, Yugoslavia. Her Croatian Bible, she said, was almost impossible to read, although she was a university graduate. Like Lydia on the other side of the world, she told me she read *The Living Bible* in English for any real understanding of God's message of love. In time she and her husband, Branko, who is a doctor, became the translators of the Croatian Living New Testament.

We did not have to go to Ethiopia to find our Ethiopian translator. One day Jim Johnson asked me to speak to one of his classes in the Wheaton Graduate School of Communications. I told the story of the beginnings and progress of *The*

Living Bible, and of the development of similar translations in other languages.

A few days later, Betta Mengistu, one of Jim's graduate students from Ethiopia, came to see me. At the time I thought it was a pleasant and interesting visit, but now I know that it was the beginning of a magnificent event in the progress of God's work in Betta's home country of Ethiopia and throughout Africa. Betta was brought up speaking the Amharic language and was converted when he came across a Bible in a library. It was an old Amharic translation, very difficult to read, but it helped to satisfy his eager thirst for God. (God had also miraculously taken away Betta's tuberculosis when he believed John 10:10, "The thief's purpose is to steal, kill, and destroy. My purpose is to give life in all its fullness." Doctors had been unable to help him.)

"Betta," I asked him, "why couldn't you translate the New Testament into contemporary Amharic?" The more we talked about it, the more interested he became in the idea, and soon the work was under way. But by the time Betta had finished his Ph.D. at Northern Illinois University, and he and his wife, Sophia, were ready to return to their homeland, the doors were closed. The Marxist government of Ethiopia was closing churches, ousting missionaries, and putting Christians into jail. So Betta and his family went to Nairobi, Kenya, along with other exiles, to continue the translation there. And the task was finally finished. Thousands of copies of the Living New Testament in Amharic have now been taken into Ethiopia, and we have heard exciting reports about its usefulness.

In Ghana I once met a young Ethiopian woman employed by the United Nations. She was overjoyed to talk with me because of what the Amharic Living New Testament meant to her and her husband.

"The old Bible we have in Ethiopia is so hard to understand," she explained. "God has used you to make it possible for my people to know God through His Word."

Betta Mengistu now heads up the African work of Living Bibles International from his office in Nairobi, where he has some wonderful coworkers. They could be commanding large salaries in the secular world, but, like Betta, they feel called of God to produce easy-to-read, understandable Bibles in nation after nation throughout Africa.

Margaret and I had the privilege of attending the ceremonies when the Kiswahili Living New Testament was first published in Nairobi and the Luganda Living New Testament was published in Kampala, Uganda. Conditions were still so unsettled in Uganda, and murders so common, that we were glad to fly in and out in a private plane so that we would not have to stay overnight. At both occasions pastors who were present were invited to come forward at the end of the service to receive a free copy of the new Bible. To see their looks of thanksgiving and hear their praise to God was a highlight of my life.

In Kenya we were graciously received by President Moi at his summer home in the country, and I presented him with a specially inscribed copy of the Kiswahili Living New Testament.

The enthusiastic response to our fresh, highly readable translation in language after language has been the same. In Japan a housewife commented, "I thought of the Bible as the hardest book to read, so I never read it. But this Living Bible is easy to read, and I want to finish it."

In Korea the Living Bible is received with enthusiasm. One older pastor read it through four times in three months! The Salvation Army reports that their young people can read and comprehend the Korean Living Bible ten times faster than the old version!

Not long after the publication of the Spanish Living New Testament, I made a trip to Mexico with Bill Ackerman, general director of the World Home Bible League (now The

Bible League). We had gone to visit a Catholic bishop to obtain his cooperation in distributing this new, easy-to-read version. Under Bill's leadership, World Home Bible League had been among the first mission organizations to make wide use of the English Living New Testament, realizing that it spoke to the man on the street as well as to pastors, seasoned Christians, and new believers. Now he was pressing for the wide distribution of the Spanish Living New Testament.

On the plane returning to Chicago Bill asked me, "Why not expect some miracles? Why not ask God for a distribution of 5 million copies of the Living New Testament in Spanish?" I smiled in appreciation of his enthusiasm! Realistically I hoped for a distribution of 100,000. But Bill would not be denied. "Let's ask for miracles," he kept saying, until finally I agreed to pray with him for this to happen. And it did happen! His faith brought about the miracle, and the miracle continues.

One outstanding part of that miracle took place in Bolivia. In December 1974, Chet Schemper of the World Home Bible League went to Bolivia to meet with Dave Farah, who was Wycliffe's liaison with the government.

Dave was able to arrange for Chet to have a ten-minute interview with Bolivia's minister of education. The interview stretched to forty minutes. The minister started reading the Spanish Living New Testament that was handed to him and exclaimed, "It is so clear." He ordered fourteen hundred copies to give to all the teachers of religion in the public school system.

Several months later he telephoned Dave. "Can we have a million copies as the religion textbook for our schools?" he asked. And so, at a cost of $650,000, every school child in Bolivia was given a Spanish Living New Testament, not only to study in school, but to have as a personal take-home copy for his or her family. What a breakthrough and answer to prayer in a country where most children owned no books and even school materials were often mimeographed.

Evangelicals in Bolivia feel that this was the turning point in their ministry. Until then they had had to be cautious about distributing Scriptures. That suddenly changed!

Because of God's laws regarding sowing and reaping, a million copies of the Living New Testament cannot be sown without reaping a harvest for God.

Eventually the minister of education and the president of Brazil heard about what had happened in Bolivia. Knowing that the students in their country could stand a big dose of religion and ethics, they requested 25 million copies of the Portuguese Living New Testament for Brazil's high school students. An order that large would take several years to fulfill, but The Bible League, in cooperation with Living Bibles International and Bibles To All (a Swedish organization), has now delivered 17 million copies. Plans are in place to deliver another 8 million copies before 1995. We pray that this will be a powerful antidote to the spiritism that is rampant in Brazil.

Living Bibles International is also cooperating with Bibles To All in a large distribution of Living New Testaments to schools in Sweden, Norway, Tanzania, and the Soviet Union.

I am frequently asked how the work of Living Bibles International relates to Wycliffe Bible Translators. Is there any overlap or duplication? Not at all. Wycliffe translators often use the same principles of making thought-for-thought, easy-to-read translations, but they are working in languages that have never previously been reduced to writing. Translators under the LBI umbrella are working in major languages that in most cases already have Bibles. The problem is that these Bibles are often not easy to understand.

It is impossible to describe adequately the grave problems some of our translators face. One of them lives in a country in the Middle East closed to the gospel. Of the millions of people living there, perhaps only about a hundred are Christians. No official government persecution of Christians takes place, but it is a Muslim nation, and ex-Muslim Christians have great fear of being found out as believers. A man might easily lose his job, or his wife might divorce him and his children be taken from him.

This translator is a professor at a national university, where he holds a high academic position. I had arranged through an intermediary to meet him at a downtown hotel for dinner one evening, but he did not show up. The next morning, Saturday, I called him at the university. He apologized and suggested that I come out to the campus that afternoon, when most of the students and faculty would be gone.

A colleague accompanied me, and when we arrived late in the afternoon, we found the campus deserted. We were able to find our way to his office, however, and he welcomed us warmly and served us tea.

After we had talked about this and that for awhile, I asked him how the translation was coming, as I had not heard from him for many months. He looked very troubled, then he got up and closed and locked the door. He went to the other side of the room and pulled down the window shades before sitting down to talk again.

"I can't do it," he said, "but I must. The Lord has told me to do it, but I can't." His voice revealed his anguish as he told how the translation work could not be done at home because his wife had found his manuscript and burned it. So he had started over, coming to the office at 5:30 in the morning as often as he could, working on a new translation before the day's activities of teaching and administration began.

He went to a closet and pulled out a manuscript from behind some boxes. "I have retranslated this much," he said with tears in his eyes, "but I have been afraid. No one knows I am doing this except my wife, and she has not betrayed me yet. I will continue," he said earnestly. "With God's help, I will continue."

How my heart went out to this man, whose desire to translate the Bible put him in such grave danger. If I were in his position, would I have the courage to give up everything? Or would I rationalize that I would be more useful to the Lord as a respected professor than as a homeless outcast? I thought of times in my own life when I had ignored the still, small voice of God when I had much less at stake, so I was speechless before this brother.

I have not heard from him since that day. The translation is still unfinished, and the power of Satan—the enormous power of Satan—still reigns in that land. By God's grace, however, another organization has taken up the Bible translation task for that country.

Sometimes our translators are literally sent to us. One day a friend telephoned me at my office in Wheaton to say that a young man from Sweden was in town. He wanted to meet me and thank me for *The Living Bible*. His name was Lars Dunberg, a fruitful evangelist both in Sweden and in England, where he had been working with youth groups with God's evident blessing.

"Lars," I said, after we had become acquainted, "why don't you develop a Living New Testament for Sweden?" He affably agreed. I thought little more of it until a few weeks later when I had a letter from him saying that he was well on the way with the translation! A brilliant man with a burden for his people, he worked with unusual speed. I was overcome with joy, and rather overwhelmed with amazement.

After completing the Swedish Living New Testament, he was asked to direct the development of Living Bible texts in other European languages, and he accepted. Three years later we invited Lars to replace me as international executive director of LBI. Since then the work has continued to flourish in a most wonderful way.

As the months and years went by, Living New Testaments

and Living Bibles began to be published in many of the world's major languages. As of this writing, fifty-five Living New Testaments and fifteen complete Living Bibles have been produced and distributed. Our worldwide staff now numbers more than two hundred full-time workers and eight hundred part-time. Thirty-five of these are Americans; the others are nationals working in their own countries.

One Living edition that has had very wide distribution is the Chinese. We had been told by local pastors in Taiwan that 10,000 copies would be sufficient, but the impact of the emotive translation was so great that nearly 2 million copies were in circulation within the first two years.

LBI also has a Chinese Bible for mainland China in the new simplified orthography. These are going into China at the rate of more than 50,000 copies a year.

One of the very exciting events in our translation program is the development of the Arabic Living Bible. This work was done in Beirut and Cairo. As bombs destroyed Beirut, Georges Houssney and our translation team kept steadily at their task. Once the unfinished manuscript was kept safe by the hand of God and His holy angels when a fire bomb penetrated the walls of the room where the manuscript was being worked on. The bomb failed to explode.

When that translation was finally completed, the question was how many to print. The traditional Arabic Bible was being distributed at the rate of less than five thousand a year. "Five thousand copies of a new translation will last ten years," we were warned. But a national Christian leader wrote a long article in a widely read church magazine, telling everyone of his deep appreciation for the Arabic Living New Testament.

"This recent interpretive translation as a whole is blameless," he said.

We sold 7,000 copies at the Cairo Book Fair during the first week of publication and more than 300,000 since. The book has been widely distributed through general bookstores as well as in churches. What a ministry already, and what a ministry ahead as the Holy Spirit uses His Word to smash the power of Satan among millions of Arabic speakers now held under his bondage.

Dr. Mavumi-Sa Kiantandu ("Kian"), from Zaire, personified the mission of Living Bibles International. He wrote, "My vision is that of having the Word of God translated into every African language, by Africans, in simple, readable, accurate, comprehensive, clear, and culturally adapted form. . . . Jesus must speak to them in their own dialect; He must use their local idioms, their proverbs, their enigmas, their figures of speech."

Born in a small village in Zaire, he felt called to full-time ministry at age seventeen. He graduated from an African seminary with honors and earned his doctorate in missiology in the United States. He began translating the Bible into his own language, Kikongo-Fioti, and this work eventually put him in touch with Betta Mengistu, the Africa director of LBI.

It wasn't long before Kian was named director of the LBI work in French-speaking Africa, a large area encompassing twenty-three countries and sixty-seven major languages. He wanted to see a Living translation in all of them, but he also sensed he would not have a long life.

LBI's African budget permitted him to begin his pioneer work in very humble surroundings—an old barn that had been converted to office space. How did he answer other Africans who thought he was wasting his talents and asked, "Can't you find anything better to do?"

Kian replied, "With my qualifications? Of course I can! But my job would not be as exciting and as challenging as this one. Don't forget, my friend, that when we were youngsters, our first classroom was under a mango tree. If the Swedish missionary who was teaching us under that tree had demanded a better facility before accepting the assignment of teaching us to read and write, you and I would not hold the Ph.D.'s we have today. I am in this barn because that is the price you pay when you are a pioneer."

From his deathbed in March 1990, Kian wrote, "I have happy news to report to you. We have finished the manuscripts of the Kiyombe, Lingala, Kiswahili, and Kikongo Living New Testaments. We would like to publish these as soon as possible—I have been in such poor health. Meanwhile, the work continues. . . ."

Kian died three days later, at the age of forty-five, with a writing pad in his hand as he was in the process of making final corrections on one of the chapters.

During its first ten years, Living Bibles International was supported entirely by royalties from the English Living Bible, channeled through Tyndale House Foundation. But as the work grew, I began to realize that we needed to tell God's people about it and ask for their financial support.

We bought names of subscribers to Christian magazines and began to build a mailing list of those who showed interest in our overseas translations. Contributions trickled in at first and then became a fairly steady but modest flow. Meanwhile, Garth Hunt was successfully presenting the challenge all across Canada.

Not long after beginning the mailing list, we talked with a man who had experience in asking for larger gifts. We had been asking for gifts of $10 and $25, but his idea was to ask for $25,000 from people who could afford to give it.

It was beyond my comprehension that gifts of that size might be possible. Nevertheless, our board of directors decided we should attempt it. "When you get used to the idea," one man told me, "you'll find it is as easy to ask for $25,000 as to ask for $25!"

One of my colleagues in the LBI office noticed that several people in a city in Texas were contributing rather regularly to the work. I was asked to go and meet with these people to tell them more about our translation program around the world. I hesitated, but in response to his enthusiasm, I agreed.

Before going, I realized I should take along a response card, so my secretary typed one. It merely said, "Here is my gift or faith promise," with squares to be checked indicating gifts of $25, $50, or $100. Then, as an afterthought, I added a line saying, "I will give $1,000 per month." After the card had been photocopied, I got to thinking about the comment that $25,000 gifts were possible. So I had the cards rerun with this additional line: "Here is my gift for $25,000"! With these cards in my briefcase, I went to meet with the group of Living Bible friends.

During a nice breakfast at a restaurant I told my twenty guests about the work of LBI. Then I asked them to fill out the cards if they wished to contribute. They could give them to me that day or mail them later.

Some of them handed me their cards as I stood at the door to tell them good-bye, and I was pleased to see that several had checked the $25, $50, and $100 boxes. I was quite overcome when I saw that one woman had indicated a gift of $1,000 per month! And you can imagine my inexpressible feelings when I was handed another card that said, "Here is my gift for $25,000," with a note that it would be mailed in a few days!

Recovering somewhat from the glorious shock, I noticed that the woman who had pledged $1,000 a month was the wife of the $25,000 donor. I assumed that neither had noticed that the other was signing a card. Finding the woman in the hallway, I thanked her warmly but asked if she was aware that her husband had also signed a card. I asked if perhaps she wanted hers returned to her. "Oh, no," she said, "what he does is his own business!" A few days later we received her first check for $1,000 and his for $25,000. So the Lord showed me that large giving was available, in addition to the smaller gifts we ask for and appreciate so much.

I am eternally grateful to this couple, not only for their gifts, but for showing me that God has His people in all levels of giving ability. He can direct them to bring blessing to people around the world through Living Bibles International. My vision enlarged and my praying changed to include all categories of God's givers.

Praise God for the fresh, new, easy-to-read translations in many languages. And pray that my vision from God on that early morning long ago will soon come true throughout the whole earth.

Farewell, Forever

From the airport at the city's edge,
The plane lofts quickly to the sky.
Already villages grow small
Beneath the aircraft's
Steady rising flight.

People walk through fields
Along the grassy trails
Into the darkness of the forest paths.
In each small hut, seen dimly now,
A family lives;
And in each family there are
    Boys and girls
    Teenagers
    Parents
    Grandparents.
Happy shouts come from
The smaller ones at play.
But those of longer years
Walk slowly, with uncertainty
And growing fears.

I leave them now forever.
I'll think of them no more.
My love is far too small
To take them in.
Farewell.

                K.N.T.
                October 1977

Chapter 30
Tithing and Hospitality

THE OLD TESTAMENT is quite clear that tithes were an obligation for God's people. Giving a tithe means giving 10 percent of one's income to the Lord's work. In addition to the tithe, God's people gave freewill offerings—not required, but appreciated by the Lord.

In the New Testament the principle is not so simple. Now we are not required to tithe, for it is not only 10 percent that belongs to the Lord. Everything we have and are belongs to Him—our money, our time, our talents, etc. How much are we to use for ourselves and our families, and how much should we give to the church or other Christian organizations? How much to individuals who are in need? Do we buy a new piece of furniture or send the five hundred dollars to a missionary? How large a house do we buy? What kind of car should we buy, and should it be new or used? If we buy a smaller house or an older car, should we immediately give the difference to God's work? These are questions that each of us needs to ask of the Lord after a lot of prayer and being saturated with the Scriptures. What one person decides correctly may not be what another person decides is right—though both are operating within the will of God as He instructs them.

Nevertheless, it may be helpful or at least interesting to tell how Margaret and I have handled these questions.

We believe that a tithe of our gross income is a minimum, and that we should add thank-you gifts to the Lord as frequently as possible. I was brought up to be a tither, meaning that even when I was a child, at least 10 percent of all income from my paper route and odd jobs went to the church or other benevolent work.

While Margaret does not remember particular emphasis on tithing, her parents were known to be generous givers to the church and other Christian causes—so well known that any inter-church evangelistic campaign had her father on the planning committee. The Gideons, the Union Gospel Mission, Central Bible Church, and Multnomah School of the Bible benefited from his generosity and wise counsel.

Even in the grimmest years financially, as our family was growing, Margaret and I felt it was both a privilege and an obligation to take 10 percent of our income, before taxes, "off the top" for benevolence.

But was this fair to the family? In our opinion, yes. We believed that God would take care of us, and we could thankfully commit the tithe to Him. We knew He would appreciate this. Isn't it amazing that He personally notices and cares what we do with the money He gives to us? We believed He would see to it that our many needs were met. And this is indeed what happened.

This does not mean that all of our desires were met, but they wouldn't have been met anyway, even if we had used the Lord's money for ourselves. And we would have had far less peace of mind, for it is our desire and obligation to do our best to follow His principles. We are told in God's life instruction book (Eph. 5:10) to "learn as you go along what pleases the Lord." Our giving is one of those ways to please Him, and it has given us pleasure too.

Another aspect of our tithing is to help individuals we hear about who are in need, rather than channeling everything through the church or other organizations. We used to make these gifts anonymously, but recently a friend who had received financial help from someone told me it was an extra blessing to see that someone he knew cared about him. He felt it was a double blessing because it was not an anonymous gift. I am still trying to think that through. Perhaps it should sometimes be one way and sometimes another.

One incident regarding giving to the Lord's work is given in detail in a long letter I wrote to Margaret from the Ivory Coast on my first trip to Africa. Family finances were particularly tight in the middle 1950s, and we were expecting our eighth child in a few months. At Margaret's urging, I will quote from the letter:

February 1, 1954
Abidjan, Ivory Coast

Darling,

The plane to Bouaki was canceled yesterday, so we were left here to await tomorrow morning's flight. Air France is a noble institution, and the accommodations here at the Grand Hotel are the best. . . .

I have a copy of Book Two of Hudson Taylor's biography with me, and although I disagree with some parts of his philosophy [that missionaries should never ask for money, but only "pray it in"], I have been impressed by his thought that going into debt was dangerous because it meant taking things into one's own hands without waiting for God's approval as shown by providing the means. Surely God could direct one to go into debt, and so I disagree with his universal prohibition (and also as to what debt is—I would think a fully protected mortgage on a home is not the same species of animal), but in general the idea sounds quite reasonable that God will usually provide in advance, and it is safer for knowing the Lord's will.

But so far as this trip is concerned, it has made me realize that Evangelical Literature Overseas had $450 and Africa Literature Committee $200 available for the trip when I left, and a request for further funds was included in the latest ELO bulletin. So if it has not been added to, the money will run out at Lagos, Nigeria (after reserving enough to come home via Brazil), and I have concluded that I ought not to go on to Leopoldville and Johannesburg unless Pete [Gunther] wires me that more has come in. For some reason this was a hard decision to make—not to tell Pete to have ELO borrow the money and wire it to me so that I could extend the trip.

A mistake at the hotel switchboard set my telephone ringing wildly at 4:00 A.M. this morning. (No one seems to understand English in these parts so I couldn't explain—hope someone made his plane!) So I had my quiet time a little earlier and longer than usual and could seem to reach no other conclusion than that mentioned—that I did not feel free to have ELO borrow the money so that I could extend the trip. It was a relief to get it decided, even though disappointing.

The Lord spoke further, I felt, when some time later as I was praying about our housing situation and your need for clothes, etc., suddenly there came to mind without warning the frightening question as to whether I would be willing to use part—or all—of the royalty check [from my first children's book] for this trip, thus being able to go on to Leopoldville. Of course I certainly was *not* willing to do any such thing and felt a bit ill and prayed that this fanatical idea might quickly depart. If one went around doing such things, where would one stop? We need the money for so many things, as I explained to the Lord.

Darling, I hope you won't be disappointed and that you won't feel that it is a wrong thing to do, but I seemed driven by the Lord to tell Him yes or no. If He wants me to use the money for this purpose, will I? And of course I could only finally tell him yes.

That money has somehow been an especially glittering toy to me—at last, after these many years we could have a substantial sum to decide what to do with instead of having to spend it to keep out of debt. It could be used in so many ways—maybe even a trip together somewhere. But the Lord and His will are more important than my plans. It has been a long time since I have felt that I have made any personal sacrifice—for the most part it has been a very joyful experience to serve the Lord together.

If the money comes in to ELO from other sources, I do not know whether our money should also be given; but if the ELO money doesn't come in, I plan now to go on to Leopoldville anyway and will repay ELO with the royalty money when I get home. Whether to go beyond Leopoldville I don't know yet—but the basic decision is made, the agony over (for me, anyway) and the money is there (even with increasing cheerfulness) if the Lord wants it. I'm sure that His further direction will become clear as I proceed.

With all my love,
Ken

P.S. Hmm! Come to think of it, the Lord has promised to open up the windows of heaven in response to this readily given gift. Not a bad bargain!!

The promise I referred to is in Malachi 3:10, "Bring all the tithes into the storehouse so that there will be food enough in my Temple; if you do, I will open up the windows of heaven for you and pour out a blessing so great you won't have room enough to take it in!" Not a bad bargain indeed!

The royalty check mentioned in the letter was $350, my first royalty income from Moody Press for my book *Stories for the Children's Hour,* published a few months earlier.

As my salary has increased through the years, and the children are now out of the nest and in their own homes, we are able to give away 50 percent or more of our pretax income, as well as 10 percent of Tyndale House's pretax profits. But the Lord was as pleased when we were unable to give as much. He appreciates the widow's mite as much or more than large sums. We have had the joy of giving in each phase of our lives and have received our full share of joy in return.

I have mentioned these financial details without knowing whether others should do as we have been led to do. We have made some provision in our wills for our children and grandchildren, but most of our estate will go to the Tyndale House Foundation, including all of the stock of Tyndale House Publishers, which Margaret and I still own. (It is more complicated than that as far as the legal steps are concerned, but that is the net result, so that the Foundation will own all the publishing profits.)

How I thank God for the privilege Margaret and I have had in seeing the work of God being helped throughout the earth.

Another aspect of stewardship, we believe, is hospitality. Margaret enjoys entertaining guests for dinner, and a few weeks after our marriage we started inviting other seminary couples over—one couple at a time, which was all the room we had, and even then someone had to sit on the bed. We became particularly close friends with Alan and Gerry Hamilton and enjoyed having them join us for a meal. Alan was a fellow student and Margaret worked with Gerry in the business office.

It was more difficult to entertain during the year we lived in Chicago. We had two babies, and John was very fussy because of his illness. Margaret's parents came through Chicago on their way to a convention and we squeezed around a tiny table for dinner. Years later Margaret's father told us that her mother cried when she got back to their hotel, because of our dingy quarters and because we had no kitchen sink. Fortunately she was able to visit again two years later when we were more comfortably situated in Mother Welsh's home in Wheaton. She commended Margaret on how well she was managing with three babies.

After we moved into our own home in 1948, we entertained quite regularly, beginning with friends for Thanksgiving dinner just a few days after we moved in. Our family, with its five children, wasn't invited out to dinner very often, so Margaret took the initiative by inviting others into our home. This worked out well, for by the time we had ten children, it was a rare occasion indeed to be invited out!

We made a special effort to have the missionaries from our church over for a picnic or dinner when they were in town. If out-of-town guests visited me in my office at Moody Press, I always felt free to invite them home for dinner. I eventually learned that Margaret liked to have a few hours' notice if possible, but it wasn't always possible. Either way, she welcomed them warmly.

After building our new home in 1966 we saw a complete turn-around as far as the children were concerned. No longer embarrassed by our old, dilapidated house, they now felt free to invite their friends in. They might have the whole youth group over for a meeting or party. Cynthia in particular brought friends home from college.

Two of Doug and Betty's children stayed with us for extended periods of time. Ginny came from South Africa right after high school and lived with us for a couple of years while she commuted to college. Later her brother, Charlie, lived with us after he graduated from Wheaton College and worked for a while in our shipping room at Tyndale House.

Steve Van Oss lived with us for his last semester in high school after his parents, Paul and Barbara, moved to California.

Our daughter Mary Lee dated Tim Bayly, son of Joe and Mary Lou Bayly, during high school. When Tim felt too inhibited in his own home during his hippie days, Mary Lee wrote to us from Westmont College to ask whether Tim could live with us awhile. We agreed he could, just as we would have wanted Christian friends to take in a son of ours in a similar situation. We did not hassle him about his smoking (he never smoked in the house) or his late hours, but simply accepted him.

He says this was a time of rethinking God's call upon his life. As a consequence of our taking him in and accepting him, we have a mutually loving relationship. Later he married Mary Lee and finished college and seminary. They now have four wonderful children and Tim pastors two United Presbyterian churches in a yoked parish in Wisconsin.

Wendell and Nancy Hawley and their three young girls stayed with us for several weeks when Wendell joined Tyndale House to be assistant sales manager under Bob Hawkins. A contractor who was building a new house for them in Carol Stream, near Wheaton, promised it would be ready when they arrived from Fort Polk, Louisiana. Wendell kept in touch with the contractor by phone and was told that the house was ready. But when he and the family arrived, they found that construction had barely started!

It was a good time of sharing meals, fellowship, and fun as they stayed with us until their house was finally ready. We have been Uncle Ken and Aunt Margaret to their girls ever since, and now that they are married and have babies of their own, we will cherish being called that by the next generation.

Something similar happened when Ken Grafham came with his family from Portland to join our sales staff. They stayed with us for ten weeks while they were waiting for their house to be completed. It was a good time of making new friends and cementing relationships.

Our house fills up with children and grandchildren at Christmas, some staying for as long as ten days.

We have a list on the kitchen bulletin board of friends and acquaintances we plan to have over for a meal when we can fit it in. Margaret feels no need to serve special meals to our guests. The menu may be just soup and salad, perhaps with her good pie for dessert. In recent years we have begun inviting friends over for Saturday breakfast. Margaret wishes others were informal in this way too. She feels that hospitality is for talking and sharing, not for gourmet food. Sometimes people allow their concern about an elaborate menu to stand in the way of doing any entertaining at all.

In 1964, after the Muirs had moved on to a larger house, we bought the house across the driveway for the purpose of renting it to missionaries on furlough, particularly if they had several children. Many missionary families come to Wheaton to attend the Wheaton College Graduate School, and they often find it hard to find houses to rent. We charge only moderate rent and do not have a fixed length of stay. It could be a few weeks, a year, or two years. So we always have congenial neighbors living next door and sharing the same driveway. A family from HCJB in Quito, Ecuador, will be coming soon for their fourth stay.

Empty Nest

The nest is empty now,
our children scattered—
not eight or nine, but all.
It's hard, of course,
but right, because we know
that so the generations come
and go,
and we bless them
in their going.

But there is One who stays behind—
no child, yet both a Child
and Elder Brother,
giving strength and joy,
a warm companion for
our solitude.

He stays with us, yet goes
with each one gone,
guarding, loving,
linking us at home
with our family gone afar.

And is He in your home
with you?
We'll share Him!
Then we'll all be brothers—
He, and we, and you—all of us
children together,
and all in His care.

K.N.T.

Chapter 31
Thoughts about Prayer

PRAYER HAS ALWAYS been an important part of my life. I know my parents prayed for all of their sons even before we were born. I can clearly recall the family prayers we had together each day, sometimes before breakfast and sometimes in the evening. These were never rushed times. Dad was extremely serious about the importance of making sure his children grew up knowing God and becoming familiar with His Word. After he had read and explained a Scripture passage to us, we would get down on our knees beside our chairs, which were set in a circle around the wood-burning kitchen stove, and each of us took a turn praying aloud. Then Dad would conclude the session with a fervent, and usually lengthy, prayer. By his example, he taught us to pray expecting God to answer.

I'm sure I tried to pray beside my bed each night during my childhood and teens, but I can't recall that my prayers were specific. I think they were more of the "God bless everybody" variety before I jumped into bed.

While I was in seminary, I developed what was for me a new method of prayer. When I had a troublesome problem, I went for a walk alone, thinking and praying it through. That was the beginning of what became a habit of taking frequent prayer walks, although I didn't consciously think of using that term then. Even in my seminary days my prayer habits were sporadic and undeveloped, but gradually the prayer walks became more frequent, and I began to spend more time praying than pondering.

After seminary, when I began my active working career, I finally realized that prayer and daily devotional Bible reading were of utmost importance, and that knowing God through these two means of grace was essential to my spiritual well-being. So I began to get up at five o'clock instead of six, so I could read my Bible and pray. Someone told me about the value of writing down on a three-by-five-inch index card the items that should be remembered in prayer, then checking them off when the answers came. This system proved to be very helpful to me.

As I look back, I think this was a good system as far as it went, but it omitted major elements of prayer: worship and praise, and then thanksgiving for answers received. I've always found it easier to ask God for things than to remember to thank Him for answering. But what a joy it is to be able to cross off the answered petitions from the prayer card! Now, instead of immediately crossing off the answered item, I put a check mark beside it, and for several days I take time to give thanks before going on to other items.

Even harder for me than giving thanks is the practice of worship. Worship is much deeper than words of praise, though that is part of it. So I can at least begin there, thinking of the incredible, unimaginable greatness of God, the Creator of the limitless eternity of time and space. I remember trying to explain eternity to one of my daughters, who was five years old at that time. As I talked she began to cry, overwhelmed and unable to take it in. I have often felt this way myself while on my knees before the infinite God. One thing that has helped to expand my mind and heart and loosen my tongue is reading some of the Psalms before the Lord.

One of the great lessons I have learned through the years is that a regular prayer and Bible reading time is not possible without a lot of determination and discipline. "The world is too much with us," and the routines of life take a lot of time. We can become absorbed with reading the newspaper and doing other perfectly legitimate kinds of mind-improving reading. I have disciplined myself to spend only about ten minutes each day on the newspaper and about a half-hour each week on the current news magazines to keep me up to date. I also read *Christianity Today, Moody Monthly,* and *Evangelical Missions Quarterly.*

There are books to be read and manuscripts to be written, yard work, entertaining, travel, church functions, spending time with our children and grandchildren, writing or telephoning the absent family members—all these are important, but I am convinced none of them is as necessary as spending time alone with God. If I really believe this, why do I sometimes skip a day or several days? I think it is because this special time with God is so essential that God's archenemy, Satan, makes it easy for me to forget under the pressures of daily life.

After many years of ups and downs in my devotional life—of success mingled with failure—I realize there is no solution except to make a regular appointment with God and to stick to it. This means doing more than my best—I must ask God to help me stay on a regular schedule. When I don't, I know I have missed the greatest privilege and opportunity of that day. My own time with God is usually before breakfast, although I sometimes keep my appointment late at night or even during the night.

I enjoy reading biographies and have often profited from learning how others have thought and lived. As a young man I read a biography of George Mueller of Bristol, England.

Mueller lived about a hundred and fifty years ago—a time when the insane asylums and poorhouses in England were like prisons, and hundreds of street urchins lived without homes or adequate care. Mueller was deeply moved by the plight of orphan children, and he opened his first home for girls in April 1836, when he was thirty years old. He decided to pray the money in to pay the bills, rather than to ask for it from prospective donors, so he didn't reveal specific needs as they arose.

For the next thirty years he continued to open more orphanage homes in Bristol for both boys and girls, to feed and educate them. In answer to his earnest prayers the money came in from unexpected sources. God honored his faith and sent the necessary funds day after day, and sometimes even meal by meal.

George Mueller often spent two or three hours each day on his knees or walking back and forth in his study—praising, worshiping, and imploring God to supply the orphans' needs. And God did. Mr. Mueller was also responsible for sending funds to China to support the China Inland Mission in its early days.

I have learned much, too, from other biographies of godly men and women who seemed to have a special ministry of prayer. "Praying Hyde," as he became known, was a missionary to India about eighty-five years ago. He spent his time praying instead of teaching and preaching. His biographer says Hyde sometimes prayed for four or five hours at a time, and a great spiritual movement began in the areas for which he prayed. I have often wondered how a person could pray so intensely and for such a long time.

Just a few years ago a Christian organization in which I am deeply interested and involved faced significant financial needs. We desperately needed money to carry out the ministry, and I became troubled in my spirit about whether God really wanted the work to succeed and grow. All of us involved were committed to God, so why didn't He do the miracles we needed, including sending in the needed sums of money?

It occurred to me that one reason might be the need for more prayer, even though all of us already were praying for the work. I wondered how much prayer was required. Then I decided it wasn't my place to try to develop a mathematical formula or equation (X amount of prayer = Y amount of dollars!), for I do not believe God does things in a mechanical manner. Yes, George Mueller prayed much, and God answered by caring for two thousand orphans; but Mueller had prayed just as much when the first twenty destitute children were brought in.

I continued to ponder what I knew about prayer, both from the Scriptures and from my own experience, and a frightening thought came to me. What would I do if God clearly showed me that He wanted *me* to pray for long periods of time? I wouldn't want to refuse to obey God, but I felt I was incapable of that kind of prayer, even though I applauded such devotion in the lives of Mueller, Hyde, and other well-known prayer warriors.

The idea continued to come to my mind, and finally—with real dread—I decided God was calling me to more extended times of prayer. I knew I must do my best to obey, whether or not I felt suited to the task and whether or not I had time, and regardless of how much I dreaded it! The next step, of course, was to decide just how much time God wanted me to spend in prayer each day. After some soul-searching I decided that for me, "longer prayer time" meant one hour a day on my knees, rather than praying while walking. Incredible! I felt I couldn't possibly do it, and yet I must. I resisted for several days, but at last I knew I must start the next morning, so I built that hour into my schedule and waited with trepidation.

I did it. And it was just as bad as I had feared. After five minutes I couldn't think of anything more to say. (I have read a survey that reveals the average Christian's daily prayer time is about three minutes—and that of a pastor about seven minutes.) I stuck with it, and the hour finally came to an end, but my relief was tempered by the knowledge that I must repeat the process the next day!

But I persisted, with the help of a prayer list and some favorite Psalms of praise. I was being welcomed into God's presence, His very throne room, and I began to feel at home. As the days went by, the terror of that time with God gradually changed to anticipation, and I now regret it when I miss my appointment.

Then, as should certainly be expected, my prayer list items began to be checked off. In fact, some quite amazing things began to happen—even things I had not prayed about. So, in addition to becoming better acquainted with my Lord and Savior, I had the added encouragement of seeing my prayers answered.

As my devotional life developed, I learned that prayer brings power, but character grows through reading and obeying the Word of God—the Scriptures. I learned this by the strange experience of coming from prayer tired, in a sense, and finding myself easily upset by minor household affairs, instead of being quiet and stable. Amazed at this condition, I took stock and realized that even extended prayer could not fulfill my need for regular spiritual food from the Bible, ministered by that same Holy Spirit of prayer. My extended prayer times had edged out my Bible reading, leaving me spiritually undernourished, so I began again to make time for regular reading of the Scriptures too.

I doubt that all of God's children should have the same kind of devotional life. I am only stating my own experiences for whatever value they may be to others. But my perception is that not enough praying is going on. God, for reasons of His own, wants His will and work known and empowered by the Word and by prayer, so these disciplines should occupy a place of great importance in our days.

We saw many answers to prayers in our family while the children were growing up. During our family devotions each evening we prayed for one another and for general family needs, and always for Uncle Doug and Aunt Betty in Africa.

A dramatic answer to prayer came one Christmas in the mid-1950s. We had been unable to put aside any money for gifts for the children, but I had hoped there would be a generous check from Margaret's sister Ruth and her husband, Bill, in California, as there had been the previous two years. Thanksgiving came and went, and Christmas was fast approaching. We finally had to tell the children there would be no presents under the Christmas tree, but we could, and did, pray about it. We remembered how God had answered our prayers for a new car not long before. God heard those prayers for presents and answered in unexpected ways.

One day I received a twenty-five-dollar check from *Reader's Digest* in payment for a clipping I had mailed two or three years earlier for "Life in These United States" or a similar column. The item had been used in a recent issue, but my name and address had been overlooked until that issue's material was filed. With the check was a letter of apology for not sending it sooner, but it had come at the right time to be an answer to prayer.

A few days later a check designated for Christmas gifts came quite unexpectedly from a friend who had never before had this special thought. And then, as a final and wonderful provision, the letter and check we no longer expected came from Ruth and Bill, but it was dated several weeks earlier. A note on the back of the envelope said that Bill had just found it in his coat pocket, having forgotten to mail it before Thanksgiving. What a Christmas that turned out to be as the children enjoyed their toys and other gifts. And what a powerful impression that experience made on the minds and hearts of the children—and their parents, too!

In these ways my own faith in the power of prayer was strengthened, and our children received demonstrations of God's willingness to respond to His people's needs.

We have had some great answers to prayer in our family regarding health. Although we had few accidents and illnesses, a couple of experiences were serious.

Once when I was traveling in Costa Rica, a letter came from Margaret saying that Becky—then ten years old—had confided to her that her urine was blood red. The next day she was hospitalized, and after tests the doctor diagnosed the disease as acute nephritis and gave sulfanilamide, the wonder medicine of those days. Soon she was out of danger, but there were many weeks of bed rest at home. We raised the living room couch up on blocks to make it easier for Margaret, who was pregnant, to care for her.

When Becky was fourteen years old she was sent home from summer camp with a severe sore throat. This developed into a mysterious ailment that the doctors could not diagnose. She was taken to the hospital and lay there for many days, white faced and listless. How frightened we were, knowing only that the doctor said she wasn't at all sure what was happening to Becky, as first one organ and then another seemed to be affected.

One Sunday morning as Becky's condition worsened, I sent the family off to Sunday school and church and stayed at home to pray. I spent the time imploring God for my child. Again, as at Janet's birth, I reminded myself that my children were a trust from the Lord. They were His, and if in His love He took them Home, I had to be willing—although I really wasn't. Finally my heart was settled and I felt released to pray, perhaps as I seldom had before, for God's will to be expressed regarding Becky's healing. I lay prostrate on the floor, crying out to Him.

Just at that moment the telephone rang. It was Becky's doctor. "I have good news," she told me. "Becky is much better!" And from then on, she gradually grew stronger. Her illness was finally diagnosed as polyserositis, a disease so rare that our doctor had never before seen a case. This disease weakens the immune system, so for a long time afterwards Becky was on a daily dose of penicillin to protect her from other infections. We were grateful it was provided by the public health department.

Another physical healing occurred a number of years later. In 1963 Peter, then sixteen, had rheumatic fever. I remember the year not only because of Peter's long convalescence in bed, but also because I had just left my employment at Moody Bible Institute, where employees and their families were well protected financially by hospitalization insurance. Employees who left the organization could elect to continue the insurance, but they would of course pay personally for the coverage.

I had elected not to continue the coverage, because of our tight budget and uncertain income. We would just pray for health and put our trust in God's care. Any actuary would have told me this was a poor decision to make when ten children were involved! And the results were not what I expected, for it was soon after the insurance expired that Peter became seriously ill and was hospitalized. The chances were great that he would be handicapped for life with a weak heart. He gradually recuperated and lived a fairly normal life, but he was quickly tired and any exertion left him short of breath.

When he enrolled as a student at Southern Illinois University, the campus doctor listened to his heart as part of the routine entrance physical examination. He shook his head and said, "No gym classes for you." Later Peter's number came up in the Vietnam War draft lottery and he reported for duty, but his heart condition was serious enough to place him in a 4-F classification, and he was sent home.

After Peter was married and he and Sharon were farming in Wisconsin, Peter would have to lie down in the field or hedge row to give his heart a rest from the physical exertion.

They attended a charismatic home church and grew under the excellent teaching of God's Word. When a visiting British evangelist with the gift of healing was ministering to the group, he announced one night, "Someone in this room has a heart condition that God wants to heal. We will now pray for the healing." Then he prayed. Peter did not consider that he might be the one who was being prayed for, but Sharon felt sure he was being healed. And sure enough, from that time on, his chronic tiredness and shortness of breath were gone. The very next day, when he maneuvered a refrigerator down the basement steps, he came back up with the glowing report, "Sharon, I'm not even panting!" This was a wonderful, life-changing miracle, completely unsought. It built up my faith.

I tried to let the children be adventuresome, although sometimes it was very hard. Mark was fourteen when he and a friend the same age decided to go on a bicycle trip to a scenic campground fifty miles away. Their route led over very busy roads, with hundreds of cars that would go whizzing past them. My heart sank at the thought. But my folks had let me out of their sight without ill effects, so I let him go. How relieved we were when they returned safely.

Mark carried his adventurous nature to an extreme when he was eighteen. He was spending a summer vacation building houses in Alaska. On a weekend he decided to build a raft and take a solo trip down the Tanana River. Using metal barrels as floats, and wiring them to a wooden platform, he started off. All went well until he was twenty miles into the wilderness, where he slammed into a log jam. The raft collapsed, and the barrels floated away. He managed to scramble across the logs to shore, swimming part of the way. There he waited, watching for a boat that might be going by and hoping to attract its attention and get a ride back to civilization. However, after several hours no boats came.

Finally, about nightfall, a fisherman and his sons came by, going in the wrong direction. They shared their provisions with Mark and let him sleep with them for the night. In the morning they pointed him toward a road ten miles away through the brush. He started out, without a compass, and on a cloudy day so there was no sun to guide him. He hiked all day, and, long after he should have arrived at the road, he realized he was completely lost. Apparently he was going in circles. Finally he went to the top of a hill and climbed the highest tree he could find. And there, in the distance, was the river. Mark remembers it as one of the most thankful moments of his life. When he arrived at the river, he still had to spend a cold night and another long day before a boat came by and took him back to civilization. When he got back to town, he found that his boss, Jim Congdon, had rented a small airplane to look for him along the river. Jim had seen the metal barrels far down the river and thought that Mark was no more. He was just ready to contact us when Mark walked in.

With the family being such a major part of my existence, I found it hard to see them leave the nest, one by one. And I was not prepared for the late 1960s and early 1970s when the Baby Boom generation, born just after World War II, came of age and headed into the Vietnam War era with all of its riots and turmoil on the campuses throughout America. Many of the young people in those days were disgusted with their elders for getting them into a war. Public and personal rebellion swept the campuses and affected many young people. My children were not unscathed by that unsettled era, and some of their marriages did not last. So my conviction as the children were growing up, that family devotions would be a stabilizing factor under every circumstance, had to be abandoned. But God was very gracious in eventually bringing much stability out of much turmoil in the lives of our children.

One night during those troubled years, I returned home from the airport at two o'clock in the morning after a business trip. I was in deep distress. I had been with one of my daughters for the evening meal, in New York, and observed her spiritual confusion. I did not know how to help her. On the plane coming home, as I thought and prayed about her plight, I thought about another six of my children and their unhappiness—marital problems and antagonisms or indifference to the church or to the family. They were walking down dangerous roads, heading for disaster. As I arrived home and entered the silent house, I was in tears, overwhelmed with helplessness, and devastated.

I had tried so hard to help them from their earliest years but had failed. I sank to my knees and once again I prayed for them one by one in their particular situations, just as I had so many times before. "O God, my God!" I cried out within my heart, my head buried in a chair. "What shall I do? What can I do? Will you not help them? Do you not care? My prayers bounce against the ceiling. I hear no voice to encourage me; there is no dream to instruct me. O God, my God!"

I stood up in despair, and as I turned off the lights to go upstairs to bed, I noticed two Bibles on the table, left there after a group Bible study Margaret had had that evening. In my anguish I picked up one of the Bibles and opened it at random, praying for some word from God. The verse I put my finger on said, "The Lord your God has blessed you." This was a tremendous encouragement to me, but I was still concerned.

"All right, Lord, thank you," I said. "But what about the children? Am I to be blessed by their suffering?"

Then, in as much despair as ever, I picked up the other Bible and put my finger down. This verse said, "The children will return." I fell to my knees before God in deep thanksgiving for this personal promise, and I held God to it. One by one the children have become settled in the faith or back in harmony with the family, one of them after twenty-three years away.

How kind God was, and is, to answer our prayers, some even before we ask them or know what to pray about.

One of the most recent of these experiences happened in the summer of 1989. Margaret and I had just returned from our annual reunion with our children and grandchildren. Our daughter Janet, who is a family counselor in Salem, Oregon, extended her vacation to be with us for a few days longer and to visit friends in Wheaton.

The morning after our return, Janet went out at eight o'clock for half an hour of jogging, and I left for the Tyndale House office. Margaret, having slept poorly during the night, was still sound asleep.

On the way back from her run, Janet passed Mark and Carol's home, which is in the same block with ours. She thought of stopping and having a cup of coffee with Carol but decided not to. As she opened the back door of our house, she was met by a great blast of smoke. Taking a deep breath of fresh air, she plunged into the darkness and found her way up the stairs, yelling, "Mom!" She found Margaret still asleep, despite the smoke alarm that was sounding outside the bedroom door. Holding each other by the hand and trying not to breathe, they groped their way back downstairs and outside again.

Janet ran to the neighbors' to call the fire department, and Margaret went across backyards to Carol's to get something to wear over her nightgown.

As I sat in a meeting at Tyndale House, a note was passed to me that there was a fire at my home, but that the fire equipment was there and not to be alarmed! I rushed home to find the street blocked with fire trucks. As I parked on the street and ran across the yard, I was thankful to see Margaret standing on the lawn with Janet and Carol. Smoke was pouring out of the upstairs bedrooms.

The firemen were efficient and quickly located the source of the smoke in the basement, where a room fan had been left on during the night. The fan motor had overheated, and the flames from the motor had set the plastic fan blades afire. The fire traveled along the electric cord to the outlet on the wall, and it set fire to one of the wall panels. The smoke had quickly poured through the heating ducts into every room of the house.

The fire inspector said that if Janet had arrived five minutes later, Margaret would not have survived.

And so the ifs begin—if Janet had not come home to spend a few days with us; if Janet too had slept late that morning; if Janet had decided to stop and have coffee with Carol; if she had not been able to make it through the smoke to find her mother. . . . And what if God had not spared Janet's life at the time of her difficult birth years before?

We had not been praying for safety from fire, but God brought about this concurrence of events for His glory and for our joy.

The Accident

The servant of God,
Preoccupied with higher things,
Drove along the busy street
And at a left hand turn
Forgot to calculate the speed
Of an oncoming car.

In heaven,
His guardian angel stood,
Poised for action
And uncertain what to do,
An eager smile of hope upon his face.
Could it be that now at last
This protege of his could come
And see the Gloryland?
(What fun to introduce him all around!)

But a quick glance
To the Eternal Throne
Told him, "Not yet,"
So he swooped down upon the intersection
Just in time.
A squeal of brakes, an angry horn—
And the servant of God
Went home unscathed
To eat his supper and regale his family
With the day's events,
The incident forgotten.

But as his guardian angel
Returned above to hear a kind, "Well done,"
Another's guardian, filled with joy,
Arrived with one entranced with rapture
At the glories all around—
One from another intersection
Whose time had come
To enter in.

 K.N.T.
 Dedicated to the memory of Paul Little

Chapter 32
The Past Ten Years

WHAT HAVE I been doing for the past ten years? That question came to mind recently as I was thinking of the wonderful blessings of the Lord upon our family and upon His work at Tyndale House and Living Bibles International.

A few years ago we were able to purchase an eleven-room summer house in Michigan, just half a mile from the beautiful sandy shore of Lake Michigan. In August of each year most of the family gathers there for a few days, some coming from the East and West coasts to enjoy beach activities and the retelling of childhood adventures. The grandchildren, now numbering twenty-seven, add their vitality and fun to these occasions.

Distribution of Bibles, books, and magazines has increased year by year. This means reaching out to more and more people for God. After Tyndale House Publishers almost ended its existence in the financial disaster of the 1970s, it has now operated profitably and has strengthened its financial base in each succeeding year.

Mark proved himself a capable executive during those difficult years, so I began to think seriously of appointing him president of the company. For a long time I could not seem to take that step, but one morning in my devotions this Bible verse leaped out at me: "Now I will relieve your shoulder of its burden; I will free your hands from their heavy tasks" (Ps. 81:6). A few days later I asked Mark to become president and chief executive officer of Tyndale House Publishers, Inc., and in May 1984 his appointment became official. He is a member of the board of directors of both the Foundation and Tyndale House Publishers, as well as Living Bibles International and other organizations.

Our wonderful team of coworkers has been augmented in significant areas by young people of great abilities, including Paul Mathews, Doug Knox, Cliff Johnson, Ron Beers, and Joan Major. One part of my work has certainly been constant prayer for my leadership team.

Tyndale House now has 190 employees—a long step forward from the beginnings around the dining table! And although we have grown so much, we are still a family. We have an annual Christmas party for the entire Tyndale staff and their spouses or guests. Since this requires a hotel banquet facility, it obviously can't be as homey as when Margaret and I could host everyone in our home, but it is always a wonderful evening. A summer picnic is another annual event we all look forward to.

Through the years we have published books for children, several of them from my pen. Recently, to my great joy, we have created a children's division, and we are producing children's book from a variety of talented authors. I myself want to write several more children's books. I hope the Lord will allow me to do this to benefit my grandchildren and other children all over the world. God has given me this particular gift, and I want to use it as long as possible. I believe that children read more than most adults and learn more from what they read. So I want Tyndale House to supply them with life-changing reading material.

With thanks to God we moved into a new three-story office building in the fall of 1990. We are especially grateful to Paul Mathews and LeRoy Elliott for their planning, as well as to our excellent architect and builders. The new building contains 40,000 square feet and is attached to the 65,000-square-foot warehouse and distribution center we built in 1984 and expanded in 1989. This new building is on nine acres immediately south of the building Tyndale had occupied since 1967. The grounds are beautifully landscaped, with a small lake for water retention.

Much of the increasing usefulness and financial progress of the last few years can be directly attributed to divine serendipities—opportunities that came to Tyndale House unexpectedly and without our planning (although requiring much hard work to bring them to fruition).

One of these serendipities was a special edition of *The Living Bible* called *The Book,* used by Pat Robertson's Christian Broadcasting Network. Pat's purpose was to get people who had never read the Bible to become its readers. His plan was immensely successful, and several million copies of *The Book* went out across America in 1984 and 1985. It was advertised heavily on "The 700 Club" and on network television, reaching people who had never read the Bible before, or who had tried to read older versions and had given up.

Another of these special events that seemed to come directly from the throne of God was *The One Year Bible.* For several years I had been asking God in prayer to tell me how to get more Christians to read the Word of God. I realized that many had never read the Bible through even once. I knew from personal experience how easy it is to read through the books of Genesis and Exodus, then get bogged down and quit.

Thinking about this problem, I remembered that Billy Graham had once said he tries to read some chapters from the Old Testament each day, some from the New Testament, and a

Psalm or two, plus a few Proverbs. The Lord seemed to say to me, "Why not publish a Bible with 365 daily sections—with each day's reading selected from those four parts of the Bible?"

The opening page of this Bible would be headed January 1, and for that day the reading would be the first chapter of Genesis, the first chapter of Matthew, the first Psalm, and the first few verses of Proverbs. The reading for January 2 would include the next chapter of these books, and so on day by day to December 31, when the entire Bible would have been read during that year.

I took an old Bible, cut it apart, and pasted up a few sample pages in this dramatically different form. I convinced myself that the idea was practical and that it would take only fifteen minutes a day for the average reader to read through the entire Bible in a year. Surely anyone would be able to invest such a minimal amount of time to accomplish what they had always wanted to do—read the Bible through.

To my surprise, the Tyndale House executives were not excited about my great idea! In fact, there was almost unanimous dissent. They felt that people simply would not use such an unusual organization of the Bible, and the project was resoundingly voted down. I asked for further consideration, and we consulted a group of managers of large Christian bookstores. They too were sure that it would never work.

Now we all look back with amusement at the meeting when the report from our select committee of bookstore managers was presented to me. The publications committee was relieved that the matter was settled and we would not proceed. Mark, by then the president of the company, explained the many reasons why I should forget it and asked for my agreement to drop the matter.

"No," I said. "Let's go ahead anyway."

So we did. Our sales manager, Doug Knox, who had felt all

along that the idea might have possibilities, proposed the title *The One Year Bible.* Since then several million copies have been distributed, and many, many people have written to say they have read the entire Bible for the first time. Many others said they had never read the entire Old Testament until *The One Year Bible* came into their hands.

Still another of these divinely planned but hard-earned serendipities began several years ago, before anyone at Tyndale House knew about it. Ron Beers, then director of publishing at Youth for Christ/U.S.A., saw the need for an entirely new kind of study Bible—not one with notes that explain the meaning of a phrase or verse, but one with notes that apply the Bible verses to everyday Christian living. What does the verse teach us about how we should live today?

No such study Bible was available, so Ron set out to create one. He called upon scores of Youth for Christ leaders to find "life applications" from verses in each chapter throughout the entire Bible, from Genesis to Revelation. Writing the notes required thousands of hours of research and hard work.

How pleased we were when Ron declared that no other text was as suitable for this project as *The Living Bible.* Tyndale House enthusiastically agreed to publish this new study Bible, and we called it the *Life Application Bible.* It is enormously helpful to its readers. Now it is available not only with the Living Bible text, but with the New Revised Standard Version, the King James Version, and the New International Version. Hundreds of thousands of copies are already in print. And now these life application notes are being translated into other languages for worldwide use.

Ron and several of his associates later joined our editorial staff at Tyndale House, so we received a double blessing—the life application notes and the talented writers.

Another of our delightful serendipities is the children's video series, *McGee and Me!* that is now in a million homes.

This project began when Paul Van Oss, representing Living Bibles International, approached a large foundation with a request for financial assistance in developing readable Bibles in languages overseas. It soon became evident that the foundation's greater interest was to provide outstanding Christian video material for children in America.

"Why are Christians unable to produce children's videos of top professional quality?" they asked.

Mark, who was with Paul, replied that excellent Christian video could be developed, but the cost was prohibitive, probably around $400,000 for a half-hour program. The foundation's representative responded, "If you can find the people to produce a truly top-quality video that communicates biblical values, we will pay for it." So Living Bibles International, Focus on the Family, and Tyndale House Publishers teamed up to produce professional quality programs. Dan Johnson, the executive producer, put together an outstanding team of professionals to use the latest Hollywood techniques and facilities. Live action was combined with animation produced in Korea.

Within two years, a million copies of the *McGee and Me!* videos have been distributed. A wonderful idea became a reality, and once again Tyndale House was God's chosen instrument to make it all come true.

Since the recent growth of Tyndale House has been greatly aided by these serendipities, I look forward with eager anticipation to what God will do next.

Another significant project is the revision of *The Living Bible.* Twenty years ago, when *The Living Bible* was first published in one volume, I indicated that it would be updated every few years to reflect changes in language usage and to correct any verses that did not adequately express the original Greek and Hebrew texts.

For several years, with all the rush and excitement of the

immense popularity and distribution of *The Living Bible,* this revision did not happen. Then, as related earlier, I spent years on a revision—only to decide in the end that the revisions did not improve upon the original Living Bible text.

Several years ago, Ron Beers proposed a different way of accomplishing my goal of complete accuracy. He suggested that we find eighty top Christian scholars to identify verses that needed improvement, and then I could work with the scholars to retranslate those verses.

It was a wonderful idea, far better than my trying to find the inadequate words or verses by myself. So I threw away my many years of effort and enlisted some of the best scholarship of America to work with me and our editors on a revised Living Bible. We hope to have it ready to print in 1994.

And what do I plan to do from now to eternity? I want to see many things happen, and daily I take these concerns to the Lord in prayer. One of these prayers is to see more and more easy-to-read, understandable, contemporary versions of the Bible in hundreds of languages overseas. I have written in another chapter about the wonderful work of Living Bibles International. Several other Bible translation organizations, such as the United Bible Societies and Wycliffe Bible Translators, are also hard at work.

But hundreds of other languages, each spoken by a million or more people, need new translations of the Bible. At the present rate of translation, millions of Christians overseas will not have easy-to-read Bibles until well into the coming century, if ever. Surely this is not God's will. May God give wisdom to all concerned, to know how to speed up the solution to this tragedy.

There are 150,000 Protestant churches in America. If 1,000 of these would "adopt a language" and contribute $10,000 a year for five years, every major language in the world could have an understandable Bible before the end of the 1990s.

I hope many will join me in praying that this will happen.

Simultaneously there is the need for Bible commentaries and devotional books in other languages. Hundreds are published each year in English, but many other major languages have only a trickle of such books, or none at all. With the vast resources of the churches of America, where a billion dollars a year goes into new church buildings, we need also to be developing and supporting Christian publishing houses throughout the world. They will produce ammunition for our missionaries and for the national pastors and congregations in every nation. I have a dream that God will cause this to happen with speed and success. I pray that God will give wisdom and leadership ability to someone so that this work can be accomplished, whether or not I myself have a part in it during these latter days of my personal ministry.

How shall I conclude this brief description of my life? What more can I say than this—"The boundary lines have fallen for me in pleasant places; surely I have a delightful inheritance" (Psalm 16:6, NIV). Margaret and I often speak of this. God has given me incredible opportunities of service and a deep desire to serve.

My life has indeed been a guided tour. Many people equally committed and equally guided have been led through dark valleys and rough roads we have not had to travel. I hope I would trust God as much if I had been called upon to walk those difficult paths.

With the years now closing in upon me, opportunities for God remain and I have a responsibility to use them. My deep prayer is that I will continue faithful to the end.

Kenneth N Taylor

This powerful poem captures my feelings. It was written by my friend Robertson McQuilkin, president emeritus of Columbia Bible College, Columbia, South Carolina.

Let Me Get Home before Dark

It's sundown, Lord.
The shadows of my life stretch back
   into the dimness of the years long spent.
I fear not death, for that grim foe betrays himself at last,
   thrusting me forever into life:
Life with you, unsoiled and free.
But I do fear.
I fear the Dark Spectre may come too soon—
   or do I mean, too late?
That I should end before I finish or
   finish, but not well.
That I should stain your honor, shame your name,
   grieve your loving heart.
Few, they tell me, finish well . . .
Lord, let me get home before dark.

The darkness of a spirit
   grown mean and small, fruit shriveled on the vine,
   bitter to the taste of my companions,
     burden to be borne by those brave few who love me still.
No, Lord. Let the fruit grow lush and sweet,
   A joy to all who taste;
Spirit-sign of God at work,
   longer, fuller, brighter at the end.
Lord, let me get home before dark.

The darkness of tattered gifts,
   rust-locked, half-spent or ill-spent,
A life that once was used of God
   now set aside.
Grief for glories gone or
Fretting for a task God never gave.
Mourning in the hollow chambers of memory.
Gazing on the faded banners of victories long gone.
Cannot I run well unto the end?
Lord, let me get home before dark.

The outer me decays—
   I do not fret or ask reprieve.
The ebbing strength but weans me from mother earth
   and grows me up for heaven.
I do not cling to shadows cast by immortality.
I do not patch the scaffold lent to build the real, eternal me.
I do not clutch about me my cocoon,
   vainly struggling to hold hostage
   a free spirit pressing to be born.

But will I reach the gate
   in lingering pain, body distorted, grotesque?
Or will it be a mind
   wandering untethered among light phantasies or
   grim terrors?
Of your grace, Father, I humbly ask . . .
Let me get home before dark.

                    Robertson McQuilkin, 1981
                    Columbia Bible College

Epilogue

Nearly three centuries ago, John Lee gave this dying charge to his children and to all of his descendants. I am one of those descendants, so this charge is for me and for my children and grandchildren. And now I pass it on to include you:

John Lee's Charge to the Lee Posterity
I charge my dear Children, that you fear God and keep his Commandments and that you uphold his public worship with diligence and constantly as you can and that you be constant in the duty of secret prayer, twice every day all the days of your lives and all you that become to be heads of families that you be constant in Family Prayer, praying evening and morning with your Families besides your prayer at meal and that you in your Prayers you pray for converting grace for yourselves and others, and that God will show you the Excellency of Christ and cause you to love him and believe in him and show you the evil of sin and make you hate forever and turn from it and that you never give over till you have obtained converting grace from God.
Furthermore, I charge you with that you chuse Death rather than deny Christ in any wise or any degree and . . . serve God in the way you was brought

up in and avoid all Evil Company lest you be led into a snare and temptation. Also be careful to avoid any Excess in Drinking and all other sin and prophaneness and be always dutiful to your mother and be kind to one another.

This I leave in Charge to all my posterity to the End of the World charging every person of them to keep a copy of this my charge to my Children. This is my dying Charge to my Children.

John Lee
January 13, 1716

An Appreciation
By V. Gilbert Beers

One of the foundations of the modern missionary movement is translating the Bible to break down the walls of communication between God and human beings. How can people understand what God wants if they cannot read what He says? Living Bibles International, which Ken Taylor began, is a major force in Bible translation work worldwide. But it flowed, of course, from the core work of translating *The Living Bible* in English. That achievement is a remarkable story of breaking down walls within the English language.

The process began with John Wycliffe in the fourteenth century. Listen to him as he proclaims, "I have mine eghen in hilles to se, whethen sal come helpe to me." This made perfect sense to English-speaking people of Wycliffe's time, but today we don't even recognize it as Psalm 121:1.

William Tyndale's sixteenth-century translation is not much clearer to English-speaking people today. Would you recognize "For all have synned, and lacke the prayse that is of valoure before God," as being Romans 3:23?

English is not always English, at least understandable English!

By the mid-point of the twentieth century, the world was ripe for a new kind of Bible translation. The venerable King James Version had been a mighty force for God for 350 years, but its *thees* and *thous* and complex sentences were not easy to read.

There was great need for a new translation that not only expressed the Word of God in contemporary English, but also expressed it in contemporary style, easy to read and easy to understand. Why obscure the truth? Say it the way God would say it if He were talking to us today in our kitchens or living rooms. That is what *The Living Bible* does.

While the Holy Spirit was moving in a great surge of evangelism and church growth during the last fifty years, He was also preparing a young man in the hayfields of Oregon. As David was taken from the shepherd's fields, anointed, and pressed into God's service, so Ken Taylor was taken from the hayfields, anointed, and pressed into this unique service for God—translating *The Living Bible*.

Why Ken Taylor? I doubt that Ken knows. Why does God choose this person for a special work rather than that person? Perhaps God chose him because Ken would faithfully stick with the task when most of us would be tempted to throw it aside. Or because He knew that Ken would channel much of the profits into worldwide Bible translation. Or could it be that God saw a heart and life that pleased Him? Did God see a man who would remain humble, and thus usable? Whatever the reason, God did anoint Ken Taylor to a worldwide ministry that Ken could never have anticipated.

As I read the manuscript for this autobiography, I felt that the story as told by the man himself is too modest. But that modesty is a mark of the humble man. I hope that someday someone will write Ken Taylor's story to show the breadth and depth of his work on the kingdom. Meanwhile, this book reveals the heartbeat of the man as he takes a candid look at himself. We are permitted to stand on the sidelines and capture some of that heartbeat.

V. Gilbert Beers
President, Scripture Press
Former editor, *Christianity Today* magazine

Chronology of Events in the Lives of Kenneth N. Taylor and Margaret W. Taylor

March 23, 1917	Margaret Louise West is born in Tigard, Oregon (a suburb of Portland), to Harry A. West and Louise Trappe West.
May 8, 1917	Kenneth Nathaniel Taylor is born in Portland, Oregon, to George Nathaniel Taylor and Charlotte Huff Taylor.
September 1930	Ken Taylor meets Margaret West in their high school algebra class.
June 1934	Ken and Margaret graduate together from Beaverton High School, Beaverton, Oregon.
Summer 1936	During his college years, Ken is deeply challenged by reading *Borden of Yale '09*.
June 1938	Ken graduates from Wheaton College, Wheaton, Illinois, with a major in zoology.
June 1939	Margaret graduates from Oregon State College, Corvallis, Oregon, with a major in home economics.
1939–1940	Ken serves on the staff of Inter-Varsity Christian Fellowship in Canada.

September 13, 1940	Kenneth N. Taylor and Margaret L. West are married in Portland.
1940–1943	Ken receives his seminary training at Dallas Theological Seminary, Dallas, Texas.
December 5, 1942	Rebecca Louise Taylor is born.
1943–1944	While finishing his seminary training at Northern Baptist Theological Seminary in Chicago, Ken works part-time at InterVarsity Press as editor of *HIS* magazine.
December 8, 1943	John Alan Taylor is born.
June 1944	Ken graduates from Northern Baptist Theological Seminary with the Th.M.
June 1944	Immediately after his graduation, Ken is ordained at Central Bible Church, Portland, Oregon.
1944–1946	Ken works full time at InterVarsity Press in Chicago as editor of *HIS* magazine.
January 29, 1945	Martha Ann Taylor is born.
1946–1947	Ken works at Good News Publishers in Chicago.
November 26, 1946	Peter Waldo Taylor is born.
1947–1963	Ken serves as director of Moody Literature Mission, a division of the Moody Bible Institute in Chicago.
1948–1961	During most of his years with Moody Literature Mission, Ken serves concurrently as director of Moody Press.
1948	Ken's first publication, *Is Christianity Credible?* is published by InterVarsity Press.

January 16, 1948	Janet Elizabeth Taylor is born.
November 1948	Ken and Margaret buy a home of their own—an old farmhouse on the outskirts of Wheaton.
September 1950	Ken's vision is instrumental in the founding of the Christian Booksellers Association.
January 16, 1951	Mark Douglas Taylor is born.
May 11, 1952	Cynthia Ruth Taylor is born.
1953	Ken's first book for children, *Stories for the Children's Hour,* is published by Moody Press.
September 1953	Ken is a founder of Evangelical Literature Overseas and serves as chairman of the board until 1970.
June 23, 1954	Gretchen Marie Taylor is born.
1955	In order to help his own children understand the Bible, Ken begins paraphrasing the New Testament Epistles.
September 7, 1955	Mary Lee Taylor is born.
November 16, 1956	Alison Margaret Taylor is born.
1957–1959	Ken's father lives with Ken and Margaret and the ten children until his death.
December 1961	Ken is asked to concentrate solely on Moody Literature Mission, leaving the directorship of Moody Press in other hands.
Spring 1962	On an extended trip to Europe and Africa, Ken loses his voice, a problem which will plague him for the rest of his life.

July 1962	Tyndale House Publishers is started as a dining-room table operation. Ken, Margaret, and several of the children are the part-time workers. The first publication is *Living Letters,* Ken's paraphrase of the Epistles.
Fall 1963	Billy Graham uses *Living Letters* as a television premium; his endorsement helps establish the paraphrase's popularity.
Fall 1963	Tyndale House Foundation is established to receive the royalties from the sale of *Living Letters.*
October 1963	Ken takes a step of faith by leaving his responsibilities at Moody to work full-time at Tyndale House.
October 1963	Tyndale House launches a dream of Ken's: *The Christian Reader.*
1965	Ken founds Short Terms Abroad and serves on its board until 1975.
May 1965	Wheaton College bestows upon Ken the first of his honorary doctorates.
June 1965	Tyndale House moves from the Taylors' home to rented offices on Washington Street in Wheaton.
Spring 1966	Ken and Margaret build a new home in their front yard and demolish the old farmhouse.
1967	Coverdale House Publishers (later Kingsway Publications) is launched in the United Kingdom.
January 1967	*Christian Times* begins publication, continuing until 1969.
June 1967	Tyndale House purchases its own building in Carol Stream, Illinois.

July 1967   *The Living New Testament* is published.

February 1968   Living Letters Overseas (later Living Bibles International) is formally established to create and distribute easy-to-read translations of the Bible in the major languages of the world.

July 1971   *The Living Bible* is published in one volume and becomes the fastest-selling book in America in 1972, 1973, and 1974.

April 1972   Ken purchases West Coast Distributors (Unilit) from Multnomah School of the Bible.

August 1972   The first Tyndale Bookshop is opened— in Carol Stream, Illinois.

March 1975   A consortium of banks calls for repayment of Tyndale House's $2.8 million loan, nearly forcing the company into bankruptcy.

July 1977   Another financial crisis occurs when Tyndale's year-end inventory is found to be valued at one million dollars less than had been expected.

November 1977   A board of directors for Tyndale House Publishers is established.

May 1979   Kingsway Publications is sold to Kingsway Trust.

March 1981   Margaret retires from her responsibilities in the finance department of Tyndale House—after serving the company for nineteen years.

February 1982   Ken undergoes double-bypass heart surgery.

August 1982   The Tyndale Bookshops are sold to the Zondervan Corporation.

September 1982	Unilit is sold to Spring Arbor Distribution Company.
March 1984	*The Book,* a paperback edition of *The Living Bible,* is launched in conjunction with the Christian Broadcasting Network.
May 1984	The mantle of leadership is passed to the next generation as Mark Taylor becomes president of Tyndale House Publishers.
October 1985	*The One Year Bible,* Ken's great idea that no one else believed in, is published in the Living Bible text. It becomes a smash best-seller.
April 1989	A scholarly review and revision of the text of *The Living Bible* is begun by a large group of world-class Bible scholars.
August 1989	Janet Taylor rescues Margaret from a fire in Ken and Margaret's home.
August 1990	Tyndale House builds a new office building in Carol Stream.

Books Authored by Kenneth N. Taylor

INTERVARSITY PRESS
Is Christianity Credible? 1948

MOODY PRESS
Stories for the Children's Hour, 1953
Devotions for the Children's Hour, 1954
Lost on the Trail, 1954
The Bible in Pictures for Little Eyes, 1956
Living Thoughts for the Children's Hour, 1958
  (originally, I See)
A Living Letter for the Children's Hour, 1968
  (originally, Romans for the Children's Hour, 1959)
The New Testament in Pictures for Little Eyes, 1989

TYNDALE HOUSE PUBLISHERS
Living Letters, 1962
Living Prophecies, 1965
Living Gospels, 1966
The Living New Testament, 1967
Living Psalms and Proverbs, 1967
Living Lessons of Life and Love, 1968
Almost Twelve, 1968

Living Books of Moses, 1969
Living History of Israel, 1970
Taylor's Bible Story Book, 1970
The Living Bible, 1971
Living Bible Story Book, 1979
Lost on the Trail (revised edition), 1980
What High School Students Should Know about Creation, 1983
   (originally, Creation and the High School Student, 1969)
What High School Students Should Know about Evolution, 1983
   (originally, Evolution and the High School Student, 1969)
Big Thoughts for Little People, 1983
Giant Steps for Little People, 1985
Wise Words for Little People, 1987
Next Steps for New Christians, 1989
   (originally, How To Grow, Oliver-Nelson Books, 1985)
My First Bible in Pictures, 1989
The Good Samaritan, 1989
Jesus Feeds a Crowd, 1989
The Lost Sheep, 1989
The Prodigal Son, 1989
The Bible for Children (coeditor), 1990
Good News For Little People, 1991
My Life: A Guided Tour, 1991

Positions Held by Kenneth N. Taylor

Inter-Varsity Christian Fellowship
  Staff member, 1939–1940, 1943–1946
  Board of directors, 1950–1959
Wheaton College Alumni Association
  Vice-president and chairman of Alumni Fund, 1944
  President, 1945–1946
Good News Publishers, staff member, 1946–1947
Moody Literature Mission, director, 1947–1963
Moody Press, director, 1948–1961
Evangelical Literature Overseas, chairman, 1953–1970
College Church in Wheaton, elder, 1958–1961, 1964–1967,
  1982–1985, 1987–1990
Tyndale House Publishers, Inc.
  Board of directors, 1962–
  President, 1962–1984
  Chairman, 1984–
Tyndale House Foundation
  Board of directors, 1963–
  President, 1963–1979
Short Terms Abroad, board of directors, 1965–1975
Coverdale House Publishers/Kingsway Publications,
  England, chairman, 1967–1979

Living Bibles International
  Board of directors, 1968–
  President, 1968–1977
  International president, 1977–1990
  International chairman emeritus, 1990–
Unilit, Inc., chairman, 1972–1973
Christian Library Service, board of directors, 1972–1976
Living Bibles Foundation, England, chairman, 1973–1979
Gordon-Conwell Theological Seminary, board of visitors, 1974
Fuller Theological Seminary, trustee, 1974–1980
InterSkrift Forlags, Sweden, board of directors, 1974–1980
Campus Crusade for Christ Christian Embassy, advisory
  board, 1976–
Association of Christian Prison Workers, board of refer-
  ence, 1978–
Eurovangelism of Canada, board of reference, 1978–
Christian World Publishers, board of reference, 1980–
Daystar, Nairobi, board of reference, 1982–
Probe Ministries, board of reference, 1982–
Inner City Impact, board of reference, 1983–
Children's Haven, Inc., advisory council, 1984–
Chicago Bible Society, advisory board, 1984–
Hellenic Missionary Union, Greece, board of reference, 1984–
Middle East Media, board of reference, 1985–
Fellowship of Christian Unions, Uganda, board of refer-
  ence, 1986–
Evangelical Church Library Association, advisory board,
  1988–
International Bible Reading Association, advisory board,
  1989–
Ethiopian Evangelical Christian Association, advisory
  board, 1990–

Special Distinctions, Honors, and Awards for Kenneth N. Taylor

1938 Wheaton College Scholastic Honor Society
1965 Doctor of Literature, Wheaton College
1965 First inclusion in *Who's Who in America*
1967 Recognition, Evangelical Child Welfare Agency
1971 Citation, Layman's National Bible Committee
1972 Special Award, National Awards Program, Religious
    Heritage of America
1972 Doctor of Literature, Trinity Evangelical Divinity School
1973 Distinguished Service Citation, International Society
    of Christian Endeavor
1973 Nelson Bible Award, Thomas Nelson, Inc.
1973 Alumnus of the Year, Northern Baptist Theological Seminary
1974 Better World Award, National VFW Auxiliary
1974 Distinguished Public Service Award, Messiah College
1974 Doctor of Humane Letters, Huntington College
1977 Recognition Award, Urban Ministries, Inc.
1977 Alumnus of the Year, Wheaton College Alumni Association
1977 Appreciation Award, Bibles for the World, Inc.
1980 Christian Service Contribution Award, Crusader Club,
    Wheaton College

1980 Achievement Award, Christian Booksellers Association

1980 Achievement Award, Allied Paper

1980 Achievement Award, Kingsport Press

1981 Gutenberg Award, Chicago Bible Society

1983 Christian Service Contribution Award, Evangelical
Literature Overseas

1983 "Man of the Year" Award, The Committee for
International Goodwill

1983 I.C.E.A. Award, International Sunday School Convention

1983 Induction into the DuPage Heritage Gallery

1984 Service Award, YFC/USA, 40th Anniversary Observance

1984 Gold Medallion Life Achievement Award, Evangelical
Christian Publishers Association

1989 Doctor of Humane Letters, Taylor University

1989 Induction into the Christian Booksellers Association
Hall of Honor

1990 Angel Award for *My First Bible In Pictures*

1990 Platinum Book Award, Evangelical Christian Publishers
Association, for one millionth copy of *The Bible in
Pictures for Little Eyes*

1991 Angel Award for *The Bible for Children* (coeditor)

Index

Ackerman, William 263, 323
Africa Christian Press 286
African Challenge magazine 183
Albany College (Oregon) 13, 80
Alliance Witness magazine 292
American Cancer Society 287
American Scientific Affiliation 287
Ammerman, James 287
Answers to prayer 155, 219, 242,
   263, 267, 353, 354–360
Apocrypha 272
"Are All the Children In?"
   (Elizabeth Rosser) 205
Autobiographies, value of ix

Baden, John and Harriet 143
Baden, Margaret 153
Barnum and Bailey Circus 14
Bayly, Hannah (granddaughter)
   photo section
Bayly, Heather (granddaughter)
   photos
Bayly, Joseph VI (grandson) photos
Bayly, Joseph IV and Mary Lou
   342, photo
Bayly, Mary Lee Taylor
   (daughter) photos

Bayly, Michal (granddaughter)
   photo
Bayly, Timothy (son-in-law) 342,
   photo
Beaverton Congregational
   Church (Beaverton,
   Oregon) 13
Beckwith, Paul 128
Beers, Ronald 364, 367, 369
Beers, V. Gilbert 375–376
Benjamin, Lydia 321
Benson, Paul 216
Benson, Ted and Mary Lou 86,
   127, 132, 148, 201–202
Berean Bookstore (Bakersfield,
   California) 234
Berghouse, Wes 49
Best-seller lists 258–259
Bible distribution
   Bolivia 324, 325
   Brazil 325
Bible in Pictures for Little Eyes, The
   (Kenneth N. Taylor) 208–209
Bible League, The 325. *See also*
   World Home Bible League
Bible reading
   daily 348, 365–367

Bible reading (*continued*)
importance of 162–163, 210, 347
Bible translation principles 138, 320
Bible versions
American Standard Version 212
Douay Version 257
King James Version 96,
210–212, 215, 239, 246, 258,
268, 270–271, 273, 276,
278-279, 303, 367, 375
New International Version 367
New Revised Standard Version
367
*The Living Bible. See Living
Bible, The*
Bibles To All 325
Bibliotheca Sacra magazine 292
Bierly, Ivan 32–33, 35
Billy Graham Center (Wheaton,
Illinois) 189
Billy Graham Crusades 159, 256
Billy Graham Evangelistic
Association 238, 240, 284,
287–288
Biographies, value of 349
Birkey, Donna 245, 295
Boardman, Donald and Betty 76,
143
Bolinder, Robert 310, photo
Book, The (*The Living Bible*) 365,
382
Books by Kenneth N. Taylor
383–384
Books, value of reading 193
Bookshorts magazine 299–300
Booth, William 261
Borden, William 63–64
Borden of Yale '09 (Mrs. Howard
Taylor) 63, 377
Bradshaw, Jerry 309
Braker, Grace 292
Bright, Bill 268

Brown, Cynthia Taylor
(daughter) photos
Brown, Kenneth (grandson)
photo
Brown, Nathan (grandson) photo
Bruce, Professor and Mrs. F. F.
photo
Burton, Jeanne 292
Bush, George 250
Buswell, J. Oliver 48
Butler, Phill 188

Campbell, Sandy 72–73
Camping 200–201
Campus Crusade for Christ 9,
188, 268
Carlsen, Odd 245
Carmichael, Ralph 262
Catholic Living Bible, The 272
Central Bible Church (Portland)
39, 336, 378
Chafer, Louis Sperry 103, 209
Chicago Tribune 258
Child Evangelism Fellowship 122
China Inland Mission 350
Christian Booksellers Association
154, 174, 209, 227, 229–230,
233, 238, 246, 255, 292–293,
379
Christian Broadcasting Network
365, 382
Christian Reader, The 291–294,
299–300, 380
Christian Times 295–296, 380
Christian workers, encourage-
ment for 20, 96
Christianity Today magazine
75–76, 292, 349
Chrouser, Harv 39
Church Around the World, The
295–296, 300
College Church in Wheaton
(Illinois) 129, 131

Colson, Charles 301
Columbia Bible College 371–372
Congdon, Jim 357
Constable, Robert 171, 178, 242
Coverdale House Publishers 303–304, 380. *See also* Kingsway Publications, Ltd.
Coverdale, Miles 303–304
Cox, Claude 259–260
Crawford, Don 245, 295
Cross and the Switchblade, The (David Wilkerson) ix, 244
Crowell, Henry P. 7
Culbertson, William 215
Cunningham, Loren 288

Dallas Theological Seminary 103, 109, 126, 317
Dare to Discipline (James Dobson) 252, 298
Daystar Communications (Nairobi) 287
Decision magazine 292
Denney, Bill and Ruth West 353; Ruth West, 105
Denney, Bob 35–36, 42–44, 51, 53–56, 77, 83, 92
Dennis, Clyde and Muriel 133–135, 138
Devotions for the Children's Hour (Kenneth N. Taylor) 209
Dickinson, Bertha Taylor (aunt) 23, 47
Dickman, Margaret 33, 36
Dobson, James 252, 287, 298, 300
Domeko, Manuel 208–209
Doubleday 258
Dr. James Dobson's Focus on the Family Bulletin 300
Draper, Edythe 255–256
Dunberg, Lars 327, photo
Durham, Wilf 160

Ecklebarger, David 309
Elliott, Ed 297–299
Elliott, LeRoy 365
England, Edward 303–304
Erickson, Wallace 187
Eternity magazine 292
Evangelical Alliance Mission, The (TEAM) 187
Evangelical Foreign Missions Association 181, 187
Evangelical Literature Overseas 183–185, 338–339, 379
Evangelical Missions Quarterly magazine 349
Evangelism Explosion (James Kennedy) 252
"Every-Member Campaign, The" 7
Evolution 131

Falwell, Jerry 268
Family devotions 16, 192, 358
Farah, David 324
Ferguson, Claude and Ruth Taylor (uncle and aunt) 23
Ferries, Frances 143
Ferwerda, John 320
Fischer, Howard 171–172
Fitz, Earle 258
Focus on the Family 287, 300, 368
Ford, Henry 4, 70
Foreign language Bibles
  Amharic 322
  Arabic 328
  Chinese 328
  Croatian 321
  Japanese 323
  Kikongo 330
  Kikongo-Fioti 329
  Kiyombe 330
  Kiswahili 323, 330
  Korean 323
  Lingala 330
  Luganda 323

Foreign language Bibles
(*continued*)
  need for 320, 369
  Norwegian 325
  Portuguese 325
  Russian 325
  Spanish 318–319, 323–324
  Swedish 325, 327
  Tamil 321
Forsberg, Malcolm 187
Frame, John 49, 67, 75–76, 112
Fraser, Gordon 29, 161
Frizen, Edwin L., Jr. 187
Fuller, Charles E. 108
Fuller, Hugh 304
Funerals, value of 136

Gambling 6
Garnett, Arnie 35
Gary-Wheaton Bank 309
Gideons 336
Gifts, financial 337–340
God's Smuggler (Brother
  Andrew) ix
Godspell 261
Good News Publishers 133,
  137–138
Graciousness of God 18, 52, 65,
  358–360, 363
Grafham, Ken 343
Graham, Billy 237–240, 245, 246,
  256, 283, 365, 380, photo
Grosman, Art (son-in-law) photo
Guidance from God x, 62, 71, 77,
  82, 90, 242, 280, 358–359
Gunther, Peter 148, 158–160, 175,
  241, 338

HCJB (Ecuador) 343
Hall, J. D. 139–140, 157–158
Hamilton, Alan 122; Alan and
  Jerry, 340–341
Hamilton, Alex 42

Hansen, Ken 310, 312; Ken and
  Jean, 249
Harrah, Bob 71–73
Harris, Eglon 120–121
Harris, William Wade 162–163
Harvest House Publishers 295
Have a Good Day 296–297
Hawkins, Bob 245, 249–251,
  255–256, 258, 293–295, 304,
  342
Hawley, Wendell 249–250, 310,
  314, 342, photos
Healing 356
Hemwall, Gus 222
Henry, Carl F. H. 75–76
Henry VIII, King of England 229,
  303
Hiding Place, The (Corrie ten
  Boom) ix
Hill, Ray 141, 149
HIS magazine 122–123, 128, 133
Hitt, Russ 139
Hodder & Stoughton 303–304
Hooten, Dwight 245; Dwight and
  Jean, 297
Horton, Bill and Doris 238
Hospitality 340–343
Houssney, Georges 328
How to Be Happy Though Married
  (Tim LaHaye) 245
Howard, David 208
Hudson, Angus 208
Huff, Isaac (grandfather) 23–25
Hunt, Garth 330
Hyde, "Praying Hyde" 350–351
Hymns (Paul Beckwith) 128
Hywel-Davies, Jack 161, 303–304

Intercristo 188
Interdenominational Foreign
  Missions Association 182,
  187
InterSkrift (Sweden) 307, 309, 313

Inter-Varsity Christian Fellowship
xi, 86–87, 111, 122
camps in Canada 89, 103, 112
InterVarsity Press 129, 131
Ironside, Harry 46
Irwin, James B. 260–261
Is Christianity Credible? (Kenneth
N. Taylor) 130–131, 378
Is God Dead? (Richard Wolff) 246
Israel, Act III (Richard Wolff) 246

Jacobsen, Margaret Bailey 76
Jesus People movement 247, 257
John XXIII, Pope 257
Johnson, Cliff 364
Johnson, Dan 368
Johnson, Elman 35–36
Johnson, James 183–184, 321
Johnson, LeRoy 172
Judson, Doug 237–238

Kaufman, Paul and Freeda 127
Kawano, Fran 292
Kennedy, James 251
Kennedy, John F. 186, 243
Kiantandu, Mavumi-Sa 329–330
Kingsport Press 256
Kingsway Publications, Ltd. 304,
312, 381. *See also* Coverdale
House Publishers
Kinote, George photo
Knox, Doug 364, photo
Kraft, Katie (granddaughter)
photos
Kraft, Lee photo
Kraft, Rebecca Taylor (daughter)
photos

La Cruz y al Puñel (David
Wilkerson) 244
LaHaye, Tim 245
Late Great Planet Earth, The (Hal
Lindsey) 298

Lee, John 373–374
Leetz, Paul 283, 310
"Let Me Get Home before Dark"
(Robertson McQuilkin)
371–372
Life Application Bible 367
Lindsay, Thomas 21, 74, 76, 104
Lindsell, Harold 74–75
Lindsey, Hal 298
Lingo, Alison Taylor (daughter)
photos
Lingo, Erin (granddaughter)
photos
Lingo, Jim (son-in-law) photo
Lingo, Jordan (grandson) photos
Lingo, Tara (granddaughter)
photo
Linkletter, Art 262
Literature distribution, importance
of 161, 184, 369–370
Lithocolor Press 216–217, 232
Little, Paul 362
Living Bible, The 297, 304, 306,
308, 365, 367
accuracy of 277–280
advertising campaigns 262–263
Anglicized edition 304
broadcast on radio 260
commendations for 260,
267–275, 277, 278–279
criticism of 275–278
distribution in general market
298–299
endorsement by Billy Graham
256–257, photo
fastest-selling book in America
259, 381
publication 255–262, 381
publication in United Kingdom
304
revisions of 279–280, 368–369,
382

Living Bible, The (continued)
  royalty paid to Tyndale House
    Foundation 286
  timeliness of 257
  translation of 211–215,
    219–220, 241, 243, photos
Living Bibles International 138,
    320, 325, 329, 330–332,
    363–364, 368–369, 375, photo.
    See also Living Letters
    Overseas
Living Books of Moses 250
Living Gospels 246, 249, 295
Living History of Israel 250–251,
    255
Living Lessons of Life and Love 249
Living Letters 198, 249, 283–284,
    291, 293, 295, 303, 317–318
  endorsement by Billy Graham
    237, 238, 256–257, 380
  publication of 216–219,
    227–241, 380
  royalty paid to Tyndale House
    Foundation 283–284, 380
  writing 211–215, 379
Living Letters Overseas 320, 381.
    See also Living Bibles
    International
Living New Testament, The 248,
    270, 275, 379
Living Prophecies 245, 249, 295
*Living Psalms and Proverbs with
    the Major Prophets* 247–248
Lofton, Jim 299
Lovrec, Branko and Marianne 321
Luther, Martin photo

Mack, J. B. 74, 77
Mackenzie, Del 76
Major, Joan 364
Malone, Ed 259–260
Marcos, Ferdinand 261
Mason, Joseph (grandson) photos

Mason, Lee (granddaughter)
    photo section
Mathews, Paul 313, 364–365
McGee and Me! 367–368
McLean, Donna 245, 295
McMinn, Elaine 105–106
McMinn, Ray and Janie 30, 52
McQuilkin, Robertson 371–372
McShane, Roger 74, 76
McVety, Kenneth 320
Media Associates International
    184
Medill School of Journalism 112
Mengistu, Betta 323, 329; Betta
    and Sophia, 322
Mennonite Brethren Herald
    magazine 222
Miller, Ted 245, 293; Ted and
    Jeanne, 291
Miracles 95, 100, 324, 356
Missions Advanced Research
    Center 189
Mitchell, Gordon 230, 258
Mitchell, Jack 105–106
Moffett, Howard 76
Moffett, Sam 76
Mohr, Gordon 306
Moi, Daniel arap 323, photo
Moody Bible Institute ix, 108,
    139, 157, 166, 191, 199,
    207–208, 215, 241, 305, 355
Moody Colportage Library 172
Moody Literature Mission
    139–140, 160, 177–179, 183,
    187, 241, 379
Moody Monthly magazine 349
Moody Press 171–179, 187, 208,
    215, 229, 297, 340, 341, 379
Moon, Irwin 108
Moore, Bill 171, 173–176
Moral corruption in America 16,
    34, 194

Mortimore, Don 105–106
Mortenson, Vernon 187
Mount Hood (Oregon) 98–99
Mouw, Paul 299
Mueller, George 349–351
Muir, Douglas and Virginia
    147–149, 154, 156, 240–241;
    Virginia, 243, 245, 256
Multnomah School of the Bible
    (Portland) 306, 336, 381
Murray, Carson 35

Naitermians (literary society) 74
New Deal 50
*New Testament in the Language of
    the People, The* (Charles B.
    Williams) 176–177
"New Twenty-third, The" (Ralph
    Carmichael) 262
New York Times 258, 260
Newsweek 260
Niles, Kathy 199
No Turning Back (George
    Verwer) 160
North Central College
    (Naperville, Illinois) 48
Northern Baptist Theological
    Seminary (Chicago) 123–124
Norton, William 175–176
Nystrom, Clarence and Gertrude
    73, 138

"Old-Fashioned Revival Hour" 108
Oliver, Victor 309–310
One Year Bible, The 365–367, 382
Operation Mobilization 159–160,
    188, 261

Palmer, Bernard and Marge 157, 239
Paraphrased Perversion, The 276
Paraphrases, accuracy of 278
Peace Corps 186
Pearl Harbor 113

Pera, Elsie 192
Philgreen, Irving 187–189
Phillips, McCandlish 260
Pocket Testament League 20
Prayer 15, 118, 347–360, 373
Praying for missionaries,
    importance of 165
Prison Fellowship 301
Protection by God 167–168
Publishers Weekly 208, 258–259

Quaye, Philemon photo
Queen Anne Hill United
    Presbyterian Church
    (Seattle) 1

Rack jobbers 299
Reach Out (*The Living New
    Testament*) 270
Reagan, Ronald photo
Reeves, John 244–245
Riverside Book and Bible
    Distributors 258
Roberts, Dayton 76
Robertson, Pat 314, 365
Rodgers, Bill and Emily 292
Rodgers, Robert 292
Rodgers, Cynthia 292
Rojas, Juan 319
Roosevelt, Franklin D. 50, 113
Rosser, Elizabeth 205
Rudes, Bud 287

Salvation Army 261
Sawyer, John 148
Schemper, Chester 324
Scofield, C. I. 103
Scofield Reference Bible 8, 50, 103
Scott Foresman Publishing
    Company 262
Screen, Robert 300
Scripture Press 291, 305
Segregation 118, 158

Selassie, Haile 220–221
"Sermons from Science" 108
ServiceMaster 198, 310
"700 Club, The" 314, 365
Shantymen 161
Shaw, Harold 245, 255, 308, photo
Shaw, Luci (Mrs. Harold Shaw) 214
Shipley, Jerry 105
Short-term missionaries 186–189
Short Terms Abroad 187–189, 380
Smith, Donald 320
Smith, Howard 245
Social Security system 50
Soltau, Mary 72–73
Southern Baptist Radio and
    Television Commission
    259–260
Spanish House 309, 313
Spasmodic dysphonia 222
Spirit-Controlled Temperament
    (Tim LaHaye) 245
Spring Arbor Distribution
    Company 313, 382
St. John, Patricia 192
Stalder, Marvin 35
Stories for the Children's Hour
    (Kenneth N. Taylor) 209,
    340, 379
Street, Harold 183–184
Strong-Willed Child, The (James
    Dobson) 252
Successful Living 299
Sudan Interior Mission 183, 187
Summer Institute of Linguistics 121
Sunday school 19, 206
Sunday School Times magazine 292
Swindoll, Charles 268

Tarr, Leslie and Catherine
    296–297
Taylor, Alison M. (Alison Taylor
    Lingo) (daughter) 155, 168,
    201, 379, photos

Taylor, Ariele (granddaughter)
    photo section
Taylor, Carol R. (Mrs. Mark
    Taylor) (daughter-in-law)
    285, 359–360, photos
Taylor, Charles (nephew) 342
Taylor, Charlotte Huff (mother)
    1–37, 42, 76, 81, 87–88, 106,
    134–136, 210, photo
Taylor, Christopher (grandson)
    photos
Taylor, Clyde 187
Taylor, Cynthia R. (Cynthia Taylor
    Brown) (daughter) 150, 159,
    194, 234, 341, 379, photos
Taylor, Douglas H. (brother)
    105–106, 135, photo
and Betty 168, 341, 353
childhood 1–25, photo
graduation from college 76
high school 27–37
Ken's wedding 105–106
missionary doctor 168
preparing for college 39–44
student at Wheaton College
    45–57, photo
Taylor, Elizabeth Waldo
    (grandmother) 23, 47, 109
Taylor, George N. (father) 1–37, 39,
    42–43, 76, 106, 347, 379, photo
birth 6
death 203–204
"Every-Member Campaign,
    The" 7
lives with Ken and Margaret
    202–204, photo
marriage 7
pastor 1, 13
personal witnessing 2
unemployed 80–81
writes newspaper columns
    10–11

Taylor, Gretchen M. (Gretchen
Taylor Worcester)
(daughter) 153, 155–156,
168, 194–195, 379, photos
Taylor, Hudson 337–338
Taylor, Janet E. (daughter) 145,
150, 155, 239, 359–360, 379,
382, photos
Taylor, Jeremy (grandson) photos
Taylor, John A. (son) 127–129,
132, 143–144, 148, 154–155,
159, 195, 198, 209, 341, 378,
photos
Taylor, Jonathon (grandson)
photos
Taylor, Kenneth and Margaret
build a new home 341, 380
camping as a family 200–201
church attendance 194
family devotions 16, 192, 207,
209–213, 228, 358
family life 191–204
gifts, financial 337–340
hospitality 340–343
limousine as a family car 199,
photo
live in Chicago 124–129
live in Dallas 108–123, photo
live in Lake Geneva, Wisconsin
134–138
live in Wheaton, Illinois 129,
147–156
live in Winona Lake, Indiana
141–145
purchase a summer house
363
purchase their first car 142
purchase their first house 149,
379
resolving conflicts 151–153
tithing 336
vacations 199–202, 249–250

Taylor, Kenneth N.
answers to prayer 155, 294,
314, 353, 354–360
attends Medill School of
Journalism 112
author 130, 131, 364, 383–384
avoiding a critical spirit 114
avoiding pride 296
Bible reading, difficulty in xi,
20–21, 96, 227–228
birth 1, 377
books written 383–384
childhood 1–25, photo
Christian Booksellers
Association 379
chronology of events 377–382
church responsibilities 194
concern about children's
college tuition 195–196
debate competition 32–33,
73–74
devotional life 191, 349, 352
edits *HIS* magazine 122–133
engagement to Margaret West
85–88, 95, 98–100
Evangelical Literature
Overseas 379
fails medical aptitude test 75
gambling, views on 6
graduate work at Oregon State
College 83, 86
graduation from college 76, 377
graduation from high school
37, 377
graduation from seminary 378
grandchildren, relationship
with 204
heart surgery 223–224, 381
high school 27–37
high school valedictorian 36
high school Bible class 29–30,
42, 87

Taylor, Kenneth N. (*continued*)
  honors 380, 387–388
  hospitality 14
  investments 196–198
  journalism, interest in 11, 81, 111
  learns business lessons 296
  learns to take advice 42
  leaves Moody Bible Institute 242, 380
  life verse x
  marries Margaret West 105–106, 378, photo
  media, views on 28
  meets Margaret West 27, 377
  miracles 95, 100, 324, 356
  missions, interest in 18, 118–122, 124, 133
  observance of Sunday 25
  oratory 34, 36
  ordination 378
  personal witnessing 9, 51, 54, 69, 111, 117
  positions held 385–386
  prayer 358, 364, 369–370
  prayer for Tyndale House 311–312
  prayer life 118, 152–153, 347–353
  praying for his children 144–145, 355, 357–358
  preparing for college 39–44
  public affirmation of faith 22
  public speaking, importance of 31
  Scholastic Honor Society, election to 75
  sees a vision 317–318
  starts Tyndale House Publishers 227–235, 379–380
  struggles with covetousness 16
  struggling with lust 33
  struggling with the love of money 309, 339
  student at Dallas Theological Seminary 108–123
  student at Northern Baptist Theological Seminary 123–124, 378
  student at Wheaton College 45–76, photos
  television, views on 52, 193–194
  tithing and generosity 128
  translates *The Living Bible* 211–215, 219–220, 241, 243, photos
  travels 119–122, 157–168, photos
  voice problems 217–224, 379
  works as dining hall manager 114
  works as editor of *HIS* magazine 122–133, 378
  works as journeyman carpenter 115
  works at Good News Publishers 133–138, 378
  works at Moody Literature Mission 139–140, 157–168, 171, 378
  works at Moody Press 171–179, 378
  works for Inter-Varsity Christian Fellowship 89–92, 95–97, 103, 111, 377
  works in hayfields 41, 52, 73, 77
  works on iris farm 40, 77
  wrestling 49, photo
Taylor, Kristen (granddaughter) photos
Taylor, Lyman W. (brother) 22, 43, 135, photos; Lyman and Jeanetta Mae, 150

Taylor, Margaret
(granddaughter) photos
Taylor, Margaret West (wife). *See
also* West, Margaret L.
chronology of events 377–382
hospitality 340–343
proofreading *Living Letters*
217–218, 227
rescued from a fire 359–360, 382
travels with Ken 323, photo
works at Tyndale House 231,
245, 310–312, 381, photos
Taylor, Mark D. (son) 150, 154,
159, 234, 239, 243–245, 285–286,
300, 310, 312–313, 357, 363–364,
368, 379, 382, photos
Taylor, Martha A. (daughter)
132, 143–144, 155, 198–199,
209, 213, 234, 239, 378, photos
Taylor, Mary Lee (Mary Lee
Taylor Bayly) (daughter)
155, 168, 194, 342, 379, photos
Taylor, Peter W. (son) 135, 143,
145, 154–155, 159, 195, 209,
239, 355–356, 378, photos
Taylor, Preston (grandson) photo
Taylor, Rebecca (granddaughter)
photos
Taylor, Rebecca L. (Rebecca
Taylor Kraft) (daughter)
116, 119, 123, 127, 129, 132,
135, 143, 148–149, 155, 195,
199–200, 209, 234, 354–355,
378, photos
Taylor, Sharon (Mrs. Peter
Taylor) (daughter-in-law)
356, photos
Taylor, Stephen (grandson)
photos
Taylor, Virginia (niece) 342
Taylor-Grosman, Alexi
(granddaughter) photos

Taylor-Grosman, Kyra
(granddaughter) photos
Taylor's Bible Story Book
(Kenneth N. Taylor) 261
Television 193–194
Thompson, Elizabeth 175–176
Time magazine 260
Timyan, Gordon 185, 188
Tithing 335–337
Townsend, Cameron 121, 221
Troutman, Charles 97, 100
Tyndale, William 228–229, 303,
375, photos
Tyndale Bookshops 304–305,
309, 313, 381
Tyndale House Foundation 187,
283–288, 308, 330, 340, 364,
380
Tyndale House Publishers, Inc.
board of directors 310, 381
children's books 364
Christian encyclopedia 309–312
distribution in general market
297–299
early years 228–252, 379–380
financial crises 307–314, 381
InterSkrift 307, 309, 313
McGee and Me! 367–368
moves out of Taylors' home
245, 380
named after William Tyndale
228–229, 234
new office building 365, 382,
photo
operates out of Taylors' home
231–245
ownership 340
publishes best-sellers 252
publishes periodicals 291–297,
299–301
purchases first office building
248, 380

Tyndale House Publishers, Inc.
(*continued*)
Spanish House 309, 313
successful operations 363
Tyndale Bookshops 304–305,
309, 313, 381
Unilit 306–308, 313, 381–382
Unirack 299

Unilit 306–308, 313, 381–382
Union Gospel Mission (Portland)
80, 336
Unirack 299
United Bible Societies 369

Van Kampen Press 173
Van Oss, Paul and Barbara 342,
368
Van Oss, Steve 342
Vanderpoel, Grace 75
Verwer, George 159–160
Victory Press 304
Vietnam War 356–357
Vila, Samuel 160
Volle, Arthur and Ruth 76
Voskuyl, Margaret 76

Walker, Don 35
Walker, Robert 122
Wall Street Journal 260
Way, The (*The Living Bible*) 288
Welsh, Evan 129, 133
Wesley, John 313
West, Charlie 36, 105–106;
Charlie and Rachel, 98
West, Louise Trappe
(mother-in-law) 107, 341
West, Harry A. (father-in-law) 27,
79–80, 87, 106, 112–113, 145,
156, 336, 341
West, Margaret L. *See also* Taylor,
Margaret West
birth 377

engagement to Kenneth Taylor
85–88, 95, 98
graduation from college 87, 377
graduation from high school
36, 377
high school 27–37
high school valedictorian 36
marries Kenneth Taylor
105–106, 378, photo
meets Kenneth Taylor 28, 377
school leader 32
student at Oregon State
College 53, 83, photo
student at Wheaton College 65
West Coast Distributors 306, 381.
See also Unilit
*What Wives Wish Their Husbands
Knew About Women* (James
Dobson) 252
Wheaton Alumni Association 132
Wheaton, City of 44
Wheaton College (Illinois) 39, 40,
69, 380
chapel services 56
class of 1938 47–48, 66–67,
75–76
evangelistic meetings 45–46, 54
Graduate School 343
Graduate School of
Communications 183, 321
literary societies 46, 65, 74
Naitermians (literary society) 74
Whipple, Grant 39
Williams, Charles B. 176–177
Wilson, George 240, 246
Wolf, Norm 231
Wolff, Richard 187, 245–246, 303,
320
Wonderling, Harold 245
Woods, Stacey 86, 91, 132
Worcester, Gretchen Taylor
(daughter) photos

Worcester, Keri (granddaughter) photos
Worcester, Kimberly (granddaughter) photos
Worcester, Lindsey (granddaugher) photos
Worcester, Robert (son-in-law) photo
Worcester, Stephanie (granddaughter) photos
World Evangelical Fellowship 208
World Home Bible League 263, 275, 323. *See also* Bible League, The
Worship 348–349
Wright, Paul 138, 140, 147–148

Wycliffe Bible Translators 121–122, 164, 221, 324–325, 369
Wycliffe, John 375, photo

Yehling, Mary Kleine 286
Youth for Christ 239, 367
Youth With A Mission 288

Zahlout, Al and Verna 142–143
Zondervan, Bill 305
Zondervan Corporation 313, 381
Zondervan Family Bookstores 305
Zorn, Loren 130
Zullinger, Sid 175